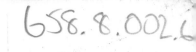

BRANDS

THE NEW WEALTH CREATORS

Edited by

Susannah Hart
and
John Murphy

Foreword by Tom Blackett

 Interbrand

First published 1998 by
MACMILLAN PRESS LTD
Houndmills, Basingstoke, Hampshire RG21 6XS
and London
Companies and representatives
throughout the world

ISBN 0–333–65908–2 hardcover
ISBN 0–333–65909–0 paperback

A catalogue record for this book is available
from the British Library.

10   9   8   7   6   5   4   3   2   1
07   06   05   04   03   02   01   00   99   98

Copy-edited and typeset by Povey–Edmondson
Tavistock and Rochdale, England

Printed and bound in Great Britain by
Antony Rowe Ltd
Chippenham, Wiltshire

▌Contents

List of Figures, Tables and Plates

■ Figures

■ Tables

■ **Plates**

The eight-page plate section comprises images depicting the following brands:
Virgin, Orange, Marks & Spencer, Daewoo, Zeneca, Kodak, Kit Kat, Bass,
Listerine, Jhirmack, Dark & Lovely, Sony, The Body Shop, Castlemaine
XXXX, Marlboro, McDonald's, Honda, Coca-Cola, Migros, Mars, Sains-
bury's, Tesco, Imigran, Apple, Bic, Red Tribe.

The editors and publishers would like to thank all those brand owners and their
agents and associates who have supplied information and illustrations for this
book. It should be mentioned that virtually every product or corporate name
mentioned in the book is a registered trade mark and virtually every logo
reproduced in the book is the specific property of a company.

Foreword

This book is about brands and the branding process. It might equally be said to be about the 'branding revolution', a relatively quiet affair by the standards of the rumbustious world of advertising and marketing, but a revolution none the less.

This is almost certainly because the last ten years has seen a train of events which, to use the language of marketing, have re-positioned brands. Brands are no longer of interest because they provide their owners with a colourful way to compete; they are now recognised widely as business assets of genuine economic value and as such have attracted the attention of a much wider audience. Brands are now centre stage: they drive major mergers and acquisitions; they appear frequently in the balance sheets of their owners; they have vexed legislators involved in updating archaic trade mark law; their application now extends to organisations who a few years ago would never have considered themselves as 'brands' (charities, utilities, sport's associations, cities, etc.); and they have changed irrevocably the way in which many major companies organise and run their businesses.

Twelve years ago Macmillan's published our first book on brands, *Branding, a Key Marketing Tool*. The title of this volume, *Brands: The New Wealth Creators*, underlines the fundamental shift that has occurred. It contains a series of essays by experts on brands, each of whom explains, from their own professional perspective, why it is that brands and the management of the branding process have acquired such importance in the world of business. In content *Brands: The New Wealth Creators* is broader than its predecessor – understandably, in view of the much wider role that brands now play. This said, however, while the role of brands may have expanded, the basic principles of successful branding have not. We hope therefore that readers will find as much solid advice on how to develop and manage strong brands as they will on such highly contemporary issues as brand exploitation, brand valuation and the battle against counterfeiters. Above all we hope that readers enjoy this book and that it adds to the fund of knowledge about one of the most dynamic, increasingly pervasive and influential trends in business today.

May 1997   TOM BLACKETT

▌ Notes on the Contributors

David Andrew founded Interbrand Pacific Pty Ltd in Melbourne in 1988 and moved the office to Sydney in 1989. He has been Managing Director of the company since its inception. His 9 years with Interbrand coincide with its ascendancy as the leading exponent of brand valuation worldwide, and during this period he has had extensive experience in valuing brands in Australia and New Zealand, as well as providing the full range of Interbrand services to clients in the region. Prior to joining the Group he was managing partner of Andrew Burberry Ireland, a Melbourne marketing consultancy, but the greater part of his marketing communications career has been spent in the international stream of advertising agency business – initially with McCann–Erickson and subsequently with Ogilvy & Mather – with assignments in New York, London, Tokyo, Milan, South East Asia, and Australia.

Alex Batchelor started his business career as a graduate trainee in Marketing with Unilever in 1987 after graduating from Oxford University with a degree in Modern History. Whilst there he worked on a number of major personal products brands, including Calvin Klein and Timotei.

In 1994 he joined Saatchi & Saatchi as a Board Strategic Planner. Whilst at Saatchi & Saatchi he won awards for both strategic planning and advertising effectiveness and helped develop a number of successful approaches to branding in services businesses. In 1996 Alex joined Interbrand as a Project Director in the Brand Evaluation team. Although based in London he has travelled extensively and already worked with clients in the FMCG, services and telecommunications industries.

Katriona Campbell is the Director of Research for Interbrand, one of the world's leading International Branding Consultancies, where she is responsible for the design and coordination of all research activities. She has been involved at a senior level within research and marketing for 11 years. Her previous roles include European Marketing and Research Manager at Quaker Europe, Head of Research at Eden Vale, Senior Brand Planner at Unilever's Brooke Bond Foods. Katriona holds the MRS diploma as well as a postgraduate degree in marketing from the University of Bristol.

Vincent Carratu is Chairman of Carratu International. He is a former member of the company fraud squad at New Scotland Yard and has been involved in the investigation of counterfeiting and international property abuse since 1963.

David Cullwick joined Ernst & Young in 1987 and is a Partner in the Wellington Office. He leads the Strategy Consulting practice, and works with many of New Zealand's leading international marketing organisations. He was previously a Director of the New Zealand Wool Board and Foundation Professor of Marketing at the University of Wellington. David had a PhD in Management, from the Kellogg Graduate School, Northwestern University, USA.

Adrian Room is a compiler of reference works on the origins of words and names, including brand names. He is the author of *Corporate Eponymy* and *Trade Name Origins*.

Janet Fogg is Chairman of Markforce and has been with the company since 1985. She is a qualified (by examination) Trade Mark Attorney, and is a Fellow of the Institute of Trade Mark Agents and a Registered Trade Mark Agent. She has a wide range of experience within private practice and has represented a large number of clients with varied activities. She is also a member (and former Chairman) of the Joint Examination Board, the body which administers the examinations for entry onto the Registers of trade Mark and Patent Agents.

Richard Gerstman is a founding partner of Gerstman & Meyers Inc., one of the nation's leading marketing-oriented design consulting firms and now part of the Interbrand group. An industrial designer and graduate of the University of Cincinnati, he formed Gerstman & Meyers with designer Herbert M. Meyers in New York City in 1970. The firm assists corporate, industrial, consumer product and service-oriented companies in shaping the identity of their brands and packaging. Richard himself has won numerous design awards and holds several design patents. He is a member of the Board of Directors of the Package Design Council.

Susannah Hart is a director of Interbrand UK Limited with special responsibility for brand strategy and name development. She has advised a wide range of clients both in the UK and internationally. She is a regular speaker at conferences and joint editor of *Naming*, an Interbrand publication.

Michael Jary and Andrew Wileman, of OC&C Strategy Consultants, work as strategy advisers to the boards of major corporations in Europe, the USA and Japan. Michael Jary leads OC&C's European practice in retail and consumer goods. He holds an MBA from INSEAD in Fontainebleau. Andrew Wileman has previously been Group Strategy Directory at Sears, the UK retail group. He holds an MBA from Harvard Business School. They are also co-authors of the book *Retail Power Plays: From Trading to Brand Leadership*.

Jo Kennelly is a policy advisor in the Department of the Prime Minister and Cabinet, Wellington. She was previously a Manager in Performance Improvement Consulting, Ernst & Young, Wellington. She previously held a

Research Fellowship at the Royal Free Hospital, London and Centre for Health Economics at the University of York. She holds a PhD from Cambridge University.

Chris Lightfoot is Creative Director of Interbrand's UK and European Business. Chris graduated from Canterbury College of Art and, prior to joining Interbrand, gained experience at Kennedy Brookes plc, King & Associates and Michael Peters Limited. Since joining Interbrand Chris has been responsible for creatively directing a number of corporate identity, brand identity and packaging projects including clients such as Mobil, Bass, Unilever, Volvo, and Zeneca.

Andy Milligan is a Director of Interbrand UK. Having graduated from Oxford in 1987, he worked in sales with VNU Business Publications, before joining Interbrand 7 years ago. At Interbrand he has worked on a wide range of brand development projects including brand valuation exercises, packaging and corporate brand development for Belgacom. His project work is international and he has worked in the US, Europe and Singapore offices. Andy has lectured in Europe and Singapore on brand development issues, is a frequent conference speaker and makes regular TV and radio appearances.

Simon Mottram is a Director of Interbrand's UK design business with particular responsibility for corporate identity. Having graduated from Sussex University, Simon worked with Price Waterhouse in London for 5 years and is a Chartered Accountant. At Interbrand Simon has worked on a wide range of brand strategy and international corporate identity projects for clients including IBM and Volvo. Simon also worked for 2 years on Brand Evaluation assignments for a variety of blue-chip clients. A frequent speaker at conferences, Simon has also published a number of articles on branding and identity matters.

John Murphy, founder of the world-wide Interbrand consultancy practice, is one of the world's leading experts on the theory and practice of branding. He is author/editor of several textbooks and has handled major brand consultancy assignments for companies in the USA, the UK, continental Europe and Australia. He is Visiting Professor of Marketing at The Open University Business School.

John Murray is a graduate of Cambridge University. He joined the Mars Corporation in 1973 and has worked for Mars in the UK, France, Belgium, Holland, Germany and the USA. Since 1991, he has been responsible for Global Branding development across all product categories of Mars, Incorporated, which sells snackfoods, petcare products, main meal foods, drinks and electronic products worldwide. He has taken a particular interest in Mars' dynamic expansion in emerging markets including China, the CIS, Central Europe, Africa and Latin America.

Raymond Perrier is a Director of the Interbrand Group and has responsibility for Interbrand's brand valuation activities worldwide. He joined Interbrand in 1987 after studying Philosophy and Theology at New College, Oxford from where he graduated with an MA (Hons). He began his professional career in the area of brand development and new brand creation and gained experience of market research, brand positioning, competitive analysis and strategic planning. For the past 6 years he has worked for Interbrand in the area of brand valuation and has valued many hundreds of brands.

Valuations conducted by Raymond have been used in submissions to the UK Monopolies and Mergers Commission, the UK Inland Revenue, the US IRS and the Australian Tax Office. They have been audited by most of the Big 6 accountancy firms and have been used also in expert witness testimony in the UK (Gucci) and Ireland (Kerrygold). He frequently speaks at conferences on the subject of intangible assets, and is also a member of the European Commission working party on the subject of intangible assets and the impact on competitiveness. He has recently joined the board of Interbrand Group plc.

Joe Pope, a New Zealander, has had a career in Marketing and General Management in the Textile, Liquor, petrochemical and Fruit industries, based on his academic training in Economics and Marketing.

From 1984 to 1996 he was CEO of The New Zealand Apple & Pear Marketing Board taking it from a small distributor to the leading international marketer of fresh apples. Joe is now on the boards of a number of public and private companies operating in the rural, international trade, and sports and entertainments industries.

Pam Robertson has been involved with brand and product development for most of her career, mainly within specialist consultancies but also within major companies such as Unilever and Brooke Bond Oxo. Her own particular focus has been on the strategic side of brand development and Pam's mission in life has been to put innovation and development on top of the business agenda. Working on household brand names like BP Mobil, Barclays, Tesco, Duracell and many other well known brands Pam has the opportunity to explore and develop the brand strategy before getting on with the bit that most clients find interesting – the new product development. Pam merged her previous company Redwood with Interbrand in 1996.

Andrew Seth is a businessman with over 30 years' experience in worldwide marketing and general management. Educated in Ireland, he has an Oxford law degree, a Kingston University Honorary Doctorate in Business, and studied and was class valedictorian at the Harvard Business School Advanced management programme in 1980–1. He worked for Unilever until taking early retirement as a company marketing Director and Chief Executive in the UK, Mexico, Europe and twice in the USA. Now engaged in a range of activity his interests are competitive strategy in business, brands and their marketing, business process and people, and change management. In 1995 he became Non Executive Chairman of the Added Value Group, a unique 8-year-old and highly successful London based marketing agency. The company started life in the UK but has now established itself in France and Germany. Added Value has design and internal communications subsidiaries – Brown Inc. and Avicom – that are themselves growing quickly in Europe.

Andrew Taylor joined McDonald's in November 1979, became Regional Vice President in 1989, Main Board Director in 1991, and Senior Vice President and

Chief Operations Officer in 1993, he served on the US Corporate Board of Directors for a 1-year term in 1995, and became President and Chief Operating Officer in 1996.

William (Bill) Tragos is the 'T' of TBWA. he is co-founder and chairman/CEO of TBWA International. After graduation from Washington University, St Louis, Missouri, Bill joined Young & Rubicam, where he stayed for 13 years. In 1964, he was appointed the youngest general manager in Y&R's history and started their operations in Brussels and then Amsterdam. In 1967, Bill took over Y&R's Paris office and helped make Y&R the first American agency to succeed in France. In 1970, Bill founded TBWA in Paris with three partners. Their founding philosophy was to build the first truly international agency.

In May 1993, TBWA joined the Omnicom Group Inc. Concurrently, Bill joined Omnicom's Board of Directors. In January 1995, TBWA announced a merger of its US company with Chiat/Day.

CHAPTER 1

What Is Branding?

John Murphy

Interbrand

■ Introduction

Since the earliest times producers of goods have used their brands or marks to distinguish their products. Pride in their products has no doubt played a part in this. More particularly, by identifying their products they have provided purchasers with a means of recognising and specifying them should they wish to repurchase or recommend the products to others.

The use of brands has developed considerably, especially in the last century. Indeed, the words 'brand' and 'branding' are now such common currency that their original meaning is in danger of being weakened. However, the function of a brand as distinguishing the goods of one producer from those of another and of thus allowing consumers freedom of choice has remained unaltered.

Brands have developed over the years in a number of significant ways. First, legal systems have recognised the value of brands to both consumers and producers. Most countries in the world now recognise that intellectual property – trade marks, patents, designs, copyright – is property in a very real sense and therefore confer rights on the owners of such property. Second, the concept of branded goods has been extended successfully to embrace services and other less tangible types of offering. Thus the providers of financial, retail or other services can now generally treat them as branded products, provided they are distinguished from those of competitors. Service brands now generally enjoy the same statutory rights as product brands. Third, and perhaps most importantly, the ways in which branded products or services are distinguished from one another have increasingly come to embrace non-tangible factors, as well as such real factors as size, shape, make-up and price. The brand qualities which consumers rely upon in making a choice between brands have become increasingly subtle and, at times, fickle. Cigarette A may be virtually indistinguishable from cigarette B yet outsell it 10 to 1; a fragrance costing £5 a bottle may be outsold by another fragrance with very similar physical characteristics but which sells at £20 a bottle.

Finally, as a result of all this development, it has been acknowledged by financial and marketing communities alike that brands do not merely have consumer 'values', but also financial value, and that this value can be measured. Various techniques for measuring financial brand value have now been developed, and the most widely recognised of these techniques are discussed later in this book.

■ Branding Today

Thus modern, sophisticated branding is concerned increasingly with a brand's Gestalt, with assembling together and maintaining a mix of values, both tangible and intangible, which are relevant to consumers and which meaningfully and appropriately distinguish one supplier's brand from that of another.

Intangible factors are, however, very difficult to estimate even individually. When a number of such elements are blended together to form that unique creation, a branded product, evaluation of these separate but interrelated constituents is far from easy. Prior to a brand's launch, measuring its likely success is notoriously difficult. Even after launch it may not be possible to ascertain with any certainty the reasons for the success or failure of a brand.

In a sense, branding consists of imposing one's will on the consumer. Consumers would never have conceived of a fragrance called Charlie or, more recently, a mobile phone network called Orange. Indeed, the culture of branding when Charlie was first launched was one where most new fragrances carried feminine, elegant, French names and consumers at that time would have specified that any new brand must meet these parameters. Yet Charlie struck a chord with consumers around the world which was attractive and unique. The brand embodied a set of values and attributes which were appropriate, which stimulated consumer interest, which distinguished the brand from others and created a unique piece of property for its owners. Charlie, then, might be seen as a 'power brand', a uniquely successful blending together of qualities and attributes both tangible and intangible. The brand offers a unique set of values and attributes which are appealing and which people are prepared to purchase. Furthermore, there is no doubt that Charlie represents for Revlon a valuable asset which has enduring and international appeal.

■ Power Brands

Power brands are those brands which are particularly well adapted to the environment and which thus survive and flourish. They are the ultimate examples of an organisation's marketing skills – their finest and most valuable productions. Power brands can be either goods or services, can act as corporate names as well as product brand names and can be very specific products or ranges of related products. What they have in common is that they all embrace products which are well priced and offer good and consistent quality to consumers. Hence the brand, in a sense, acts as a credible guarantee for that product or service, allowing the consumer clearly to identify and specify products which genuinely offer added value.

The term marketing mix is frequently used to describe the process of developing a new brand and it is apt. Essentially, a provider or service assembles a series of attributes and blends these together in a unique way. It is a little like cooking – part of the skill is in the selection of the elements in the mix, part in the blending and cooking and part in the presentation. A good cook produces good and consistent results which are constantly in demand.

The ingredients in a brand constitute the product itself, the packaging, the brand name, the promotion, the advertising and the overall presentation. The brand is therefore a synthesis of all the elements, physical, aesthetic, rational and emotional. The end result must be not only appropriate but differentiated from the brands of competitors – the consumer has to have a reason to choose one brand over all others.

Branding consists, then, of the development and maintenance of sets of product attributes and values which are coherent, appropriate, distinctive, protectable and appealing to consumers. Marketing is a broader function which includes branding and concerns the development and implementation of strategies for moving products or services from the producer to the consumer in a profitable fashion. Advertising is a narrower function within marketing, which is concerned with the use of media to inform consumers that products or services, branded or otherwise, are available for them to purchase and to stimulate them to do so.

■ The Importance of Brands

Companies which invent new brands are able generally to defend them from blatant copying in a variety of ways, though not normally from broad imitation. If a brand is a good one then consumers will purchase it and it becomes a valuable asset. But its asset value derives from more than just its ability to attract sales. The very fact that consumers perceive a brand as embracing a set of values which they can specify means that they will reject, or tend to reject, alternatives which are presented to them that perhaps may not possess all these values. Brands are therefore enduring assets as long as they are kept in good shape and continue to offer consumers the values they require.

In practice producers of goods or services generally do not interact directly with their consumers. Kodak films are normally sold through chemists or kiosks or mail order; Formica laminates are sold by hardware stores or as components in fitted kitchens; British Airways airline tickets are retailed through travel agents. Thus the producer, the brand owner, constantly faces the possibility that, at point of sale, his efforts to develop branded products which attract strong consumer interest will come to nothing. If Heinz Baked Beans are unavailable or a penny or two more expensive than Safeway's own-brand baked beans then the own-brand product may suffice; if British Airways Club Class is fully booked then the traveller will readily settle for Virgin Upper Class; if

Ford's Mondeo is on six weeks delivery and the equivalent Vauxhall is available from stock then the Vauxhall may do just as well. Few brands are so powerful as to protect the brand owner against the persuasiveness of a substantially lower price or a much better delivery. For this reason the marketing function is normally concerned with ensuring that a company's brands are not handicapped by such factors.

But what the successful brand does is tip the balance slightly in favour of the producer or at least ensure that the balance does not rest entirely with the retailer. H.G. Wells described this process as 'reaching over the shoulder of the retailer straight to the consumer'. The brand allows the brand owner to prevent his product simply becoming a commodity which is bought by an intermediary, mainly a major retailing or distribution chain, simply on the basis of the market forces operating at a particular time.

But brands do more than just protect the producer from the depredations of the retailer – in a very real sense they add value to products.

Consumers know that it is vaguely absurd to bottle carbonated water in France and ship it across the world, yet millions of bottles of such water are drunk each year in America, Australia, Hong Kong and elsewhere. We realise too that paying £30 000 or £40 000 for an imported BMW car is a little irrational when a perfectly adequate domestic model can be purchased for one-third of the price. Yet Perrier and BMW are enormously successful. So the added and apparently intangible values afforded by the brand can in practice become very tangible indeed, such that the financial brand value can be accurately measured.

■ Maintaining Brand Values

Brand owners must constantly ensure that the qualities and values of their brands are maintained. They must continue to appeal to the consumer and should be developed in order to maintain their attractiveness in a changing society. In other words, brands can seldom, except in the short term, shield brand owners from their own failure to maintain quality, from their failure to keep their brands in good repair or even from their own rapacity or stupidity.

In the 1960s the British brewing industry, in an attempt to streamline and modernise its activities, made a concerted attempt to change the formulation and presentation of existing branded beers, arguably for the worse. Public outrage was slow to develop but develop it did. Loyalty to many of the leading brands fell considerably and the brewing industry was forced to reverse its policies.

This relative slowness of consumers to desert established brands was demonstrated too in the 1970s when the product quality and reliability at Jaguar Cars plummeted. Sales followed the product quality spiral downwards, but when a new management restored quality, loyalty to the brand returned.

Brands are therefore fairly robust and capable of surviving in adversity. But consumers are not fools and will not maintain their support for a brand once it ceases to keep its side of the bargain.

■ Brand Extension

One of the most difficult decisions facing the owners of existing brands is that of 'extend or not?' On the one hand, the brand owner foresees the possibility of endowing a new product with some or all the qualities of an existing brand. He or she can thus enter a market more cheaply, establish the new product more quickly and increase the overall support and exposure of the brand. Indeed, it has been estimated that while around 16 000 new products are launched in the US every year, 95 per cent of them are launched as extensions of existing brands. On the other hand, the brand owner faces the possibility that by extending the brand to cover a new product all he is really doing is diluting the appeal of his existing brand.

In Britain, Cadbury's, over the years, increasingly extended the Cadbury name to embrace not only chocolate and confectionery products but such mainstream food products as mashed potatoes, dried milk, soups and beverages. Over time the brand management realised that in using the Cadbury name as an endorsement of quality, origin and value on non-chocolate products they were diluting its reputation for excellence and its power in the chocolate area. The development of a new brand for mainstream food products would have taken greater effort and investment to establish in the marketplace, but it would have preserved the integrity of the existing brand – a greater risk in one sense and a far lower risk in another. Furthermore, by developing portfolios of power brands, as opposed to extending a single brand, more ready divestment is possible of activities which have become inappropriate. Also, in situations such as the contamination of Tylenol (Tylenol capsules had been poisoned and were subsequently taken off the market and repackaged in tamper-evident packaging), it ensures that potential damage is contained and does not extend to a wide number of products.

Illustration 1.1   Cadbury

Over time Cadbury's management realised that extending the brand to endorse quality, origin and value on non-chocolate products jeopardised its integrity and reputation for excellence and therefore its power in the chocolate area.

Brand extension has of course proved in many cases to be a remarkably successful strategy – it has reduced the risk and cost of new product entries, increased the exposure of brands and made brands more attractive and contemporary to consumers. Chanel, for example, has introduced ranges of male fragrances under what was exclusively a feminine brand without the slightest dilution of the existing brand, and with the new product ranges assuming all the desired attributes of the original. Certain brands – for example, Virgin – have successfully and profitably applied their name to products completely outside their mainstream business – in Virgin's case extending from music into airlines, vodka, cola, financial services and jeans. It is apparent, therefore, that brand extension is entirely practical but needs to be treated with considerable care and skill.

What then are the factors which should govern our decisions in this area? A wide number of techniques exist for producing brand inventories, for market testing and mapping and for concept development. Ultimately, a brand owner has to take a long, hard look at the brand and say, 'What is it?', 'What could it reasonably become?' 'What do I want it to become?'

What does the Lea & Perrins brand represent? An ability to enhance foods? Sauces in general? Excellence in savoury sauces? Traditional food values? Olde England? Cocktail mixers? Could the Lea & Perrins brand be extended to embrace other savoury sauces? Possibly. To embrace dessert sauces? Probably not. (Lea & Perrins strawberry-flavoured ice cream topping? Ugh!) To embrace certain foods? Possibly (for example Lea and Perrins traditional steak and kidney pie).

What does the Marlboro brand represent? Excellence in cigarettes? Style and sophistication? The modern male? Could we envisage a range of Marlboro smoker's requisites? Yes – in fact these are already on sale. Marlboro cheroots? Just possibly, but unlikely. Marlboro sports clothing? Yes – it is already on sale. Marlboro light scotch? Possibly. Marlboro stout? Probably not. Marlboro cocktail snacks? Possibly yes. Marlboro doughnuts? Probably no.

Which, of course, all seems perfectly logical and sensible. Yet a leading savoury sauce manufacturer *did* introduce under its name a range of ice cream toppings – it was a disaster. Rolls-Royce *did* supply car engines to a manufacturer of limousines selling at one-third of the Rolls-Royce price and allowed their brand name to be used in the promotion of these cut-price limos. So the moral in brand extension is to act with great caution and remember that it may not be extension at all – simply dilution. But if you decide to go ahead, look at your brand very carefully. Consider the qualities of real value to the consumer – and these may not be immediately obvious. Look too at opportunities outside your normal sphere of activities – a cigarette manufacturer does not need to manufacture clothing to derive an attractive income from activities in the clothing area. Indeed, increasingly power brands derive their strength not from product features but from values and beliefs – Virgin is able to extend into completely different product areas because it stands for cocking a snook at authority and challenging the *status quo*.

■ Own Label

Producers of branded goods and retailers necessarily live together in a state of mild mutual tension. The manufacturer needs the retailer in order to market his brands yet wants to control margins, selling prices, volumes, how far his brand is discounted, where it is displayed, how it is displayed, the breadth of the range stocked and so on; the retailer, on the other hand, wants to be able to shop the market for the product he sells, determine his own selling prices, arrange his own store layout and be free, when it suits him, of pressures from the brand owner.

The brand owner, therefore, frequently feels that the retailer is destroying his brands and failing to appreciate their inherent values. The retailer often accuses the brand owner of failing to support his brands, of overvaluing them and of other similar misdemeanours.

But in the end the brand owner and the retailer generally need each other and usually compromise. But not always. One option open to the retailer is to develop his own brands and this most retailers do. Such own brands, besides offering benefits to the consumer, serve as a sort of warning to the brand owner by the retailer that perhaps he is not essential. Also, because the manufacture of own-brand products is often undertaken by companies with spare manufacturing capacity on a marginal or quasi-marginal basis, they are frequently cheaper and can be used by retailers to attract customers and to establish price points in their negotiations with brand owners.

Thus conventional own brands are the tactical weapons of the retailer. In so far as such brands embrace common sets of product attributes, even if they are no-name brands in white boxes, they are every bit as much brands as those produced by manufacturers. The original, price-fighting, white-label brands of the retailers have given way in markets such as the UK to high-quality, value-for-money product ranges which are endorsed by the values of the parent retailer brand.

In Britain, for example, the corporate name Marks & Spencer and the product brand St Michael have come to represent excellence, quality and value across a very wide range of clothing products, household textiles, foodstuffs, toys and so on. Marks & Spencer sell only own-brand merchandise. They specify what they require, conduct their own market testing (normally simply by putting products onto the shelf in a few stores to see if they sell) and exercise tight quality control. The intangible brand values of Marks & Spencer – which we might see as quality, value for money, reliability, accessibility and approachability – allow the brand to extend into new and different product areas, their most recent attempt being financial services. Other retailers, such as Tesco and Sainsbury, have also announced plans to extend into consumer banking, hoping to build on their strong relationship with the consumer.

Perhaps the ultimate example of the appeal of own brands is the Harrods brand. Harrods have allowed cigarette and other manufacturers to produce goods under their name for sale through other retail outlets. Thus the own brand has come full circle and become a manufacturer brand, albeit on a licensed basis.

It is important then when considering own brands to see them not as an alternative to branding but rather as a different way of using branding, in this case by retailers.

■ The Lifecycle of a Brand

In practical terms most brands need have no lifecycle at all. Such major world power brands as Kodak, Coca-Cola, Gillette, Schweppes and IBM have been with us for generations and are all still thriving and enormously successful. Indeed, it is the potentiality of such long life which makes new brand development so exciting and important, and existing successful brands so valuable.

But like anything else, brands survive only if they are looked after. If Kodak had stopped product development and innovation with the Box Brownie, the Kodak brand would have been of interest only to historians; if Coca-Cola had a generic name like sarsaparilla or soda rather than a proprietary trade mark then it too would not be in such powerful use today.

The potentially indefinite life of a brand is recognised in law. Whereas patents have a finite life of, generally, fifteen to twenty years and then expire (indeed, once a product is patented it may take many years to get to market, so the practical market life of a patent may be only a few years), registered trade marks, if properly maintained and renewed, can go on indefinitely.

■ International Branding

Another important characteristic of most major brands is that they are international in scope – McDonald's is as likely to appeal in Brazil as in Hong Kong. The developed countries, whose inhabitants are the major consumers of branded goods, have shown in this century an enormous coming together of consumer tastes and expectations. Regional and local tastes, attitudes and preferences remain and these must be taken into consideration. Nevertheless, brands successful in one market are increasingly likely to have appeal to consumers on an international basis.

The reasons for this are many and include improved communications, increased travel and greater language tuition in schools (particularly of English). The most important reason, however, is that wherever we live, whatever our colour and whatever our culture we are all very much the same. Coca-Cola tastes as good to a teenager in Kowloon as to one in Chippewa Falls, Wisconsin. A couple in Tokyo take as much pleasure in looking at their Kodak wedding photographs as a couple in Nairobi. Wherever we live and whatever our background we will respond to well-produced, attractive branded products.

The possibility of developing new international brands rather than simply national brands is an appealing one to brand owners. International brands are reassuring to consumers, take advantage of the enormous and growing promotional overlap between countries brought about by travel, sports sponsorship, satellite TV, and so on. They also give brand owners substantial economies in such areas as production, inventory and promotion.

Most importantly, international brands provide companies with a coherence to their international activities. International companies which permit, or are forced to accept, a proliferation of local brands often find a fragmentation of their activities. In theory each of these brands should be more ideally adapted to particular local conditions; in practice the appeal, coherence and power of competitive international brands makes it difficult for the local brands to compete.

■ Developing New Brands

Perhaps the most appropriate and successful approach to the development of new brands is the pragmatic one – try to identify new brands with some measure of distinctiveness and consumer appeal, which are not simply me-too products, use appropriate research techniques to measure the brand's likely market success, recognise that branding does have a strong creative element and encourage creativity and flair. But recognise too that successful new brands, due to their very intangibility, can never be guaranteed to be successes. The chances of success can however be significantly increased.

Successful brands, whether they are national or international, offer consumers something of value which is different from that offered by competitive brands, and which they are prepared to purchase. Once satisfied they will continue to purchase until their needs change, the brand changes or they are offered a product which better suits their requirements.

What are the implications of this? Surely that in developing new brands one should seek those which are meaningfully differentiated from competitive products, which afford consumers a reason to change, will continue to meet their requirements on an ongoing basis and which are difficult to imitate? First Direct, for instance, launched 'banking without branches' in the UK, initially providing a very strong point of differentiation for the new brand against existing high street banks. However, First Direct was not difficult to imitate, and over the course of the next couple of years all the competing high street banks brought out telephone banking services.

first direct

Illustration 1.2   First Direct

First Direct launched 'banking without branches' in the UK, initially providing a very strong point of differentiation against existing high street banks. All the high street banks now have telephone banking services.

In practice, most branding is concerned with products which are relatively undifferentiated in terms of product specification or performance and where consumers are relatively satisfied with existing brands. It would seem logical that, under these circumstances, manufacturers would seek out those components of the brand which are susceptible to innovation and look to create meaningful differences there.

It is estimated that seventeen out of twenty new brands fail. The reasons for failure can sometimes be attributed to product problems, at other times to distribution problems, to changes in legislation, to bad luck or to bad management. Most commonly, however, the reason for failure is simply that the new brands do not offer the consumer anything of interest that he or she does not have already – they are not differentiated meaningfully from existing products. Most new brands are simply approximate facsimiles of those in existence – they are as close as they can be to existing brands within the constraints imposed by trade mark law, passing off, copyright and corporate pride.

Why is it that organisations constantly launch new brands which are banal and imitative, which are initially supported by heavy advertising, coupons, give-aways and sweepstakes but which once such support is removed, disappear into obscurity? The reason is partly that research tends to push in this direction. After all, when seeking the views and opinions of consumers these tend to be formed by their current terms of reference. The manufacturer is advised that if he wants a successful new brand it should possess the qualities of the existing market leader.

Another factor is simple risk-avoidance. By imitating an existing brand or brands the new brand can be shown as being not too far wrong, even if it proves a failure! Lack of imagination also plays a part. Brand owners as well as consumers are subject to the influences of the existing brand culture and find it difficult to think beyond that culture. Equally important, however, is a genuine wish on the part of manufacturers to imitate directly successful competitive brands. Today's consumer markets are tough and rugged. Competition is fierce. The urge to tackle the competition head-on in their territory is a real one even if it might be more sensible to avoid a set-piece battle and take on the opponents on one's own ground to develop completely new weapons or even to revert to guerrilla tactics.

Some brand owners, however, deliberately set themselves up to appeal to the myopic shopper, the shopper who recognises products by generalised shape or colour (in Britain all bottles of tonic have yellow labels, soda black-and-white labels, ginger ale brown and green labels, and so on). Perhaps the major exponents of this art are the retailers.

Producers of such me-too brands may argue that they are merely following the category code; if everyone knows that frosted cornflakes come in a blue box (why? because that's the colour that Kellogg's makes them) then it is providing greater customer value by making all competing packs blue, too, so that the correct type of product can be purchased. Though such own branding by retailers at times barely stops short of passing off, the natural reluctance of manufacturers to face up to their major customers, the retailers, on this matter has led to such practices becoming at times virtually standard. Recently in the UK steps have been taken to try to end the more blatant examples of pack imitations by the creation of a voluntary code of practice by the Institute of Grocery Distribution. Some would argue that this does not go far enough, however, and that packaging, like brand names, requires greater protection in law.

But the remedy to dull, imitative me-too brands is not generally extreme novelty and world innovation. Indeed, opportunities seldom exist to do this even if one wishes to. Rather, anyone developing a new brand must look at the components of the brand and its totality, and ask 'Why should anyone buy this?' 'What am I offering which existing products don't?' If credible answers cannot be found to these questions then the brand is unlikely to succeed.

The corollary of this is that when you have a new product with a more than average measure of innovation be sure not to conceal its novelty by developing a brand personality similar to other, less innovative products. Furthermore, and despite the established wisdom, consumers do not in fact work hard to track down better mousetraps.

It is also inappropriate when branding an innovative product to develop a brand personality which is easy for competition to copy. The innovator simply takes all the risks of innovation and, once successful, is swamped by a mass of similar brands. Yet this too happens frequently – a descriptive and unprotectable brand name is used or a conventional packaging style adopted which encourages ready imitation.

Innovative, differentiated brands can also have a further potent advantage. Not only can they offer the consumer real benefits and thus give the consumer a reason to change from an existing brand; they can also serve to outmode existing brands. The new one not only offers the consumer a new set of values, it wrong-foots the opposition and shows it up as being unexciting and staid. In the 1950s in Britain the culture of car branding was largely 'British' in style – cars had names like Westminster, Prefect, Herald, and Oxford. Ford then introduced the Cortina. The post-war boom was getting under way, consumers were starting to take organised Mediterranean holidays and Britain's earlier insularity was beginning to dissolve. Cortina hit the mood of the moment. It was fresh, exciting, different and a little foreign and sophisticated. Not only did the brand name assist in positioning the new car in an interesting and fresh fashion, it also wrong-footed competitive products and made them look somewhat dull and old-fashioned.

■ **Conclusion**

Branding is a creative process. It uses research techniques and the skills of a number of specialists. But in the end it is about creating distinctiveness – in a consumer-relevant fashion. Unfortunately, most branding seems to be concerned not with distinctiveness but with sameness, with camouflaging the brand so that it melds in among all the other brands on the market. To be distinctive, to refuse to follow the herd takes courage – and it can be highly rewarded.

CHAPTER 2

History of Branding

Adrian Room
The Names Society

■ Beginnings

Branding began many centuries before the term acquired its modern usage. The Greeks and Romans and others before them had various ways of promoting wares or goods, whether they were wines or pots, metals or ointments. Messages would be written informing the public that this man, at this address, could make shoes and that the man who lived over there, at that address, was a scribe. The Greeks also used town criers to announce the arrival of ships with particular cargoes.

Much early advertising and marketing (in the literal sense) was thus done on a personal basis, with the name of a particular individual as important as that of his product or service. The modern development of this can be seen in the name of the private shopkeeper over his shop, and some of the best known chain store names have originated as that over a single establishment.

In the earliest days shops, as distinct from individuals, were quick to sell their wares by using pictures. In Rome, for example, a butcher's shop would display a sign depicting a row of hams (Figure 2.1), a shoemaker one of a boot, a dairy a crude sketch of a cow.

Figure 2.1 A Roman sign found at Pompeii

Hog in Armour   *King's Porter and Dwarf*   *Barley Mow*   *The Ape*

Three Squirrels   *Bull and Mouth*   *Man in the Moon*   *Hole in the Wall*
"A Guide for Malt Worms"

Goose and Gridiron   *Harrow and Doublet*

Figure 2.2   Seventeenth-century English inn signs

Such pictorial promotion was a forerunner of the many inn and pub signs with which we in Britain are familiar today (Figure 2.2). In classical times most potential purchasers of most products were illiterate and would be able to identify a particular product only from a picture. Again, in our own time the use of pictorial advertising is exploited in many ingenious ways to accompany a brand name and draw the attention of the public to it. A more sophisticated and literate age has led, too, to the use of visual puns to suggest the brand name concerned: the lance on the Lancia logo, the shell to match Shell, the bird's eye in the Birds Eye logo and the nest and nestlings that illustrate the Nestlé products.

■ **The Growth of Branding**

Modern branding and the use of individual brand names has its origin in the nineteenth century. The Industrial Revolution and the consequent development of advertising and marketing techniques made the selection of a good brand name of great importance. In both America and Europe the rapid increase in population, expansion of the railways and construction of new factories brought with them a keen public demand for a whole range of newly available products, from domestic goods such as home medicines to electrical and mechanical devices. In fact, the greater the quantity and variety of products, the greater became the demand for them, and this resulted in the need for manufacturers and marketers to choose a brand name that would be effective in as many ways as possible: memorable, pronounceable, original and, in many instances, directly or indirectly descriptive of the product it denoted. Later, of course, trade mark laws were to clarify and impose restrictions on the sorts of names that could be protected – legal protection was not given equally to all types of brand names.

The following list of American leaders in national advertising in the 1890s shows the range and variety of actual brand names that were already beginning to emerge (some of them still well known today) and enables some clear categories to be distinguished.

Leaders in American Advertising in the 1890s

Adams Tutti Frutti Gum
Aeolian Company
American Express Traveller's Cheques
Armour Beef Extract
Autoharp

Baker's Cocoa
Battle Ax Plug Tobacco
Beardsley's Shredded Codfish
Beeman's Pepsin Gum
Bent's Crown Piano
Burlington Railroad
Burnett's Extracts

California Fig Syrup
Caligraph Typewriter
Castoria
Chicago Great Western
Chicago, Milwaukee & St Paul Railroad
Chocolat-Menier
Columbia Bicycles
Cook's Tours
Cottolene Shortening
Crown Pianos
Cuticura Soap

De Long Hook and Eye
Diamond Dyes
Dixon's Graphite Paint
Dixon's Pencils

Edison Phonograph
Epp's Cocoa
Estey Organ

Fall River Line
Felt & Tarrant Comptometer
Ferry's Seeds
Fisher Piano
Fowler Bicycles
Franco American Soup

Garland Stoves
Gold Dust Washing Powder
Gorham's Silver
Gramophone
Great Northern Railroad

Hamburg American Line
Hammond Typewriter
Hartford Bicycle
Hartshorn's Shade Rollers
Heinz's Baked Beans
Hires' Root Beer
Hoffman House Cigars
Huyler's Chocolates

Ingersoll Watches
Ives & Pond Piano
Ivory Soap

Jaeger Underwear

Kirk's American Family Soap
Kodak

Liebig's Extract of Beef
Lipton's Teas
Lowney's Chocolates
Lundborg's Perfumes

Mason & Hamlin Piano
Mellin's Food
Mennen's Talcum Powder
Michigan Central Railroad
Monarch Bicycles
Munsing Underwear
Murphy Varnish Company
New England Mincemeat
New York Central Railroad
North German Lloyd

Old Dominion Line
Oneita Knitted Goods

Packer's Tar Soap
Pearline Soap Powder
Pearltop Lamp Chimneys
Pears' Soap
Pettijohn's Breakfast Food
Pittsburgh Stogies
Pond's Extract
Postum Cereal
Prudential Insurance Co.

Quaker Oats

Rambler Bicycles
Redfern Corsets
Regal Shoes
Remington Typewriter
Rising Sun Stove Polish
Rogers 1847 Silverware
Royal Baking Powder

Santa Fe Railroad
Sapolio
Scott's Emulsion
Sears, Roebuck & Co

Sen Sen For The Breath
Shredded Wheat
Smith Premier Typewriter
Sorosis Shoes
Southern Railway
Sozodont Dentifrice
Spalding Bicycles
Spencerian Pens
Standard Mfg Co. Bathrubs
Steinway Piano
Sterling Bicycles
Studebaker Carriages
Sunlight Soap

Uneeda Biscuit
Union Pacific Railroad

Van Camp's Pork & Beans
Van Houten's Cocoa
Vaughan's Seeds
Vichy Celestins
Victor Bicycles
Vin Mariani
Vose Piano

Walthan Watches
Warner's Corsets
Warwich Cycles
Waterbury Watches
Waterman Fountain Pen
Waverley Bicycles
Weber Piano
White Label Soups
Whitman's Chocolates
Williams Shaving Soap
Winchester Arms
Woodbury's Facial Soap
Wool Soap

Among the above are the following:

- Names based on a *personal name*, whether that of the investor, patentee, shopkeeper or some other person associated with the product, for example Baker's Cocoa, Cook's Tours, Edison Phonograph, Hammond Typewriter, Pond's Extract, Postum Cereal (after Charles William Post who developed it) and Jaeger Underwear.
- Names based on a *place name*, often that of the original place where the product was invented, sold or developed, for example Columbia Bicycles, New England Mincemeat, Pittsburgh Stogies (a type of stout shoe).
- *Invented scientific* names (Figure 2.3), usually based on Latin or Greek (or even both), for example Caligraph Typewriter ('beautiful writing'), Cuticura Soap ('skin care'), Gramophone (see below), Sozodont Dentifrice ('tooth saver').

Figure 2.3   First telephone advertisement

- *'Status'* names derived from fine-sounding English words, for example Crown Pianos, Diamond Dyes, Gold Dust, Monarch Bicycles, Regal Shoes, Victor Bicycles, Camp Coffee (Figure 2.4).

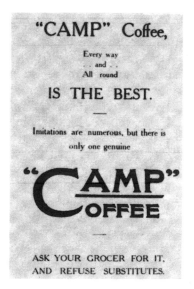

Figure 2.4   Early promotion of Camp Coffee

- *'Good association'* names, often ones that have a true or purported story of origin, for example Ivory Soap, Quaker Oats, Sunlight Soap, White Label Soups. (All the associations here are of purity and wholesomeness.)
- *Artificial* names that may or may not resemble real words, for example Kodak (see below), Uneeda Biscuit (slogan: 'Do You Know Uneeda Biscuit?').
- *Descriptive* names, for example Rambler Bicycle, Shredded Wheat (later to be the subject of legal debate as a trade mark).

Some of the names in the selection here would today not be acceptable for registration as trade marks under present trade mark laws but the distinctive categories for brand name creation had clearly already been established, and many more recent names can be readily assigned to one of the classes outlined (for example Birds Eye to Category 1, Bostik to 2 (Boston), Linguaphone to 3, and so on).

Mention has already been made of the use of pictorial advertising to accompany and support a brand name. The degree to which it does so may vary from the direct to the allusive. Many car marque logos were to be similarly indirect and the visual pun or reference not so obvious as in the case of Lancia (Figure 2.5). The Rover logo (Figure 2.6), for example showed a Viking ship and head (the Vikings were 'sea rovers') and the Volkswagen sported a device that was an oblique reference to its place of manufacture, the town of Wolfsburg (Figure 2.7). The exploitation of a brand name's potential can be extended in other directions, too, such as the famous 'Sch . . . you know who' advertisement and the wide use of apt slogans to suggest a brand name.

■ The Development of Leading Brands

The need to select a brand name that could be as effective internationally as nationally was a factor appreciated early on by companies, and it is interesting to examine the ways in which some of the most famous names originated and to see to what extent they have actually become effective in the many different languages of the world.

Two well-known brand names that were created within a year or two of each other (both in the United States) are Coca-Cola (Figure 2.8) and Kodak. The first of these is a meaningful name (descriptive, as in category 7 above), while the other has no meaning (so is in category 6).

The name Coca-Cola is based on two of the product's original constituents – extracts from *coca* leaves and from the *cola* nut. That coca leaves also yield cocaine was a factor that did not then, in the 1880s, concern the manufacturers and indeed originally the drink did actually contain minute quantities of the drug. In the early days it was marketed as an 'Esteemed Brain Tonic and Intellectual Beverage'! Sales of the drink grew so rapidly that its

Figure 2.5   The punning 'lance' logo of Lancia

Figure 2.6   The 'Viking' Rover logo

Figure 2.7   The post-war Volkswagen logo

Figure 2.8   The first Coca-Cola advertisement

name was soon popularly shortened to Coke. Although this was in effect a further reminder of the original cocaine connection, the manufacturers were keen to stake their legal claim to this version of the name, particularly as other companies were now marketing their own versions of the drink under similar names. After a rather complex legal tussle the company succeeded in its claim, but not until 1920 when the familiar version of the name had been current for several years. The product is today unique in having two equally well-known brand names, one chiefly used for the international market (Coca-Cola) and the other one mainly adopted by English-speaking consumers (Coke). Both names are, however, of identical legal status in most countries. Even so, the fact that there are now many types of cola drink on the market (the word 'cola' is not a proprietary name) constantly prompts the company to remind the public of the interconnection between the two names. Hence the clever slogan of the mid-1980s – 'Coca-Cola is Coke, Coke is Coca-Cola'.

The name has turned out to be an excellent one for the international market. It is certainly memorable, easy to pronounce and write in different languages (even in non-Roman scripts), and has the incisive 'k' sound that is often chosen for effective international use. It also so happens that the elements comprising the name are internationally comprehensible, since 'coca' and 'cola' are native words and have been adopted by most major languages in an unaltered form.

Kodak is a similarly successful name worldwide and also has the two effective 'k's. However, unlike Coca-Cola, it is meaningless, but we are fortunate enough to have on record the account of the man who created it, explaining how he arrived at the final form. This gives an important insight into the thinking behind an 'artificial' name, and one that is historic of branding standards.

The creator of the name was the photographic pioneer George Eastman, who registered it on 4 September 1888. His account of the creation is as follows:

> I knew a trade name must be short, vigorous, incapable of being misspelled to an extent that will destroy its identity and, in order to satisfy trade mark laws, it must mean nothing. The letter K had been a favourite with me – it seemed a strong, incisive sort of letter. Therefore, the word I wanted had to start with K. Then it became a question of trying out a great number of combinations of letters that made words starting and ending with K. The word Kodak is the result, (Kochan, 1991, p. 89).

The name became so popular that, like Coca-Cola, it nearly became a generic word for 'camera' in some countries, and countermeasures had to be taken to prevent this. The generic adoption of a trade name is, of course, not simply a tribute to its success but also a peril inherent in its popularity.

These two names, Coca-Cola and Kodak, were thus established at an early stage worldwide in their originally created form and have retained their prominence today. There can hardly be a single person in any country who has not heard of one or both of these names.

Sometimes, for legal or other reasons, a brand name will appear in different forms, and sometimes the same product is marketed in different countries under entirely different names. A case in point is that of Esso. The name originated from the initials (SO) of the Standard Oil Company of New Jersey which was set up as the chief company of Rockefeller's Oil Trust in 1888. When the Trust split up, however, Standard Oil was obliged to look for another name in those American states where newly formed companies were trading as a result of the dissolution of the Trust. Finally Esso decided it wished to revert to the use of a single brand name and, after extensive tests and surveys Exxon was found to be the most easily recognised and protectable name – its distinctive double 'x' makes it memorable and easy to write. The name also, of course, hints at the Esso of the original.

■ The Death of a Brand

An interesting example of a brand name that has changed several times, finally losing its legal status as a proprietary name in Britain and some other countries, is Gramophone – an 'invented scientific' name. The first Gramophone was patented by Emile Berliner in Washington, DC, on 8 November 1887. Berliner chose the name to differentiate his instrument from its predecessors (his machine used discs and earlier machines had used a cylinder). He devised the name by reversing the two elements of Phonogram, an instrument which itself had a name based on Phonograph ('sound writing'). This last name (historically the first) later became generic in America as Gramophone did in Britain. One company setting up to manufacture the instrument in the United States devised a further name based on it, Gramophone, for its own models. Meanwhile, in Britain the Gramophone Company was established. Yet another version of the instrument emerged in America as the Victrola (originally the Victor). This profusion of related names and instruments led to Gramophone or Phonograph (or a similar spelling to suit national languages) being adopted as the generic name for the machine in many countries. In Russia, however, the initial name of Grammofon (borrowed from the German Grammophon) was superseded by Patefon when a new model of the instrument with a permanent sapphire needle was introduced in the early twentieth century. This came from the surname of the French inventor, Emile Pathé, brother of Charles Pathé who founded the famous film company.

■ Some Well-Known Brands

The names of man-made fibres comprise a special category of brand names since the word nylon, on which many of them are based, is not a proprietary name. It was devised by the Du Pont company in 1938 as a generic name and was itself based on the earlier name rayon. This is also a generic name and was devised by the National Retail Drygoods Association in 1924 from the word ray. Various other names based on the word nylon, most of which are registered trade marks, have been adopted in other countries – for example Crepon in France and Dederon in East Germany.

It is significant that many brand names that have come to be known worldwide are either scientific in origin or easily memorable in different languages. Among the scientific names containing classical elements are Aspirin (now generic in Britain and some other countries), based on the German equivalent of '*acetylated spiraeic acid*', Cellophane (generic in the United States but still a registered trade mark elsewhere), Frigidaire, Klaxon (based on the Greek word meaning 'I will make a loud noise'), Linguaphone, Thermos (generic in the United States since 1963 but still a keenly protected registered trade mark elsewhere) and Vaseline, based on the German for water and the Greek for oil. Among short, memorable international brand names are Berec (the initials of British Ever Ready Electrical Company), BiC (pioneered by the Frenchman Marcel Bich), Biro (invented by the Hungarian László Biró), Decca (of uncertain origin, but said by some to represent musical notes), Jeep (believed to be from a cartoon character who made the sound 'jeep', but later associated with the initials of 'general purpose') and Xerox (based ultimately on the Greek word for 'dry'). These names are internationally known because the products themselves have been successfully marketed in different countries.

The most obvious examples of truly international names, however, are those of cars, which are exported worldwide and, even more, those of airlines, which are international in the literal sense of the word. Some, understandably, have developed as abbreviations of acronyms of the original name, so that today worldwide recognition has been gained by such names as Qantas (Queensland and Northern Territory Aerial Service, founded in 1920), and Sabena (Société Anonyme Belge d'Exploitation de la Navigation Aérienne, set up in 1923).

■ The Uniqueness of Brand Names

What makes all such well-known brand names interesting is that unlike most other words in the language they have been deliberately created, even when based on existing names. They did not develop naturally as personal names and place names have done. Moreover, although very familiar to most people, they are relatively young. Personal and place names often date back hundreds of years. Brand names, on the other hand, started to develop little more than a century ago and many of them have been in existence for a much shorter time than that. Meanwhile, the creation of new brand names continues, and although methods of devising and selecting them are infinitely more sophisticated today than at any previous time, the basic principles and categories established in the nineteenth century still hold good.

■ Further Reading

Oren Arnold, *What's in a Name: Famous Brand Names* (New York: Julian Messner, 1979).

Henry Button and Andrew Lampert, *The Guinness Book of the Business World* (Enfield: Guinness Superlatives, 1976).

Otto Klepner, *Advertising Procedure*, 8th edn (Englewood Cliffs, NJ: Prentice-Hall, 1983).

Kochan (ed.), *The World's Greatest Brands* (Macmillan, 1996).

Milton Moskowitz, Michael Katz and Robert Levering (eds), *Everybody's Business: An Almanac* (San Francisco: Harper & Row, 1980).

Tim Nicholson, *Car Badges of the World* (London: Cassell, 1970).

Frank Presbury, *The History and Development of Advertising* (New York: Doubleday, Doran & Co, 1929).

Adrian Room, *Dictionary of Trade Name Origins*, rev. edn (London: Routledge & Kegan Paul, 1983).

Marjorie Stiling, *Famous Brand Names, Emblems and Trade-Marks* (Newton Abbot: David & Charles, 1980).

UK Trade Names, 8th edn (East Grinstead: Kompass Publishers, 1984).

CHAPTER 3

New Brand Development

Pamela Robertson
Interbrand

Any successful business is generally good at new brand development; it is part of the life blood of the organisation and failures are regarded as an opportunity to learn. Many a big business that exists today has been founded on an innovative idea and has continued to thrive through having further good ideas.

Any commentary on new brand development will talk about the risks and high failure rates. The reality is that good ideas fail rarely, although they may stumble a bit at the outset as the innovators learn and modify the product or aspects of the marketing mix in order to realise opportunities.

This chapter is not intended to teach the reader how to develop new brands, but to show how new brand development is important to organisations generally and to provide guidelines for it. It takes a broad look at the development of new products both as extensions to existing brands and as new brands in their own right. In the next few pages we cover aspects such as why businesses need to develop new products at all, the risks involved, what makes success, the need for differentiation, and the NPD process.

■ Why Develop New Products at All?

With so many products available it is tempting to ask why there is a need for more. Part of the answer is to do with lack of differentiation, which means that there can often be a lot to choose from, but very little choice; more of that later.

There are however very important reasons for developing new products. In the market economy within which we live and work, for both the country and companies to grow and prosper we need new products to fuel growth, as many of the products currently available are in mature markets or growth stages.

In order to develop new products companies need to increase their financial investment in their business. This money often comes from existing or new shareholders. Shareholders tend to invest in companies that achieve higher than average growth as they obtain a better return. They will therefore look for companies with a good track record in developing new products.

A high level of successful new product development can also help a business to attract executives of the best quality. Such success usually means that the organisation is dynamic and growing, and this provides the setting within which the individual can develop.

Not only management and executive staff are attracted by an organisation that is growing and developing. New product development often motivates and energises staff, providing it is carried out in an appropriate way that involves them and takes into account the impact that it may have on their working life. Having new things to work on makes most jobs more interesting, but just having more to work on pleases nobody.

Competition is also likely to make it impossible for a company to stand still. However, rather than an organisation reacting to competitive activity, it is better for it to set the pace by developing new products and services ahead of its competitors, thus putting them on the back foot.

Nowadays many people expect products or services to improve, or they expect to be offered more real choice. In some product areas consumers' expectations are ahead of suppliers' potential to fulfil them. This is particularly true in areas like communications and financial services; how often have you asked yourself why bank counter staff can't tell you how much is in your account, when the ATM outside the bank can do this, or why the banks can't immediately link all the products and services that you buy from them?

The reality is that companies cannot survive without new products. At a minimum, existing products need to be made more relevant to today's customer, though this does not mean necessarily that all companies give new product development the emphasis and resources that it requires.

■ Risks

There is a great quote that says that nine out of ten new products fail. By whose definition? No actual research has specifically defined failure and asked people to judge their own experience on that basis.

After all, what is a failure? If a product is no longer on the market this does not necessarily mean that it is to be classified as a failure. It could be that the company has made a strategic decision to rationalise its portfolio or pursue a different direction and the product no longer fits the strategic criteria. A product may be developed to optimise utilisation of overheads and, again, having achieved its task may be discontinued once other products are developed.

Many failures deserve to fail in that the products developed add no value and can be considered 'me-too'. This does not reflect the riskiness of launching new products but the stupidity of the management that launched the products in the first place.

Of course there are risks, not least that if the product is really new and different it can be difficult to replicate a real market situation in research and therefore the risk element must be higher. However, there are often greater risks in doing nothing, because competitors are unlikely to stand still, consumers may lose interest in the current product portfolio and retailers will look to other companies for future profit growth.

Given that there will always be a degree of risk, this means that organisations need to put their best people on the development of their business and to put sufficient resources behind the initiative to ensure that failure is not due to lack of them.

■ What Makes a Success?

The key to successful new product development is to identify an unmet need or desire. Consumers or customers may not have even recognised this themselves, but they can immediately see the potential benefits when the idea is put before them.

Identification of the opportunity area is one aspect, but the other is creating a product that is different, relevant and appealing. This is achieved through a real depth of consumer and market understanding and insight, creativity to develop a solution that is truly innovative, the technical expertise to deliver the product or service, and focus to get the product to market in a *faithful* and timely fashion.

In addition to this the whole organisation from the top down must be committed to the success of the new idea and to provide the required support.

Historically there has been much talk about the need for a product champion if companies are to be successful in their quest for new products. Inevitably one person must be responsible for the development but if there is no commitment from all members of the team developing the product and in turn the company, then a lone sponsor is unlikely to achieve success.

Because of the level of commitment required for new products, companies that are particularly successful often have product development as a board-level responsibility and provide experienced and specialised resources to project-manage new developments. People who are skilled at brand management and technical product maintenance are not necessarily good product developers.

If a new product is to be launched under an existing brand then another factor to ensure success is to understand the brand essence and values and develop the new product to reflect these and enhance them.

■ The Need for Differentiation

This cannot be stressed too much. There is no reason for consumers to change their brand if a new product is a copy of what they are currently buying. It could be said that own label copies brands and offers the same product at a cheaper price, thus the differentiation is on price. Many own labels are not exactly the same, and the onus is on the brand owner to ensure that own label is not a cheaper version of the brand. Therefore if the branded product can be easily copied the brand owner will need to have a consistent programme of product evolution to ensure that this does not happen.

Although retailers are often keen to copy brands, they resist accepting new products that are copies of existing brands because they see this as trading sales from one product to another. Retailers are looking for new products that either add value or offer more real choice to their customers.

Most of the own label produced does not do this. One major retailer launched four thousand new products in a year recently. When asked, customers said that they thought the retailer had launched an average of four new products in the previous twelve months.

Products need to be different either in reality or perceptually. The former is preferable but not always achievable. But perception can be just as persuasive. An excellent example of this was the development of Timotei shampoo. The shampoo was different in that it was mild, but it probably did not require 'rocket science' to produce a product that could cleanse hair on a daily basis. The real brilliance was in the targeting and positioning of Timotei. What the Elida Gibbs team had recognised was that women were washing their hair much more frequently and were becoming increasingly concerned with the fact that they might have also been removing their hair's natural oils. Thus launching a mild shampoo for frequent washing had filled a gap in the market.

The start point for the new area of opportunity was probably the change from bathing to showering where hair inevitably gets wet. Showering is also a daily activity whereas historically baths have been taken less frequently.

By positioning Timotei as a natural herbal shampoo with the attendant visual cues, the implication of gentleness was implicit. The differentiation was much more in the positioning than in a major product breakthrough.

■ The Process

There are of course new product development (NPD) processes, but if a new initiative is breaking new ground even the process itself may need to be innovative.

In general terms an NPD programme will involve:

- Understanding the market dynamics.
- Understanding consumer habits, attitudes and motivations.
- Creating an idea.
- Assessing the potential of the idea.
- Developing the product to optimise the commercial and market opportunity.

However, there are different ways to achieve this and ensure a successful outcome to an NPD programme.

■ Setting Objectives

At the outset of any new product development programme there needs to be a clear idea of objectives, whether the ultimate goal is a new product or a service.

This may sound blindingly obvious, but often the first task of any NPD consultancy is to identify or clarify the objectives for the task they have been set. Virtually any project of any type, NPD or not, should have objectives against which the outcome can be measured.

Objectives can be relatively simple and straightforward, such as needing a new product to retain a leadership position in a market, or developing a product that targets a specific segment of consumers and therefore needs to be tailored to their particular needs. Alternatively the NPD task can be much more fundamental, such as providing the mechanism for a step change in growth and direction of the company.

Clarity in setting the objectives is a prerequisite for success because it helps to provide a focus for the NPD team.

Objectives should be both financial and commercial, and should be agreed with and by the project sponsor(s). Thus they could cover turnover and profit expectations on an ongoing basis, return on capital invested, market share or specific asset utilisation – for example underutilised plant, distribution channels and so on. Within the objectives there is also a need to consider the potential consumer/customer objectives such as added value or lower-cost products and services.

Other parameters and criteria also need to be set, such as the defined market area, investment levels, time scales and action standards for each stage of the process. These may change over the period of the development, but they will change through reasoned discussion and debate rather than by default. Many people involved in NPD talk about 'the goalposts moving'. This should not happen frequently and should only be required on the basis of more learning and understanding, which suggests a need to change aspects of the original brief.

A useful way of getting the programme off to a good start is to form a team of senior managers who will ultimately be responsible for the new initiative and then to set aside one or two days in order both to explore the area of opportunity and to hammer out the key objectives, priorities, project parameters and so on. This can then be documented and will provide the reference manual for the project.

■ Understanding the Market Dynamics

This is a task that is becoming harder and harder in many market sectors because changes are happening more and more rapidly. These changes can be anything from new channels to markets such as the Internet, to new technology and competition arriving from unexpected quarters. The first task therefore is to determine what the key market dynamics are. Consumers' needs and wants are also changing, but perhaps not as rapidly as the market around them. The task may be difficult, but it is critical to understanding the potential commercial opportunity.

The market area needs to be looked at in both its broad and narrow contexts. For example, if a manufacturer is considering developing a new cake, the market assessment should include other snacking and dessert products, both sweet and savoury, as this is where the product will ultimately be judged by consumers.

Although savoury snacking products could be judged to be another sector, in assessing trends it would be clear that savoury snacks are growing faster than sweet snacks. Maybe there is an opportunity for a more savoury 'cake' which could bring the real food values of cake with some savoury taste values.

Potential competition is another area that needs careful consideration. Assessing the strengths and weaknesses, opportunities and threats of existing competitors can help to identify areas of opportunity.

The launch of Orange exemplifies this, in that through analysis of the competitive environment Hutchison correctly identified that the complexity of pricing and the steep call charges, which could lead to unexpectedly high bills, were deterrents to many potential purchasers of mobile telephones. By simplifying pricing and providing an amount of call time in the monthly charge, Orange attracted a substantial share of the market very quickly.

Competition may not always come from the obvious competitors. Examples such as Marks & Spencer, Tesco and Sainsbury offering financial services and Marks & Spencer entering the grocery business before that demonstrate this clearly. Other examples are Daewoo, which has circumvented the traditional dealerships, and Virgin, which has moved into airlines, vodka, cola, jeans and so on. Because outsourcing products and services has become so easy, competition can come from very unexpected qualities. This is particularly true where companies' brands have a strong consumer franchise. Therefore in considering competition it is worth considering brands that would work or have relevance in the sector on which the new initiative is focused.

Understanding the benefits of new or potential technological breakthroughs is also important. If the new product will be superseded by better products in a short space of time through technological developments then the organisation will possibly not achieve the level of return on investment required.

Distribution is another important factor. It is crucial to determine which channels to market are most appropriate and additionally the potential ease or difficulty of accessing them. The initiative may be to open up new distribution channels such as home shopping. Distribution itself could be the Unique Selling Proposition – the area for innovation – as was demonstrated by First Direct in setting up the first telephone banking service.

There could be many other factors that are critical to explore, such as seasonality, economic factors and so on. Understanding these is the key to ensuring that any initiative is profitable and sustainable, but, perhaps more importantly, this understanding will lead to identifying a new area of opportunity.

■ Understanding Consumers/Customers

There is an instinct within many management teams to start any new product development programme with consumer or customer research. Prior to doing any research, the first stage should be to look again at existing consumer research that is available in-house, and to reread it without any preconceptions. In so doing the reader needs to be looking for key consumer drivers, current habits, facts or thoughts that may be surprising, aspects of communication that are important in the sector and so on.

Overall, what the reader should be looking for are clues as to consumer needs. There is a great deal of published research about consumers and how their lives are changing that again could provide insight. Government publications show how the population structure is changing and how factors such as the increase in the number of one- and two-person households and an ageing population may highlight potential opportunities. Equally, the change in consumers' expenditure patterns provides yet more clues. For example, in the last recession people became very insecure about their prospects; many either could not or would not move house and as a consequence of this were spending less on their homes and on major purchases. More money went into saving, but at the same time many people spent more money on small indulgences, including food treats such as the very expensive count line ice creams (single serve, individually wrapped ice-cream snacks), for example Mars or Häagen-Dazs, and so on. Perhaps this is surprising given the overall spending constraint, but understanding consumers leads to many insights into apparently odd behaviour.

Insecurity has also been reflected in young people. Many have found it difficult to get jobs. For some this insecurity has led to a 'live-for-the-moment' approach to their lives. Alcoholic drinks provide a quick hit for enjoying life, so high alcohol content has been important and alcopops have provided this in an enjoyable and irreverent way. Most alcoholic drinks are an acquired taste, but the young do not want to have to learn to enjoy alcohol. The sweetness of the alcopops made them easy to drink and the communication style made it clear that they were for the young.

However, looking forward, one might hypothesise that alcopops will not continue to achieve the success they have to date, as older teenagers buy products such as alcoholic drinks to appear more adult. Products clearly aimed at their group therefore may not give them the maturity that they may be looking for. This could ultimately restrict the growth of alcopops, but opens up opportunities for less overt targeting and more subtle positioning.

Having carried out an initial review of existing research and started to develop hypotheses as to how the market might develop, it may be necessary to conduct some research to gain more insight and understanding.

The first phases of consumer research are generally qualitative, to obtain a better feel for needs and motivations. However, initial quantitative research is required occasionally to understand the structure of the target market and basic habits.

If a product is to be innovative then there is limited value in asking consumers what they would like, because they tend simply to improve or expand on what they already know, which is valuable in extending existing products or improving them but rarely leads to a development with the potential to make a real impact on a market.

To help in both understanding in directing the new product process there is a real benefit in developing ideas that push the market in a variety of different directions, some of which are close to current products while others push the boundaries of the market. Understanding how these ideas are received by different target consumers will lead to a greater depth of understanding about need states and motivations and how to fulfil them.

In the early stages of research, although there will be a degree of evaluation, the process should be more about learning, development and refinement of ideas rather than necessarily throwing out ideas that have not worked well initially.

Any stage of research should generate more knowledge and understanding and develop the idea(s) being progressed. Each stage needs to have clear objectives so that it is clear what is expected to be achieved.

■ Creating the Idea

Ideas may be generated when assessing the market dynamics and in the early review of existing consumer research. However, if really innovative ideas are to be developed there needs to be a specific creative idea generation phase. There is a good chance that ideas developed through the early market and consumer assessment phases are obvious and the same ideas will occur to others who have access to data of the same type.

Creative idea generation is not brainstorming. Brainstorming tends to generate very obvious ideas, but it is an important start point for a creative session because it clears the participants' minds so that they can start to create and explore more laterally. The creative facilitator usually has a programme of imaginative techniques to help the team 'think outside the box'.

Such a session should not be expected to generate 'the big idea', because this puts unnecessary pressure on the team and so inhibits creativity. Its aim should be to create a myriad of very different ideas that will provide the stimulus for a small creative team to work through to build new product or service concepts and, indeed, to generate more ideas.

Idea development requires a team with flexible and creative minds to work through and create a variety of different ideas to develop the market. It often benefits the creative process to use a multi-disciplinary team. This helps to look at the opportunity area from a variety of different perspectives. It is also likely that the team members will be involved in the development of the product itself and therefore will have a better understanding of the essence and evolution of the idea and can help to ensure greater integrity in the development of the product itself.

The development of an idea through to launch requires careful nurturing. The product or service proposition needs to be distinctive, relevant and appealing. This can be enhanced further through the various aspects of communications. The way a product is named, the strapline, the verbal and visual cues all add to the overall appeal to the target market. Positioning development should have its own creative phase and every aspect should have separate consideration if the overall development of the new brand is to be optimised.

Once the product, positioning and communication have been developed using qualitative research at appropriate stages it is likely that the product or service will need to be evaluated on a larger scale using quantitative research.

■ Launching the New Brand

Through the developmental phases much will have been discovered about the target consumer that will help determine how the new brand or service should be launched. Should the launch be a conventional, big-budget advertising and promotional campaign, or would an approach by stealth be more appropriate? Certainly the latter is often more appropriate for youth-oriented brands. Creativity and innovation in the launch programme is very important nowadays, because of the high level of noise generated in conventional media which makes it difficult to stand out.

The critical aspect of deciding how to launch a new brand is what appeals to the target consumer and their habits and lifestyle.

Distribution is obviously – crucial – whether the channels to market are controlled externally or internally. Although a great deal of attention is paid to selling to external channels and ensuring that the product is in distribution prior to any promotion, scant attention is often paid to the internal selling, particularly where the distribution channel is owned. This can lead to a less than optimal launch, where staff already have a large product portfolio that they are expected to sell and on which their personal performance assessment relies. Internal sell-in (the process of explaining and discussing to create understanding and agreement) can make the difference between success and failure.

Success in new brand development depends on insight, intuition, creativity, attention to detail, objectivity and tremendous commitment. And, in all honesty, if you are serious about being a practitioner, it also helps to be slightly mad!

eveloping New Brand Names

Susannah Hart

Interbrand

■ What's In a Name?

The brand name is arguably the most important element of the branding mix, because it is the one element you hope never to have to change. Packaging designs will be updated, advertising campaigns will change, even product formulations may alter. But the brand name will stay the same.

The brand name performs a number of key roles:

- It identifies the product or service, and allows the consumer to specify, reject or recommend brands. In this way a strong brand name becomes part of everyday life.
- It communicates messages to the consumer. In this role the name can be either an overt communicator, for example, Rentokil or Sweet 'n' Low, or a subconscious communicator.
- It functions as a particular piece of legal property in which a manufacturer can sensibly invest and which through law is protected from competitive attack or trespass. Through time and use, a name can therefore become a valuable asset.

The brand name is therefore not only important but also complex. It must satisfactorily perform a number of quite different roles involving aspects of communication and it also has an important legal role.

■ Strategic Considerations

In view of the potentially pivotal role that the brand name must frequently play, it is amazing how often names are selected with little or no real consideration being given to the complex functions they have to perform.

Company, product or service names selected in a haphazard fashion often turn out to be unsuitable or unprotectable in foreign countries – and not infrequently in home markets too! Sometimes they focus too closely on one product benefit or attribute, which over time can become either less important or even detrimental. Or the name is so particular to one product that it actually precludes any form of line extension. Alternatively, the name is too easy for the competition to imitate or even improve upon.

What then are the key strategic questions that should be asked early on in the development of brand names?

Is the new product innovative or not?
If the answer is yes, it is probably sensible to develop a name that clearly differentiates the product from its less interesting and innovative competitors. Even if the new product is not particularly innovative there is frequently an opportunity to set it apart from competition by means of an interesting and distinctive brand name.

Is the new product likely to be an international brand in the future?
Strong international brands normally have certain common key characteristics:

- The same brand name in all countries.
- Common pack design.
- A broadly similar target market in all countries.
- Similar formulation.

Too often brand management is either not aware of plans to market a product on an international scale, or does not consider it sufficiently important to include in a brand name strategy. When this consideration is not taken into account it can later result in loss of time, considerable extra costs, and possible embarrassment and loss of business.

We can all see that fashions are now very similar in London, Paris or New York, whereas twenty-five years ago there were wide differences. Middle-class consumers in Thailand are now likely to shop in supermarkets and purchase foods similar to those used by middle-class households in Europe. Well over 50 per cent of all people under the age of 35 in western Europe can speak English, up from 42 per cent in 1969, and from less than 25 per cent in 1950. This does not mean that the national or cultural differences should be ignored. What is apparent, however, is that the international environment is broadly conducive to international brands, as opposed to local national brands, and is becoming more so.

The advantages of international brands can be very real. There are significant promotional 'overlaps' between countries – much American TV is viewed in Canada, many Irish consumers watch British TV and many thousands of Italian adults watch Swiss TV daily. Moreover, strong international brands allow companies to develop strong central co-ordination without fragmenting into a number of semi-autonomous national units. The possibility that your brand might become an international brand obviously should not be ignored.

Is the new product likely to produce line extensions, or to be part of a range?
Line extension and ranges of products are frequently more effective and less
costly methods for introducing new products then adopting separate brand
names for each individual product. Through the use of a common brand name,
the costs of package design, brand name development, launch advertising,
promotion and distribution can be sharply reduced.

Again this is an approach that must be carefully considered in the
development of a naming strategy.

What is the nature of the protection which the brand can be afforded?
If your new product is made by a proprietary process which competitors will be
unable to imitate, or if you enjoy a monopoly position, there may be little
prospect of competitive brands appearing on the market and therefore a
descriptive and hence largely unprotectable brand name may be acceptable. If,
on the other hand, powerful competitive response is likely then an inherently
strong and protectable brand name may be essential.

■ Developing a Brand Name Strategy

The strategic considerations involved in developing a brand name strategy are
similar to those involved in new product development or advertising strategy
development, and essentially, involve a series of closely related components:

- Product or service information.
- Market information, including competitors, trends, demographics, and so
  on.
- Trade mark information, including corporate requirements and policies,
  marketplace influences, legal requirements, existing company trade marks,
  and so on.
- A clear statement of brand name objectives, based not only on the new
  product under consideration but also upon the broader, long-term
  objectives for the division or the company.

Spending time and effort on these broad strategic branding questions is
critical to the development of a strong, appropriate brand name.

■ Product or Service Information

Product or service information involves examining carefully the product
concept and what the product does; its special properties and its market
position; the way it will be used; the satisfaction it brings to the user; its
relationship to competitive products; distribution and media plans; whether the
product forms, or will form, part of a range; points of sale; the relationship to
the company name and to existing trade marks, and so on.

■ **Market Information**

Market information involves the gathering together of data relating to the market, both qualitative and quantitative, so that the role of the new product and the environment in which it is to be launched are both thoroughly understood.

■ **Trade Mark Information**

Trade mark information involves determining those countries, cultures and languages where registration is to be sought, and hence where the name must be particularly appropriate; the message or messages to be communicated by the trade mark, and those to be communicated by other means (for example advertising and packaging); existing competitive trade marks; any constraints on length; the phonetic qualities sought in the trade mark; and the graphic qualities sought.

If, for example, the product in question is an inexpensive toiletry for family use then to give it an expensive or luxurious-sounding name would be inappropriate and discordant. If the product is given too feminine a name it could lead to men rejecting it. If the product is given too 'national' a name (for example an Anglo-Saxon, a German or a French name) it could hinder the international prospects of the product – unless the language chosen has strong positive associations with the product category in the other markets. Again, if the product is innovative then it might be sensible to avoid certain well-used word roots such as 'aqua' as this could lead the consumer to believe that the product is similar to the host of other products already on the market.

The length of the name is also important. For example, in the case of a toiletry that is to be sold in a bottle that will be displayed upright on the shelf it may be preferable to choose a short word.

■ **Brand Name Objectives**

Once one has become familiar with all the available information on the product, the market and on the particular role of the trade mark, one should set out clearly identified objectives for the naming of the product or service under consideration. We believe that, in addition, these objectives should be discussed and agreed by the various levels of management involved in the product – the new product or brand group, senior management, the advertising agency and package designer. It is also important to have a champion for the name development exercise – someone who will see that decisions are taken and that the project is moved onwards.

Mutually established and agreed objectives can be a strong unifying element in what can all too frequently become a highly subjective and emotionally charged decision – the choice of a name.

■ Developing Creative Themes

Let us consider the case of a hypothetical vitamin C tablet. There are a large number of possible themes around which name generation could be centred. For example, names that sound broadly ethical or pharmaceutical in origin could be developed so as to give the product some implied clinical authority; the theme of zest, vitality, energy could be explored, as could a sporting or outdoor theme. Again, a name associated with oranges and other citrus fruit, sources of vitamin C, might be appropriate, or a name associated with the countries from which citrus fruits come.

In order to choose between these alternative and quite different branding themes, it is important to decide precisely what role the brand name is to play and to relate it to the uses to be made of other means of communication, such as media, advertising and packaging. For example, a sporting name might be inappropriate because the brand name has to 'live' for many years and this particular theme might unduly constrict the media approach in the future. Alternatively, it might be found that in Spain and Italy associations with citrus fruit are inappropriate – citrus fruits could be such a commonplace item of diet as to lend little interest to a brand name for a vitamin C tablet.

Potential creative themes may well already have emerged from previous qualitative research, which can in turn enhance these themes. Certainly in our experience a variety of quite different routes are normally available, all of which have varied implications in positioning and differentiating the product.

■ Name Creation

Specialist brand name development companies are increasingly being used to develop both national and international brand names. Such consultants will normally start by examining in detail the company's plans for the new product or service, its marketing objectives and trade mark policies, and will prepare and agree a naming strategy. Once the brand name development task is clearly defined, work starts on creating new names.

One of the most productive starting points for the creative process and a useful method for exploring existing themes and searching for possible new ones is the use of carefully selected and managed creative, or focus, groups. For international projects focus groups would be organised on an international basis, and each group would be led by a trained psychologist skilled in this area. All members of a particular group are usually of one nationality and are specially chosen for their skills with language. It is more important for this task that the participants have good verbal skills and enjoy playing with words than that they are traditional target market consumers; idea generation is key. In these sessions the task is to develop words, word roots, analogies, phrases and ideas in line with the chosen themes. In the course of a two- or three-hour creation session a group of six to eight people will create a great mass of verbal raw material – perhaps five hundred names in total. Several such groups may be held.

■ Computer Name Generation

Creative consumer groups can provide a good starting point for a name generation exercise. We have also found that, in certain circumstances, computer techniques can be used productively to assist name development in a number of areas:

- To search existing databases and computerised dictionaries.
- To identify names which process the required attributes (for example, masculine, international, stylish, exotic, and so on).
- To take existing names and use phonetically based, word-splicing or modelling techniques to build new and interesting names from preferred 'core' words or name suggestions.

Many organisations have experimented in the past with computer name generation techniques. Since most brand names also need to have a qualitative element, to be associated in some way with the product or its performance or the satisfaction the product brings, the most successful computer name-generation techniques work within such qualitative parameters and take account of natural language, of phonetics and linguistics. Access to computerised synonym and foreign language dictionaries can also greatly enhance the quality of output and assist with name creation.

■ Name Development Specialists

Name development specialists (a very particular type of 'copywriter') will carefully examine all the material produced, either by the creative consumer groups or by computer techniques, for themes, words, concepts, word roots and associations of significance in the different languages. The name development specialists would then begin to build up from this raw data an extensive list of potential trade marks – often literally thousands of potential names.

■ Selecting the Name

Stage one, therefore, in developing a new brand name is to decide what job you want the new name to perform, now and in the future. Stage two is to isolate those naming themes that are relevant to the consumer and appropriate in branding and positioning terms. Stage three is to use focus groups, name development specialists, computers and an existing name library to create names. Since one focus group alone can develop five hundred or more potential names, and a short computer run can produce many thousands more, how does one cope with the super productivity of the creation process?

Brand name development necessarily invoices a careful refining process: a great deal of ore has to be fed into the hopper in order to produce a small amount of pure gold, namely the attractive, strong, protectable brand name. Thus once a vast list of names has been created, it has to be pared down to manageable proportions. To do this, those words are eliminated that at first sight have inherent defects of pronunciation, legibility, memorability or meaning. We also eliminate all those words that are unregistrable as trade marks, that are too close to existing competitive marks or that fail to meet other criteria, for example length.

In this way, the initial list of names can be reduced to perhaps forty to fifty candidate names. These would be discussed in detail with our client and a preferred shortlist of names drawn up for further testing. Though none of these words would have been checked yet for registrability, they should all appear capable of doing the marketing job in hand.

■ Testing Names

This shortlist would then be thoroughly checked in all languages to be covered by the project, for ease of pronunciation, inherent meaning or associations in each language, similarity to existing brand names and broad fit to concept. If more detailed name testing is required, it is advisable to undertake this on no more than ten names, or fewer if at all possible. It is possible to test names in isolation with consumers and name development agencies have often developed specific name testing methodologies designed to get over some of the more common pitfalls encountered in name testing. It is however always best to test potential brand names in the context of a full brand mix research programme. Testing names is notoriously difficult, as consumers tend to respond favourably to the familiar and the descriptive, leaving no room for the adventurous and the ground-breaking. Traditional name research could well have meant that names like Hob-Nobs or Virgin would never have seen the light of day. Techniques for researching names are discussed more fully in Chapter 6 by Katriona Campbell.

■ Trade Mark Availability Screening

Depending on the number of countries in which the new name is going to be launched, between six and twenty-five names will usually need to be submitted for trade mark availability screening. This may seem an extravagant number of names but in such overcrowded product classes as pharmaceuticals, food, drink and cosmetics the chances of a free international mark emerging at the end of the process are unacceptably low if one does not start with a list of this size.

Even with fifteen or twenty carefully chosen names it would be unusual to find more than two or three free marks at the end of the international legal screening process.

The next step then is full legal searching. At Interbrand we normally start by carrying out national and international searches using computer searching facilities. This service is quick and reasonably thorough. We receive a detailed listing of all apparently pertinent marks as well as those where consents may be negotiable or those where validity of title may be questionable. We then undertake detailed searches of the apparently available names plus searches, where appropriate, of unregistered marks.

Such searches and negotiations are expensive and time-consuming. It is not uncommon, for example, for a single name to encounter many apparent objections. These must all be checked; often the owners must be contacted and at times commercial agreements are necessary. In one case we helped set up an arrangement whereby the Dutch subsidiary of a British company bought flour from a French company in return for which the French company gave the British company rights to one of its trade marks. In other cases it has been necessary to conduct detailed confidential investigations to check independently if a trade mark is being used and if so on what products. Sometimes it may even be necessary to threaten legal action to have a trade mark cancelled so as to secure it in a particular country.

Trade mark availability screening is covered in more detail in Chapter 8 by Janet Fogg.

■ Is It Worth It?

The brand name is central to a product's personality. It is the one aspect of a product that never changes and is an essential prerequisite of international marketing. It can become an asset of enormous value. Obviously it pays to get the brand name right, to select one that is legally available in all the countries of interest and to remove all third-party obstacles at relatively low cost before launch rather than at very high cost after launch.

Curiously, however, such a systematic approach is often ignored. Organisations select names with profound marketing and legal defects. They spend fortunes in litigation trying to resolve inherent legal defects. They even, not infrequently, have to withdraw products from the market.

In an age in which companies spend tens, or even hundreds, of millions of dollars or pounds per year advertising and promoting a single product or product line, when the clutter and noise in most sectors increases constantly, when those magical market share points can be worth tens or hundreds of millions of dollars or pounds, the power of their brand name continues to grow. Within the brand name resides all that investment. And it is the only clear, identifiable, aspect of the product that the consumer uses in selection and purchase. Can we afford not to do it properly?

■ The Good, The Bad, The Ugly

In the early 1990s, ICI decided to split into two separate businesses, by demerging its biosciences and life businesses, which it was felt were being undervalued on the stock market by the association with the bulk chemicals business. Interbrand was employed to create an international name for the new biosciences business. This name needed to be free from serious problems of pronounceability and meaning in almost every country of the world and available to use as a trade mark for a wide range of products, and as a company name, in all those countries. Moreover, the name needed to be very different from ICI in order to cast off its past and also appropriate for a dynamic, successful twenty-first-century business. The name chosen was Zeneca, coined from the word 'zenith' with suggestions in English and other languages of peak performance. The name is easy to pronounce and distinctive internationally, is highly protectable and is not particularised to one country. The new company Zeneca has gone from strength to strength on the stock market and the name has become as familiar as ICI.

Not all names have been developed to travel. Many of us have heard rumours of such wonderful products as Sic and Pschitt (both French soft drinks), Creap (Japanese coffee creamer), Green Pile (Japanese lawn dressing), Super Piss (a Finnish product for unfreezing car locks) and Bum (Spanish potato crisps). Indeed, encountering such exotic brands is one of the more obscure pleasures of international travel. Most problem brands, however, have less obvious flaws; it may even be unfair to describe these brands as having flaws when the owners probably had no intention of marketing them outside their home markets and are not concerned that their brand occasions mirth among visiting foreigners. Rather, it is the more insidious problems that can really cause difficulties – brand names so descriptive that they are not protectable, names with so little distinctiveness they are readily copied, or names so particular to one positioning that they lock the brand into that positioning without any chance of further development.

■ The Brand Name Spectrum

The brand name Kodak, as Adrian Room has shown in Chapter 2, is a pure invention. It is a collection of letters that is short, memorable, strong, both graphically and visually and yet has no 'core' of meaning whatsoever. It was adopted by a brave marketing man and, over decades, has developed into one of the most potent brand names in the world.

Visa is a highly associative name for a credit card. It says nothing about money or finances or even about cards (unlike some of its rivals), but instead talks about travel, opportunities, passports, opening doors and crossing frontiers – a much more exciting and imaginative approach.

Bitter Lemon is purely descriptive of a lemon-based mixer drink. It shows very little invention and hence is unprotectable.

These three brand names span the brand name spectrum from totally free-standing names to completely descriptive names (Figure 4.1). All brand names fall somewhere along this spectrum. Schweppes is of course a family name with no inherent meaning, but it also has fortuitous in-built onomatopoeia which helps to convey an image of effervescence. Formica is mainly an invented name but has a core of meaning. Sweet 'n' Low is a name with a high descriptive content.

In general, the more descriptive a name the more it communicates immediately to the consumer – although only in its country of origin. Head & Shoulders may speak volumes to a Briton or an American, but would be completely meaningless to someone in Asia with no knowledge of the English language. Such names also tend to be less distinctive and less protectable. In contrast, the more free-standing a name is the less it immediately conveys to the consumer and the more the brand owner needs to invest in it to confer upon it the qualities of excellence and superiority he requires. Between these two extremes lie 'associative' names, those that are distinctive and protectable and yet communicate some appropriate message or messages to the consumer, perhaps subconsciously.

Companies tend, when developing new brand names, to seek descriptive names. It is somehow felt that such names will help sales and scant attention is paid sometimes to the longer-term implications. But why does the name need to contain an overt message? After all, the advertising, the graphics and the packaging all convey messages to consumers. So why use the brand name to describe your product? To hazard the long-term success of the brand by adopting a descriptive name that is unprotectable is clearly absurd. But this is done constantly.

The answer is not necessarily to adopt totally invented names of the Kodak, Exxon or Xerox type and, indeed, few organisations have a sufficiently innovative product or a sufficiently large promotional budget to allow 'blue-sky' branding of this type. But the middle route, the associative route, can and does result in powerful, attractive and protectable brand names. Kodak might have fared as well had Mr Eastman adopted a name such as Vista but would hardly have been in a powerful a market position today had he called his company Super-Pic or Easi-Foto.

■ Conclusions

As segments become narrower and more specialised, and as national habits, tastes and markets become more sophisticated and more international, the job of the brand name becomes more critical. Companies and their brand or new product management must become increasingly aware of both the commercial and legal realities of trade marks.

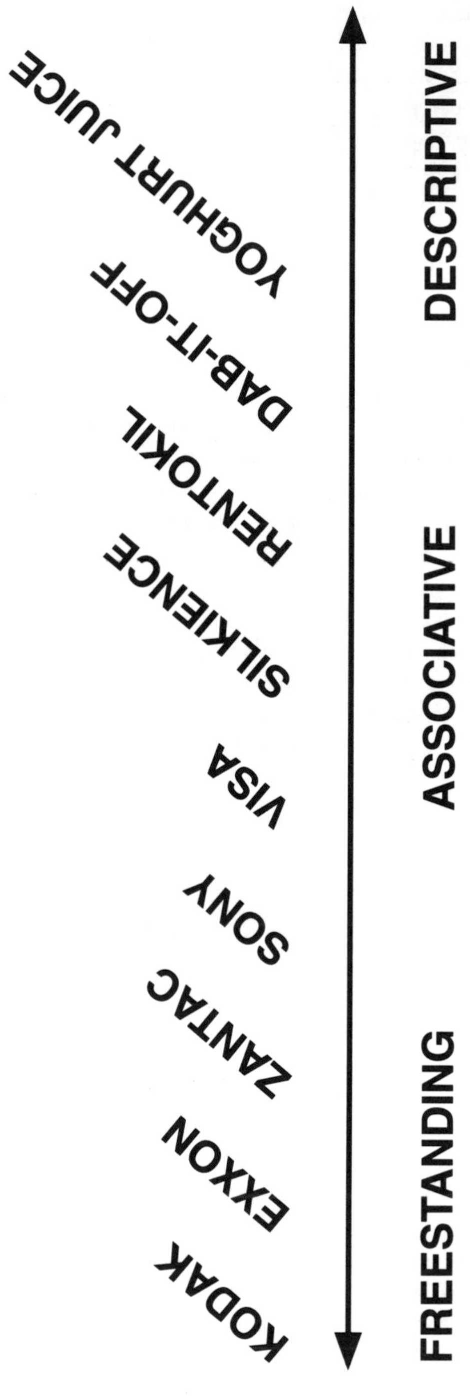

Figure 4.1   Naming spectrum

Although brand value is increasingly discussed, trade marks are still far too often under-recognised assets and under-utilised marketing and strategic weapons. A greater awareness of their potential importance, and a greater willingness to spend time and money in their development, application and protection will pay enormous dividends to those companies engaged in the daily battle for the consumer's attention.

CHAPTER 5

Brand Packaging

Chris Lightfoot
Interbrand

Richard Gerstman
Gerstman & Meyers

We are living in a world where there are ever more products available to us. In such a crowded marketplace, brand owners need to try ever harder to make their products appeal to consumers. In many situations, such as the cluttered and colourful aisles of the supermarket, brand manufacturers have very little time in which to communicate their point of difference. We have seen elsewhere in this book how differentiated brands are able to stand out from the crowd. This chapter concentrates on one particular means of differentiation – brand packaging.

■ The Importance of a Brand's Visual Identity

What do we mean when we talk about a brand's visual identity? The visual identity of a brand includes its logo or symbol and the packaging in which it appears, but it is much more than that. A brand's visual identity crosses over into every manifestation of the brand and can even include the environment in which the brand appears, among them advertising, sales promotion and point of sale.

Our first reaction to most things is visual and it is said that 80 per cent of our brain is dedicated to recognising visual stimulus. We all know that the way human beings look is an important part of the way they identify themselves and communicate messages about themselves to others. However, a human being's personality is more than just the way they look; it is also how they behave, their attitudes and values and how they fit into society. In the same way, although a brand's visual identity is not the whole brand, it is a vitally important building block in its identification and communication.

There is of course more to brand packaging than just communicating the product features and benefits; brand packaging also needs to express the values inherent in that brand to potential customers (it will be supported in this of course by advertising and other publicity). The brand needs to convey a clearer and more appealing brand personality than any another brand in its sector.

Packaging is today a part of everyday life; packs that we buy in the supermarket make their way into our bathrooms and onto our breakfast tables. As a result, many of us grow up to associate a particular pack with a particular time and place; at its most simple, this can result in sentimental attachments to brands. At its best it means that packaging can become a powerful means of achieving brand loyalty.

Packaging is a permanent and constantly visible expression of the brand and clearly therefore has an extremely important strategic role to play in brand building.

■ A Short History

Before we look in more detail at how to create great packaging design, it is interesting to review the historical development of the packaging industry. The multicoloured, glossy and innovative packaging of today has come a long way from the simple protective wrappers or containers of the past. During this century in particular, packaging has developed significantly beyond its original purpose. Once primarily functional, used to protect and transport products and to inform purchasers of the product within, it is now an important element of the branding mix.

The history of packaging dates back at least to Roman times – and no doubt further. Romans would use a particular shape of earthenware pot to identify whether the contents were water or another substance. Packaging was also needed of course to protect some goods during transport to the marketplace or shop. The decoration on these containers was also a form of identity of origin and ownership.

For centuries, most goods were not individually prepacked but were sold loose by specialist retailers, for example chemists, butchers and grocers. It would be the retailer who would recommend products to the customer. These products were usually supplied to or bought by the retailer in bulk and most were displayed without their packaging in the shop. However, over time some were put on display in cases produced by the manufacturer. On these would be written details of the manufacturer's name and address; for example, labels on wine bottles and on chemists' bottles. Thus the manufacturer's name came to have a presence in store. Eventually, consumers learned to identify the products and names of particular manufacturers and they were therefore able to ask for the same manufacturer's product again.

During the eighteenth century manufacturers began to make their wrappers or labels more decorative so that their name stood out from others on the retailer's shelf; hand printing and lithographs, for example, were often employed. The first designs to appear on labels tended to be have a purely decorative purpose rather than any specific strategic intent – they were usually just elaborations or illustrations of the origin or name of the product or both. During the 1850s colour printing began to be used to enhance label design. This had the effect of making labels more widely available and more affordable for use on packaging. It also meant that large quantities of labels could be reproduced relatively cheaply and it was this that enabled packaging design to develop rapidly .

Goods that were prepacked or labelled (often smaller items like tobacco, spirits, or toiletries) were highly decorated with intricate lithographs, coloured papers and typography. They often carried the manufacturer's name and address; many of these names and (much modified) packagings are still in existence today.

Below are some examples of classic brand packs that have been developed over a period of time but are still similar to the original packs:

Bass	Jack Daniels	CocaCola
Colman's Mustard	Southern Comfort	Camel
Brasso	Martini	KitKat
Perrier	Cadbury's	Gitanes
Lyle's Golden Syrup	Heinz	Nescafé
Swan Vestas	Quaker Oats	Marlboro
Rizla	Oxo	Kellogg's

Many of these classic brands have stood the test of time. Both the name of the brand and the design of its packaging are the same or similar to the appearance on the day it was launched.

As consumer demand grew for a wider range of products, retailers needed to supply a greater range of goods and consequently became less oriented towards service and more towards supply. Many other social trends, including the great increase in the number of working women and the corresponding need for bulk shopping, led to the development of larger and larger shops and, particularly over the last two or three decades, the supermarkets have emerged.

Supermarkets supplied a wide range of products, and because they were self-service the consumer was left to decide which product to buy. Now packaging took on an even more significant role: it had not only to identify each product but also to inform consumers about the product within and to convince them that it was the best of its type available in the store.

■ Modern Packaging Design

Manufacturers today pay particular attention to shopping habits, attitudes and choices in order to make sure that packaging appeals appropriately to different target market customers. Because of this ever increasing need for distinctive and protectable packaging design, specialist packaging design companies have developed all over the world. Design is now a sophisticated industry and all the elements of a pack design (including its shape) are carefully evaluated before a new product launch.

Packaging design has now developed a visual language or shorthand code for helping consumers to identify products of a particular type or price or usage. In many product categories, this language is so well established that consumers expect to see a particular use of colour, style and graphics on a particular product; for example, one expects to see a large amount of white and other pale colours on a pack that contains milk, yoghurt or other dairy products. This sometimes comes about because of the success of one particular brand, so that other competing products follow a style similar to that adopted by the market leader. In other cases, all products in the category focused on illustrations of the ingredients or contents, leading to a predominance of certain colours and illustrations, so that today in the UK, for example, coffee traditionally uses rich golds, reds, blues and greens accompanied by an illustration of coffee beans, images of the origin of the beans or a cup of steaming coffee.

One of the important questions that brand owners, as well as graphic designers, need to ask themselves today is whether it is appropriate for their brands to follow the language of the category or to invent their own way of speaking. Of course, the brand must not be unintelligible, but nor must it have anything new to say for itself.

While the adoption of the visual language of a category is extremely well accepted as a short cut to product communication, it is debatable whether this ever really aids true brand communication. The approach in question has been taken perhaps to its most extreme form by many of the leading retailers in the UK, with the 'visual language of the category' or, often, more accurately, the design style of the leading brand in a particular sector, tending to be adopted for the retailer's own-brand version. In many ways, this suits the needs of retailers perfectly; because they produce many thousands of product lines under their own brand, their brand communication needs to focus on the corporate, or retail, brand, rather than on the individual product items. They rely on distribution and display in order to achieve sales and if they can communicate similarity to the leading brands in the sector, so much the better. There is however a clear distinction between adopting a common language or colour coding to simplify consumer choice and slavishly aping a brand's getup. Using a certain colour palette should not be a barrier to innovative and original packaging design.

■ Creating Great Packaging Design

Great packaging design is much more than an arrangement of colour, typography and imagery; it also involves innovative and appropriate pack shapes and constructions (like the Jif lemon packaging or the new Mini Jaffas packaging). To develop such creative solutions demands expertise as well as inspiration. Today, therefore, almost every branded-goods manufacturer employs a specialist packaging design agency, both to update the pack design of its existing brand or brands and as part of new brand development programmes.

◼ Commissioning Packaging Design

Probably the single most important aspect of a successful project is the relationship between the design agency and client. If they understand each other and their tasks and expectations then the programme will run smoothly. The client must understand the agency's capabilities and expertise. Conversely, the agency must understand the expectations and needs of the client.

However, without a clear understanding of both the brand personality and the brand's target market, even the cleverest and most creative packaging design can fail. Such an understanding is not automatic. The agency and the client need to make sure that everyone understands the aims of the project in the same way, right down to the details.

Once the brief has been clearly defined and agreed, the project must be planned out in detail. Project planning and management is crucial to a successful programme.

One of the most important roles in the project team, therefore, is that of the project manager. It is their responsibility to ensure that both the client and agency are clear on all aspects of the job. There is nothing worse for a relationship, for example, than a misunderstanding about deadlines or deliverables, or hidden or unexpected costs.

◼ Briefing an Agency

Be careful not to be too broad in your specifications; provide all the information you have, so that the agency has a clear idea of the people they are designing the packaging for. Just as you would not expect someone who does not know you to choose clothes you like for you, so you cannot expect a design agency to design a pack that will appeal to a target market about which they know only the vaguest details. There are numerous physical and legal constraints placed on packaging, which vary from country to country, and this information too must be given and understood before the design starts, so that impractical designs are not produced. This will include details such as inventories, print and production methods, packing and storage, shipping and distributors, stacking and display, and so on. It is important to remember that you know a lot more about your products and product ranges than the agency.

Make sure you have a good idea of the kind of people you need on the team to complete the project and if you are not sure then get advice from the agency. Make sure also that before you start the project the team structure is clear and transparent from your point of view. The team is undoubtedly the most important part of a project and will consist of members of both the design agency and the client company, all with important responsibilities. It is, for example, not uncommon for the client to provide woefully little access to key decision-makers or to provide insufficient resource internally for the agency to progress the project. One of the most common problems is that of maintaining project momentum; this is as much the responsibility of the client as that of the agency.

■ Bringing It to Life

The following brief case histories illustrate the principles and practices described above and show how they have been applied in the highly competitive US cosmetics market, where the development and maintenance of brand personality and design equities are of critical importance.

Cosmetic products sell the promise of beauty, fashion and romance. The visual presentation must connect emotionally with the target consumer. Advertising and promotion must also work together to fully express the brand, but it is at the point of purchase where consumers make most of their buying decisions, and this is where the brand's personality must be most clearly conveyed.

With so many similar products on the shelf today, it is essential for every cosmetics marketer to have the best possible packaging, both structurally and graphically, that effectively communicates to the consumer. Cosmetics packages rely on minimal elements (shape, colour and typography) to communicate their message and therefore these elements must make emotional connections with the consumer and form the essence of the brand's image.

There are several reasons why a manufacturer might wish to redesign a piece of packaging: competitive pressure, product repositioning, product reformulation and line expansion. Every company strives to be number one in its category and does not want to be perceived as offering the same benefits as its competitors. When considering redesign, a good place to start is to look at how the brand is packaged in comparison with the competition. Gerstman & Meyers recommends the following 'brand essence methodology':

- Assess the brand personality profile. Define what the brand's character is and define the essence behind the person that the product appeals to. Gerstman & Meyers takes its cues from fashion and from the environment of the consumer (that is, the magazines they read, their aspirations, and so on) and constructs 'lifestyle exhibit boards' that relate to the brand character. These boards reveal the image of the people who use this product, where they are today and where they want to be in the future. The personality profile helps determine a design direction.
- Find out if the package matches the profile by performing the 'yesterday, today, tomorrow' (YTT) test. Look at the brand's current packaging to

determine if it is related to yesterday's brand character, today's or tomorrow's. Do the elements of the current packaging reflect the brand personality profile? This will reveal what may have changed and what has made the current packaging inappropriate.

- Conduct retail audits. Thoroughly assess the retail environment to determine what competitors are doing and see how your brand stacks next to the competition. What feelings do you get when you look at your package on the shelf next to its competitors? Which one really evokes the right feeling? Does your package look current? Is it bold enough? Soft enough? Elegant? This is the environment where cosmetic products in particular must really speak to the consumer.

- Research. Conduct focus group research to determine the brand's visual equities – elements that consumers relate only to your brand and that allow them to recognise your brand. Also, conduct separate interviews with retailers to find out what they think about your brand and the category. If consumers are consistently singling out positive aspects of the brand's equity, incorporate these essential elements of the brand's identity. If there are no apparent equities (which is rare), then you may need to completely redesign or relaunch the product in order to be competitive.

- Design the unexpected. Do not settle for obvious solutions if you want uniqueness and memorability. The knowledge you gain from the brand personality profile, the YTT test and research will drive the design process. With the right package, consumers should be able to close their eyes and envisage what your brand looks like without having the package in front of them. Just the mention of the brand name should evoke the messages and feelings you are attempting to communicate through your packaging and graphics.

Even if a brand is successful in the marketplace, it is imperative for the brand management to update the image periodically. In the cosmetic industry, trends and fashion prevail and so it is a good idea to redesign every three to five years, even if it means just slightly modifying the design, or upgrading the image without losing the equities. Otherwise, packaging that appears dated will erode sales. Also, one should monitor new competitors in the category *before* sales begin to slide.

How do you redesign the shape of a package to achieve an emotional connection with your consumer? On the one hand, consumers usually require recognisable, physical cues that quickly identify the product category – the package must fit in. On the other hand, when you are selling an aspiration or promise of romance or beauty, the package must stand out from the crowd. That is, the package shape must emphatically express at least one feature possessed by no other product in the category. For cosmetics, this one feature is paramount to success.

For example, the simple shape of the Chanel perfume bottle evokes messages of elegance, simplicity and premium quality – long-term equities that define the product. While other fashionable perfumes and their bottles come and go, the image of Chanel is timeless.

The leading feature may be a germane product difference (for example greater effectiveness); or, it may be a better method of using the product (for example an improved dispenser); it might be a symbol of the product (the Chanel bottle shape, for instance) or the promise of a desired trait (for example elegance, energy, youthfulness). Thus, the process of creating a contemporary structure that 'fits in' and 'stands out' can be subtle yet complex.

How do you find a structural design that will support a cosmetic brand's strategy? To do so, a designer can use the brand essence methodology. A designer must examine every package in the category to find the underlying forms that identify the category. For example, mouthwashes are described by their makers as either breath-freshening or therapeutic. Upon analysis, most breath-freshening products are in 'banjo-shaped' packages, whereas the therapeutic mouthwashes have rectangular shapes. When Gerstman & Meyers redesigned the classic Listerine bottle, we determined, through research, that much of its equity was in its barbell-shaped glass bottle. We decided to use a hard-edged rectangular barbell shape that echoed the shape of the old glass bottle, yet said 'strong', 'hardworking' and 'effective' to the consumer. Other physical features that may define the abstract characteristics of a category are colour, opacity and specific materials.

■ The Graphic Elements

Colours come and go in cosmetic packaging. Today, cobalt blue is in, but tomorrow it will be something new and bold. When redesigning, keep in mind that you are making a fashion statement with your brand. Brands can look old and tired if they are packaged in yesterday's colours. The use of colour trend research can help you catch the next trend before a competitor. Remember, the colours you choose could become your strongest equity because they tend to give your product more personality than any other design feature.

Lettering styles can also establish a mood, an era or a gender. They can be bold, sophisticated or playful. A typeface can define the buyer as youthful, passionate or spirited; it can denote high quality, high price or a bargain. By carefully choosing a style or typeface appropriate to your target market – one that will integrate well with the other design elements on your packaging – you are creating a valuable visual equity.

■ Repositioning Strategy

Cosmetics marketers sell hope and promise in their bottles. When a cosmetic brand is reformulated or repositioned, it must communicate these attributes to its current customer base as well as to potential users. There is no better place to start than with the packaging.

When Jhirmack, the first salon brand to go mass-market (1979), watched an array of competitors enter the category and erode its market share, company executives decided to reformulate and reposition the entire product line. Gerstman & Meyers created a new brand identity that focused on the brand's new positioning strategy.

Since the product reformulation included the addition of vitamin E, an ingredient known for its therapeutic properties, the packaging needed to reflect this new image and communicate the added benefits to the consumer. We created a new graphic device that represents an abstract of hair in the process of mending. The Jhirmack brand name was made legible by removing it from a square black background and changing it from red to black lettering, thus emphasising the familiar Jhirmack signature while at the same time giving it a more feminine image. The 'Reduces Breakage' claim was prominently positioned under the graphic device, along with the 'Made from Vitamin E' wording. This design concept scored extremely high in consumer research next to other category leaders, while also reinforcing the key positioning benefit – 'Reduces Breakage'.

The new graphic device was colour-coded for each product in the line, along with a matching cap, to facilitate purchase decisions and create a strong billboard on the shelf. The bottle structure was also modified by changing to a more elegant, smooth-surfaced bottle. To further differentiate the products in the line, bottle colours were also changed: white for shampoos, light grey for conditioners and pale green for Jhirmack Plus (shampoo and conditioner in one bottle). The result was an energised new look for a brand that has increased sales, improved visibility on the shelf and attracted new buyers.

■ An Eye Towards the Future

Successful brands allow cosmetics marketers to leverage into new products that enable them to cross-sell and grow. But as cosmetics marketers add products to their lines, it is imperative that they continually monitor the look of the brand to remain consistent, effective and attractive to their target consumers. A graphic approach that works for a single product may not be the answer for a full line of products. Gerstman & Meyers helped the Carson Products Company, makers of the Dark and Lovely hair care line, create a cohesive brand identity system that worked effectively across the current product line while allowing for future product introductions.

Although Dark & Lovely had a well-known name and credibility with its target consumers, black women, the application of its branding became inconsistent as it added new products to the line. Before the design process began, focus groups revealed the visual inconsistency across the line, resulting in a lack of shelf impact and less cross-usage among the products.

The graphics were redesigned to clearly and consistently identify the products and effectively differentiate the lines. The logo was modified to make it more colourful, graphically impactful and feminine. Working with the existing logo style, the modification features the Dark & Lovely name stacked in white lettering within a consistent, colourful panel. To further link the products together, a pink cap or lid adorns each package. Packaging graphics and copy are similar across the line, which creates a billboard effect at retail. To assist product selection, different brightly coloured brush strokes are placed behind the logo, enhancing the cosmetic image. The result is a unique, modern, new look that has dramatically increased sales and has promoted cross-selling through the line.

■ Summary and Conclusions

Packaging design is crucial to the success of a brand and without giving it the right investment in time, money and resource you will miss the potential for your brand's success. And irrespective of whether your product is being relaunched, repositioned or reformulated or if it just looks tired and needs an update, you should not lose sight of your design equities. Believe it or not, it can happen very easily. In the process and excitement of conveying your new message, you may be tempted to diminish or even abandon trade mark design equities – the features your customers look for and are reassured by every time they reach for your product.

When choosing a packaging design company to help develop your brand, select one that not only can meet the creative objectives of the brief, but also can really understand the values and aspirations of your brand. Discussions with the design agency should centre around the brand's personality, its current, former and future brand character, any relevant research findings, the strength of the brand equities, the brand's heritage, its shelf impact and level of brand recognition, its perceived strengths and weaknesses versus the competition, its sales performance and the positioning in the marketplace you wish to achieve.

Finally, if there is a single thought we would like to leave you with it is this: be realistic about the amount of time needed to develop brand packaging. One of the most common phrases we designers hear is 'I need it tomorrow'. Although physically the deadlines might be achievable, great design rarely happens overnight; and as we have shown earlier, the development of a great brand takes a little longer!

CHAPTER 6

Researching Brands

Katriona Campbell

Interbrand

■ Introduction

Research has a vital role to play in the life of a brand, both at the initiation phase when the brand is brought to life and in the ongoing process that is involved in successfully maintaining a strong and relevant brand.

It is widely acknowledged that successful brands are frequently supported by a sound knowledge base; this explains what makes the brand tick and the strength of the relationship it has with its consumers.

Researching brands is a multifaceted process, involving all aspects of what constitutes the brand in the minds of the consumers. Often research is conducted in a piecemeal fashion, evaluating individual components such as the price, the advertising, the packaging, image perceptions and so on. Although it is very important to be able to progress short-term tactical issues like the next press advertisement, it is also equally important to stand back and assess the whole picture. Only then can one truly understand the brand's performance and fit all parts of the picture together.

It is impossible in one chapter to provide a comprehensive insight into every aspect of researching brands. I hope, however, to give a flavour for some of the issues that need to be considered and the pitfalls to watch out for when evaluating new and existing brands.

■ How Healthy Is My Brand?

Monitoring the performance of a brand is a widely accepted practice and in most organisations is often necessary in order to justify budget expenditure levels. However, what is measured, and how, vary significantly.

The obvious internal measures, such as sales volume targets in consumer goods industries, customer loyalty and new and existing customer retention levels in service industries, are the start point. However, the real measure of a brand goes beyond this and can be considered to be the total net impressions of the brand in the minds of the consumer. This is much harder to measure and has been the topic of many papers and much debate (Gordon and Restall 1996; Feldwick 1996). Many research agencies have proprietary techniques that claim to measure this and refer to it for example as brand equity, brand strength or brand personality. All have their merits and weaknesses and one must choose techniques and methodologies that suit the brand, the marketplace characteristics and the company. Irrespective of how one collects the facts, the information that needs to be obtained in order to understand how strong and relevant the brand is falls into three broad categories:

- Awareness, Usage, Saliency
- Brand Image and Personality
- User Imagery

■ Awareness, Usage, Saliency

This is not just about how many people are aware of your brand, or how many people use or experience it, but how relevant it is to them and how much they actually know about it. It could be that of those who are aware, very few actually know anything about the brand – or that what they do know is driven by market 'givens', rather than distinctive brand values.

By understanding what the strength of the consumer relationship is with the brand, one can start to gauge how vulnerable the brand is to new entrants or to short-term promotions and/or activities, as well as how much can be changed without 'rocking the boat' with those consumers who are key to the brand in the target market.

Collecting this type of information generally needs to be done quantitatively – that is by measurement of knowledge, habits and behaviour. In quantitative research, the views of relatively large numbers of people are sought across different geographic and demographic groups, as appropriate. Clearly the questions and survey methodology employed should reflect who the consumer groups are and how frequently one expects the picture to change.

■ Brand Image and Personality

This is a combination of all the perceptions and beliefs that the consumer holds about the brand. It can involve a number of different techniques, but the objective is to link words, statements, pictures, sounds, and/or smells to a brand. This should be done qualitatively – that is, in depth, through probing interviews. Different markets or brands obviously demand different techniques, and it is important to ascertain at the outset which form of interview will be most appropriate to discuss the relevant subject matter and achieve the relevant insights. Qualitative research can take a number of forms: focus groups, in which people are interviewed in small groups together with others who share some characteristics of lifestyle, age, gender or purchase behaviour, enabling views and opinions to be shared among the group and spark off debate; in-depth interviews, usually carried out one-on-one; and paired depths or friendship interviews, which might be used when a particularly sensitive topic is being discussed. Data gained from qualitative research can then be quantified as well.

In this way a picture of the brand can be generated that can be compared to the relevant competitive set. The exercise should lead to a good understanding of how differentiated the brands are in a particular marketplace. This of course does not necessarily tell you whether this is a 'good' or 'bad' position to be in, because other factors have to be taken into account in order to assess whether a change in direction is needed.

Many research companies have favoured ways of collecting such information, involving particular words and/or questions or visual techniques. The most important requirement is to choose an approach that will stand up to the rigours of time and work across your target market and category.

■ User Imagery

Another aspect worth considering is the consumer's perception of what the typical user is like. This adds another dimension, which can be quite insightful in some but not all markets. It can help to explain perhaps why a particular brand is not appealing to some consumers and add depth to the understanding of the values and beliefs of the consumer group being targeted.

Such analysis and information can be very useful in markets like alcoholic drinks, clothing or cosmetics, where perceived image and user identification are intrinsic to success.

Words are often not enough in this area and using good visual material, such as a library of facial or personality shots, dress styles and lifestyle shots, can help to conceptualise the words.

■ The Role of Research in New Brand Launches

Whether one is launching a completely new and distinctive brand or an extension to an existing brand, research can help. There are many examples quoted, however, of how research failed to produce the 'right' answers. I would argue there are no clear 'right' or 'wrong' answers, and so much can change from the testing situation to when the new brand is launched that it is impossible to be 100 per cent predictive of the future. However, research used sensibly can be indicative, and it is better to have asked and judiciously chosen to ignore the finding, than it is never to have asked in the first place.

There is no logical, step-by-step guide to what should and should not be researched within the new brand development process, but there are certain imperatives that can be identified as key for research and these are:

- Understand the target consumer and their needs and motivations.
- Identify the brand differentiators relative to the competition.
- Develop realistic consumer stimulus.

The first maxim concerns the depth of market and consumer knowledge that one has. This informs the choice of target market for the new brand, and research should be conducted among those consumers whose opinion you feel is important in driving trial and repeat purchase. These will not all be users; they may be the light buyers, or the buyers of one particular competitive brand, or seasonal-only buyers. What drives buyers' motivation, the reasons for dissatisfaction with existing brands, overall behaviour, attitudes and needs, will all shape the role for the new brand. Good exploratory qualitative research involving in-depth interviews, group discussions, usage diaries and consumer videos can help to formulate this understanding. It is the researcher's job to analyse all this information, filter it and order it to make sure that it is useful.

Identifying what differentiates the new brand in the marketplace is the second important maxim. Too many brands are just me-toos, and it is the job of research to highlight this. Spotting this involves identifying the key variables and important brand values that are core to the proposition. For instance if you are developing a new brand of shampoo for older women, then the product benefits, the user imagery and the brand personality must differentiate it from the competition in order to position the brand to its chosen consumer segment.

The final maxim concerns communicating to consumers in a way they understand both logistically and culturally. Consumers are becoming more sophisticated, and appropriate language needs to be geared to the level of the target market. However, marketing-speak should be avoided in research and it is always preferable to show ideas in as realistic a form as possible. Consumers are always better at building on tangible ideas than having to imagine what one means by a particular pack shape or service deliverable. The closer one gets to reality, the closer one gets to a realistic answer.

■ Researching Specific Brand Components

Sometimes it is necessary to evaluate in isolation an individual aspect of a brand mix, like the name or the visual design. We know that consumers buy entities rather than 'fragments' of brands. However, they frequently claim that the advertising has not influenced them, that the pack shape is irrelevant, and that the sponsorship of a sporting event plays no role in their likelihood to buy. This is because we all like to believe that we are logical and intelligent beings, making decisions on purely rational and tangible grounds. This reaction is found across all target market groups – from teenagers and young adults (perhaps the most sceptical group of all) to mothers and to doctors and other professionals. Logically it is clear that these reactions do not represent the true state of affairs; all aspects of a brand's identity do play a role in the decision to buy or to reject, however subliminal.

The difficulty arises in having to break down the components of the brand and evaluate what contribution the new design, the new name and so on, is likely to have on overall appeal and/or performance. Two areas that are frequently recognised as difficult to research are:

- The name.
- The design/identity.

■ The Name

When a brand name is sought for a new product it may often be the last component to slot into the mix. A wide range of options may still be under consideration and be legally available. But how can research then help in selecting the most appropriate name, not just on a local basis but also on a multi-country basis? The name is a vital part of the mix, but the brand must work as a complete entity with all aspects contributing to the development of brand values – it cannot be considered in isolation. It is important, therefore, to understand where research can help and where it cannot in name evaluation.

Name research tends to favour the descriptive and the familiar. Distinctive names are often rejected owing to strangeness and original names often lack relevance to the product category in the consumers' minds. Analysis is therefore very important. There are many techniques employed. At Interbrand we have developed a proprietary technique called Nometrics, which was devised on the basis of many years' experience of creating and testing names. The technique can be applied both qualitatively or quantitatively.

The most important test criteria in the Nometrics name evaluation approach are:

- Pronounceability.
- Scriptability (of particular relevance to the ethical pharmaceutical industry).
- Imagery conjured up.
- Negative associations.
- Likely service/product areas suggested.
- Similarity to existing names.
- Fit to brand concept.
- Memorability.

The analysis of all the above criteria in the light of objectives agreed at the start of the exercise should mean that the research can be used to help with the selection of a name. However, research must not dictate the answer, as the solutions are often not black and white; there can often be other influencing factors with a role to play in the final selection, such as legal problems, fit within current company brand hierarchy, other future launches and extensions and the future that the company envisages for the brand.

■ The Design/Identity

The visual appearance of a brand, be it pack shape, colours, graphic styles, logos, characters, is a critical part of the brand identity and a vital contributor to its personality.

Asking consumers to evaluate new designs, logos or corporate identities is very often unpopular with designers, as they see it as an opportunity for consumers to make comments like 'I don't like orange – it's a cheap colour'. Such comments, if taken at face value, can of course stop the progression of a design route and ruin an excellent creative execution. If comments like these are interpreted in context, however, there is no reason why research cannot be of great help in the brand development process. It is always important to ensure that research is used at the appropriate stage and approached creatively. Conducting research at an early stage, when design concepts and brand identities are being debated, can help identify what triggers choice in a category and this can be invaluable.

There are several key pointers that should be remembered about packaging research:

- Test with the right consumer. Who is most important to you? Brand loyalists? Or those who have drifted away from the brand? Different need states will lead to different requirements and responses.
- The research should not be about picking winners but identifying what is or is not communicating against the brief.
- Competitive comparisons are important; no brand ever exists in isolation.
- Identify early the visual elements that must be there to 'cue' the brand and those one can lose.
- Brand recognition or impact is important, but the role it plays with a new brand differs from the role it plays with a well established mature brand. This should be recognised when deciding whether this aspect of the research needs to be quantified.

Useful techniques to consider in the evaluation of packaging are:

- Accompanied shopping trips or the videoing of fixtures.
- In-home diary completion on practical usage elements.
- In-depth interviews rather than group discussions to avoid the group influencing effect.
- Mock-up fixtures or computer-generated fixtures to check pack standout.
- Decoding the brand visual cues from the design by developing phased mock-ups.

■ In Summary

Research can play a vital role in helping to understand how well a brand is performing against the objectives set for it. This applies both to well-established brands and to new brands under development, although clearly different techniques and approaches are appropriate in each of these cases.

Therefore understanding what role you wish your brand to perform is intrinsic to being able to design effective research for both evaluation and development. This understanding, coupled with a creative approach and a sound methodology, will mean that your brand research becomes a crucial part of your brand management approach and makes a significant contribution to helping the brand flourish.

■ References

Ehrenberg, Andrew S.C., 'If You're So Strong Why Aren't You Bigger? Making the Case Against Brand Equity', *Admap* (October 1993).

Feldwick, Paul, 'Do We Really Need 'Brand Equity?', Esomar in *Researching Brands* (1996).

Gordon, Wendy and Restall, Christine, 'Brands – the Missing Link: Understanding the Emotional Relationship', Esomar in *Researching Brands* (1996).

CHAPTER 7

Branding the Corporation

Simon Mottram

Interbrand

'In future, the real competition in international markets will be between companies – between company reputations.'

Martin Sorrell (Marketing)

The key challenge for companies at the end of the twentieth century will be realising the potential of their corporate brands. In today's markets, companies increasingly compete on the basis of intangible factors and the reputation of the corporation itself is often the most valuable and most misunderstood intangible of all.

For some time many have viewed the rise of corporate branding as irreversible. Already, the bulk of consumer spending is on corporate brands (motor cars, financial services, telecommunications and utilities) rather than on product brands. But important questions persist about how corporate brands should be developed and managed most effectively. Companies are realising that possessing a well-known name such as Shell, Visa or CBS does not, in itself, signify a strong corporate brand. Finding techniques for branding the corporation effectively is now more important than ever.

■ The Rise of Corporate Branding

Until recently, brands tended to be associated with everyday groceries, stand-alone products that secured demand and often a ~~price~~ premium for a manufacturer by guaranteeing consistent quality to the consumer. And yet some powerful corporate brands have existed since before the Industrial Revolution, most commonly where the name of a product and the company that produced that product were one and the same.

The success of multinational brands such as Ford, IBM and Sony since 1945 and the mergers and acquisitions activity in the 1980s led to increased awareness that corporations themselves were often perceived as brands. The increasing prominence of 'non-traditional' forms of branding (service brands, business-to-business brands and retail brands, for example) has been accompanied by a refocusing of marketing attention on the potential of corporate brands. The reasons for this attention are clear:

- The cost of creating and supporting brands has become prohibitive. It has recently been estimated that it would now cost more than $1 billion to develop a new branded franchise across Europe, the US and the Far East.
- Increasing retailer power is making it difficult for stand-alone brands to compete in some markets.
- Traditional forms of fragmented and/or distributed brand management are now seen to be inefficient and ineffectual.
- The focus of consumers and customers is moving up the value chain to the company behind the brand. This is supported by vocal pressure groups and an increasingly intrusive press.

Corporate branding is thus being discussed widely in the boardrooms of the world's most powerful companies. It is now understood to bring considerable benefits:

- A strong corporate brand attracts and inspires employees, stakeholders and business partners. Thus stronger and deeper relationships with suppliers can be developed and longer-term investment secured.
- Corporate brands connect up all the goodwill generated by a business's operations. They build public support for an organisation and can sometimes provide credibility in times of crisis.
- New product launches and brand extensions become cheaper and can be implemented more speedily. Brand support can become more efficient when it is focused on a single brand.
- Corporate branding provides a long-term, strategic rather than short-term, tactical focus for brand development.
- Most importantly, financial performance and value creation can be enhanced.

The benefits of corporate branding have been most clearly illustrated in Japan and the Far East. Companies such as Sony, Samsung and LG have built global businesses remarkably quickly by focusing clearly on the visions and values of the corporation. These brands have a global brand umbrella, which acts as the 'corporate glue' when entering new geographic markets or product areas. The corporate brand is used consistently by these companies to add 'higher' brand values to all products. Contrast this approach with that of western companies such as General Electric, Thomson and Philips who operate in similar markets. It has been suggested that western companies are ten years behind their competitors in the east when it comes to branding the corporation.

However, for a variety of reasons, it is by no means easy to brand a corporation successfully:

- Organisations can be extremely complex.
- The wide variety of audiences makes consistent communication of a brand proposition difficult.

- Many companies cover a number of businesses – it is generally easier to build a strong reputation and brand image when one is known for one product or service.
- Corporate brands tend to be led from the top, by the founder or CEO, who can be difficult to pin down on day-to-day brand management.
- Business directors and leaders historically tend to have backgrounds in finance or in the operations of a business – not in marketing.

Nevertheless, for the reasons already mentioned, more and more companies are deciding that these difficulties are not severe enough to outweigh the considerable benefits of corporate branding. Accepting that the principle of branding the corporation is a sound one, companies must address a number of significant practical issues.

■ Brand Architecture and Endorsement Strategy

A company that wants to get behind its corporate brand and use it more proactively must decide on the most appropriate brand architecture for its business or businesses. The choice is between three alternatives:

- A monolithic structure.
- An endorsed brand architecture.
- A hybrid structure.

A monolithic structure has the corporate brand right at the centre. All products and services are branded with the same name, identity and set of brand values. So, for example, the Shell brand is used across all its business, from upstream oil exploration to its chemicals and passenger car lubricants. Richard Branson has taken the Virgin brand from music and publishing to airlines, financial services, spirits and beyond. The advantages of this sort of structure include a seamless transfer of goodwill to the centre, cheaper brand building and instant credibility when launching new products or extending into new markets. The difficulty with the monolithic approach is that the corporate brand's personality has to be flexible enough to cover different products and markets while being precise enough to compete with specialist brands in each segment. Crucially, too, damage to the brand's reputation in one part of the business can lead to damage or risk to the brand throughout the corporation. One of the most interesting debates in the branding world is whether the monolithic approach does indeed result in added value or just the insecure, 'profitless prosperity' that comes from sales volume and international spread.

When a company uses an endorsed brand architecture, it aims to add the higher values of the corporate brand to the specific values of product and service brands in its portfolio in the interest of competitive advantage. Thus the corporate brand can add security, trust and credibility to the positioning of the product or service brand. This endorsement can take the form of a strong 'umbrella' brand (such as Ford, Apple or Birds Eye) or can be much lighter, putting some distance between the product and corporate brands (3M and its famous Post-it and Scotch brands, for example).

Recently, however, a number of 'hybrid' approaches have been adopted by brand owners. For example, Nestlé has recently pulled all of its products under ten global 'banner' brands (among them Perrier and Carnation). Each banner brand is targeted at a specific market or closely linked markets but, crucially, all will continue to benefit from the Nestlé corporate endorsement as well. Other companies have adopted the name of one of their brands as the corporate brand, in the hope of leveraging specific product brand attributes across the group and increasing the intangible value of the entire business in the process. So, for example, BSN is now Danone.

In practice, there is no 'right way' to structure brands in a portfolio. What is clear is that the higher up the brand ladder towards a monolithic structure a company goes, the greater become the practical challenges of moving from product-based brand equity to a higher-level brand platform. The key challenge is to persuade customers to transfer the goodwill that they have for one product or service to another of the company's products without blurring the product or corporate brands' strength in the process. In practice, this takes skilful management of the brands in the question and a clear focus on the long-term branding goals of the corporation.

■ Corporate Brand Identity

Recognition of the benefits that a consistent visual presentation can bring to a company's performance has grown steadily since the 1950s. During the 1980s there was an explosion of activity around the world as companies large and small invested in their identities in a search for competitive advantage. In the process a multi-billion-dollar industry was born. It now seems that every company has a logo that is full of personality and a corporate identity manual at least three inches thick!

In the early days of the industry, consultants, designers and their clients focused on the visual presentation of the company through publications, advertising, signage, uniforms and so forth. But justified concern has grown that the practice of stamping a logotype, symbol or even a complex identity system on all aspects of a company can often appear contrived and superficial – an example more of corporate vanity than of enlightened management and value creation.

Fortunately, things are beginning to change. Corporate identity is important because it looks at the myriad of reminders that consumers use to navigate between different products, services and organisations. Corporate identity practitioners increasingly look beyond visual materials to all those 'reminders' associated with the company, both those within and on the outside. These reminders include sponsorship and community activities. But corporate identity also encompasses the vocabulary and tone of voice used in the company's publications and by its employees, proprietary sounds (the Intel jingle) and even smells (witnessed by the rush of companies to register proprietary smells as trade marks, including Pirelli registering the smell of roses for use in its tyres!).

The next important step that corporate identity managers and practitioners need to take is to link the discipline of corporate identity more closely to the real heart of the organisation – the corporate brand. The successful corporate identities of the future will be based on a more fundamental understanding of the corporate brand; its vision, personality, culture and expression throughout the company. The starting point of corporate identity development should therefore be an appreciation of the brand, because only when such an understanding exists can the visual and behavioural style of the corporation be developed. The most coherent and effective identities of the future will be developed by looking *inside* the business to the brand, not outside to target markets and other audiences.

■ Corporate Brand Management

There are no longer any automatic models for creating and managing brands successfully and the accepted rules of brand management for fmcg products have never been appropriate for use at a corporate level. If corporate branding is to be successful then it should work for all audiences; consumers and customers, distributors and other partners, employees, investors and other stakeholders, the broader communities that it impacts. This requires investment, commitment and passion on the part of brand managers. Crucially, these brand managers should sit at the top of the organisation – in the board room.

If one thinks of the most-focused and well-managed corporate brands they are often inextricably linked to the personality and vision of their founder (Richard Branson's Virgin, Anita Roddick's Body Shop, Bill Gates's Microsoft,

Figure 7.1   Microsoft
Microsoft is inextricably linked with the personality and vision of its founder, Bill Gates

for example). When businesses are large and multinational and operate in a variety of different product markets then brand management by the CEO becomes increasingly difficult – how can one person possibly hope to direct and control the actions and personality of every aspect of the business? Of course, good corporate branding is bound to be easier for smaller companies than it is for larger ones.

For most businesses, the benign dictatorship model is unrealistic. Instead, companies need to develop a more distributed and/or networked system of brand management, for which three guiding principles should be followed:

- *Leadership*. Just because the CEO or founder may not be involved on a full-time basis does not mean that leadership can be forgotten. The brand management function in the business needs to have a senior voice. In practice, companies should appoint a board member as brand champion.
- *Buy-in*. Corporate brand management is most effective when it is practised by everyone in the organisation. Employees need to understand the brand's vision and personality if they are to communicate it and nurture it day in, day out.
- *Communication*. To secure buy-in from employees and ensure effective leadership, the corporate brand must be communicated clearly, frequently and consistently within the organisation. Company newsletters aren't enough – more sophisticated communication systems (Intranet, for example) and forums for discussion are required. Branding consultants are increasingly engaged by clients to prepare materials, 'experiences' and channels that explain and develop the personality of the corporate brand to the company's employees.

■ Branding the Corporation of Tomorrow

Corporate branding is clearly becoming more important for all manner of organisations. The benefits of corporate branding are better understood than ever before, and new techniques for corporate brand management are being developed all the time. But a sneaking suspicion persists that the whole concept might be built on sand – a marketing construct that will be dropped when the next best-selling management book hits the shelves. In my view, such concerns are understandable but misguided. And they are misguided because tomorrow's corporate brands will be different. A number of factors are conspiring to force companies to look harder at the corporate brand itself and deeper, to the vision and purpose of the organisation.

For a start, new kinds of business organisation are putting strains on traditional brand management theory. As competition in business is increasingly replaced by cooperation, and companies focus on core competencies in networks, partnerships and alliances, brands will become ever more important for each company's cohesion and motivation. The growing numbers of flatter, more flexible and virtual organisations provide still sterner challenges to traditional models of brand management. In these organisations, effective internal communication of the corporate brand is paramount.

The most important factor that shapes the corporate brands of tomorrow will be the increasing sophistication of consumers. When it comes to consumption, the public is increasingly media–advertising–design–brand–literate and, after more than fifty years of the consumer society, has lost its naïvety. It seems unlikely, therefore, that companies will ever again be able to 'dazzle' the consumers with empty promises. This has fundamental implications for all brands, not least for corporate brands.

Whereas consumers used to be satisfied when corporate brands simply added a few higher, service-based values to their product brand offerings, today they are much more cautious and sceptical. They no longer respect authority and will show trust only where it has been earned. To earn this trust, companies will have to be much clearer about the value of the product, service or concept that they offer: Would the world be a worse place without it? Is it truly different from the competition? Is the organisation really honest and sincere about the promise that is being made? In a world where these qualities seem to be held in diminishing esteem, this is immensely reassuring to the consumer.

Consumers may see upwards of a thousand commercial propositions every day, but they are learning to filter out those brand messages that they do not want to hear. They might still be attracted to a simple product or service if it is particularly innovative or well advertised but, by and large, they will look to develop relationships with corporate brands. New moves towards relationship marketing by brands such as Heinz and Buitoni are evidence of this.

It has been argued that it can be very useful to have distance between the actions of the product or service brand and the reputation of the corporation. Gone are the days when corporate leaders could hide away at their head office, distancing themselves from the effects of a failed product or broken environmental promise or public scandal.

Nor is this confident, assertive and questioning attitude just the preserve of consumers. Increasingly, alongside this trend towards consumer vigilantism, shareholder action groupings, environmental groups and other social pressure groups, the press and local community groups are taking a closer interest in the actions and objectives of companies.

Brand architecture, corporate brand identity and corporate brand management are all important considerations for company leaders today. But the key focus in coming years will be on the substance that lies behind the brand. When companies have a clear vision of their place in the world, a well-defined sense of corporate purpose and personality and a clear brand strategy, then corporate brand identity and brand management problems become much easier to solve.

■ Corporate Vision and Purpose

The corporate brand is at best superficial and at worst meaningless unless it reflects a corporate vision and purpose that creates value and differentiates it from other organisations. 'What's new?' many business leaders might rejoin; 'After all, we've been hammering on about creating shareholder value and focusing on customer service for years!'

However, although every company has a mission statement these days, most corporate visions and mission statements are dull, undifferentiated and irrelevant to building corporate brand value. Worse still, they tend to be ignored by almost everyone within the organisation. There is a world of difference between the sense of group purpose that lies at the heart of the corporate brands of tomorrow and traditional corporate strategy and mission statements. Why? Because the principles of marketing are finally becoming accepted by business leaders. A common corporate objective such as 'maximising shareholder value' is a valid aim for one discrete corporate audience – investors. But it means next to nothing to employees, business partners and, crucially, customers. To be really effective, corporate brands need a more rounded purpose and reason for being. The latter should stem from a fusion of the organisation's core competencies and, most importantly, its core beliefs. As James Collins and Jerry Porras wrote in the *Harvard Business Review* (October 1996):

> It is more important to know who you are than where you are going, for where you are going will change as the world around you changes. Leaders die, products become obsolete, markets change, new technologies emerge, and management fads come and go. But core ideology in a great company endures as a source of guidance and inspiration.

Here brand owners should consider their own brands for a moment. Would the world really be a worse place if your brand ceased to exist? After a couple of years, would any of your audiences really miss or even remember your brand? Contrast the apparent visions of many of today's companies with that of Sony when the business was first founded:

> If it were possible to establish conditions where people could become united with a firm spirit of teamwork, and exercise to their hearts' desire their technological capacity, then such an organisation could bring untold pleasure and untold bounty. (Sony's original corporate vision)

A brand vision like that of Sony provides strategic direction for the business and can increase the motivation and loyalty of all employees. The vision is given texture and personality by a company's values. But there are many different types of values, from *functional* values such as quality and affordability to *expressive* values such as street credibility and conservatism, through to more central values such as respect and trust. In practice, most corporate brands are rooted in functional values. Recently, many companies have attempted to add expressive values to position themselves more precisely for their target market. This trend is most clearly evident in markets such as financial services and motor cars. But the best brands have a balanced mixture of all three kinds of value. Central values, in particular, can be remarkably effective at binding audiences to the corporate brand.

■ New Organisations

Corporate branding is now spreading beyond the realm of the company as other organisations from charities to football clubs start to appreciate that they too possess unique intangible assets. But effective corporate brand management is further complicated when the company itself does not fit the traditional sales- and profit-oriented norm.

Powerful corporate branding becomes very important when a company no longer owns or controls all the assets and levers in the value chain. A clear personality and higher brand values help to keep the company's contribution clear in such circumstances. Corporate branding, where a one-dimensional personality is projected to all audiences, looks increasingly anachronistic.

Effective corporate branding is not just a theoretical idea. Companies in industries ranging from pharmaceuticals to construction are looking inside their organisations and focusing on the corporate brand. Good examples of companies that are already ahead of the game include Marks & Spencer (now a UK institution), Saturn (US automotive division of General Motors), Co-operative Bank (ethical UK retail bank) and SouthWest (domestic US airline).

In my view, the companies that embrace these new corporate branding techniques in the future will lead their markets and be the creators of new categories and opportunities. In tomorrow's competitive markets, only the bravest or most foolish companies should overlook the potential of their corporate brand.

CHAPTER 8

Brands as Intellectual Property

Janet Fogg

Markforce Associates

■ What is a Trade Mark?

A trade mark is defined in the UK Trade Marks Act 1994 as 'any sign capable of being represented graphically which is capable of distinguishing goods or services of one undertaking from those of another undertaking. A trade mark may, in particular, consist of words (including personal names), designs, letters, numerals or the shape of goods or their packing.' While in practice most trade marks consist of a word or words, logos, labels or a combination of these, trade marks can also consist of one or more of the following;

- Slogans.
- Shapes.
- Sounds.
- Smells.
- The overall getup of a product.

A trade mark has three functions:

- To distinguish the goods or services of one business from those of another.
- To indicate the source or origin of the goods or services.
- To serve as an indication of consistent quality (whether good or bad).

■ What can be Registered?

Although the criteria for registrability of a trade mark can differ quite substantially from country to country, the UK and other European Union (EU) countries are required to comply with a Directive intended to harmonise to a large extent (although not entirely) their laws relating to trade marks. The UK complied with this Directive through the Trade Marks Act 1994. This was responsible for some dramatic changes to the law which had previously been in force; it affected a number of areas, including what is now registrable as a trade mark.

In addition to being 'any sign capable of being represented graphically which is capable of distinguishing goods or services of one undertaking from those of another undertakings', in order to qualify for registration now a trade mark must *not*:

- Be devoid of distinctive character.
- Be recognised in the relevant trade as denoting the kind, quality, quantity, intended purpose, value, geographical origin, the time of production of goods or of rendering of services, or other characteristics of the goods or services.
- Be generic in relation to the goods or services.
- Consist of the shape of the goods themselves, the shape of goods which is necessary to obtain a technical result, or the shape which gives substantial value to the goods.
- Be contrary to public policy or to accepted principles of morality.
- Be deceptive.

However, it is possible to overcome objections from the Registrar of Trade Marks on these grounds if the trade mark owner can demonstrate that through use of the trade mark it has become distinctive of his products or services exclusively.

As well as fulfilling the registrability criteria set out above, a trade mark must not conflict with an earlier trade mark, and it is here that most of the problems arise which will be discussed later in this chapter.

■ Selecting New Trade Marks

From the trade mark owner's view the most attractive trade mark is the one which best describes his or her goods or services. The more the trade mark indicates what the product is, the less effort the trade mark owner will have to make to get his or her message across to the consumer.

From a legal viewpoint, however, distinctiveness is the key to a strong trade mark. The more distinctive the trade mark, the more likely it is to be legally available, and the stronger the rights which will be obtained through use and registration. The disadvantage of a very distinctive trade mark is the investment the trade mark owner will have to make in marketing the product and service. But once consumer awareness has been established, there should be far fewer problems in maintaining a monopoly in the trade mark. In practice very distinctive trade marks often consist of invented words, examples of which are Kodak, Zeneca and Xerox, household names in the UK and many other countries.

■ The Trade Mark Searching Process

Before adopting a new trade mark it is essential to carry out searches to make sure that the trade mark does not conflict with existing third-party rights.

While trade mark searches in one country are relatively quick and inexpensive, searching internationally is both time-consuming and expensive. This is because the trade marks registers are becoming increasingly crowded, making it more and more difficult to find attractive and appropriate trade marks which are legally available; some categories of goods and services are especially cluttered, notably the areas of toiletries, pharmaceuticals and computer technology. Indeed it is probably true to say that any obviously attractive names will almost certainly have been already registered in at least one of the relevant countries.

Consequently it is usually necessary to search a number of names before one will emerge as available for use and registration. For this reason it is wise to allow as much time as possible for the searching process. The most cost-effective way of tackling the process is first to conduct preliminary computerised searches, probably on a long list of names, in the trade marks registers of those countries which can be accessed on-line to eliminate at the outset any names which have obvious problems.

More detailed searches, which will involve obtaining the opinion of a local expert in the relevant countries, should then be carried out. Again, to keep costs down, and if time permits, it is advisable to search the relevant registers sequentially, starting perhaps with a list of twenty to thirty names (depending on the number of countries in which the trade mark will be used) in the trade mark owner's home country. The survivors can then be searched in the remaining countries of interest, which can be divided in several batches. Although this phased process will take much longer than searching all the shortlisted names in parallel, it does mean that names encountering serious obstacles can be eliminated at each stage, thereby avoiding unnecessary costs.

However, even if the searching process is handled in this way, it is unusual for a trade mark to emerge completely unscathed with no potential problems in any of the countries searched. More often, the selected name will have at least one or two minor obstacles which need to be resolved before the trade mark is brought into use. For example, it may be advisable to seek consent from the owners of a similar mark, or to check whether a conflicting mark is being used in the same or similar area of business, or whether the registration might be vulnerable to cancellation on the grounds of non-use. In cases where an approach for consent is necessary, this can often take some time, since the trade mark owner will have to wait until the party who has been approached has considered the matter internally and is ready to respond. This again illustrates the importance of starting availability searches as early as possible before the proposed launch of the new product or service.

In the UK and other common law countries, in which rights to a trade mark are acquired through use as well as by registration, it is a good idea to carry out searches not only of the trade marks registers, but also to check the index of company names, relevant databases and telephone and/or trade directories.

■ Registering Trade Marks and the Importance of Registration

Although to a limited extent rights to a trade mark in the UK are acquired through use, in most countries the rights belong to the first applicant for registration. Registration of a trade mark gives the owner a statutory monopoly in the trade mark for the goods or services covered by the registration, and in many countries for similar goods and services too. The owner can therefore take action in the courts to prevent the unauthorised use of his trade mark (or of a mark which is confusingly similar) and, if successful, will obtain an injunction and damages.

In the UK and other common-law countries it may be possible to prevent use of the same or similar trade mark by a competitor by means of an action for passing off, even if the plaintiff's mark is not registered. But to succeed the plaintiff has to establish to the court's satisfaction that he has acquired a reputation and goodwill through use of his mark, and that the defendant's use of the same or similar mark amounts to a misrepresentation, which is confusing or likely to confuse a substantial number of people, thereby damaging the plaintiff's business. Common-law rights are therefore difficult, time-consuming and expensive to enforce and the outcome of passing-off actions is often unpredictable.

By contrast the rights granted through registration of a trade mark are relatively straightforward and inexpensive to enforce, and the outcome tends to be more certain. The advantages of registering a trade mark may be summarised as follows:

- The trade mark owner obtains a statutory monopoly which is legally enforceable against infringers.
- Filing a trade mark application reserves a trade mark before it is brought into use.
- A trade mark registration can act as a strong deterrent to competitors considering the adoption of the same or similar name, because it will be entered on the trade marks register and revealed by searches as a potential obstacle.
- The owner of a trade mark registration can lodge a notice with customs authorities to prevent the import of infringing goods by specifying the expected time and place the consignment will arrive.

■ The Registration Procedure

The procedure differs substantially from country to country even in the EU, notwithstanding the Harmonisation Directive. In the UK once an application has been lodged at the Trade Marks Registry and a filing receipt issued, it will then be examined as to inherent registrability according to the criteria outlined earlier in this chapter, as well as for conflict with earlier trade marks. An examination report will be forwarded to the applicant or his or her attorneys stating either that the application has been accepted or, more often, that official objections have been raised. It is sometimes possible to argue successfully against official objections through correspondence with the Registry, although if these arguments fail the applicant has the option of attending a hearing before one of the Registry's more senior officials at which the objections are reconsidered.

Following examination and subsequent arguments, the application is either rejected, in which case the applicant can appeal to the High Court, or accepted, when it is then ready to be published in the *Trade Marks Journal.*

Following publication there is a period of three months within which anyone may object by filing formal opposition. Provided no oppositions are lodged the application will be registered and the registration certificate issued. Typically this procedure takes about a year to eighteen months, assuming there are no serious problems. Once a trade mark is registered (but not while it remains pending) it can be used as the basis for an infringement action, and because the rights obtained are backdated to the date of application, it may be possible to claim damages for the period in which the application was pending, provided the infringer was placed on notice.

Provided a trade mark is used within five years of registration and use does not cease for any continuous period of five years or longer, the registration should remain valid and can continue in force indefinitely, provided the appropriate renewal fees are paid every ten years.

Many countries have systems which are similar to the UK and which provide for a full examination as to inherent registrability and conflict with prior marks. At the other end of the spectrum, however, there are countries such as Belgium, the Netherlands, Luxembourg and Italy which operate deposit systems of trade mark registration, whereby the application is filed, there is no official examination or opposition procedure, and the registration certificate is issued whether or not the trade mark is inherently registrable according to their laws or in conflict with earlier trade marks already on the register. In the absence of an opposition procedure anyone wishing to raise objection in these circumstances has to wait until after registration and then apply for cancellation.

■ Protecting and Monitoring Trade Marks

To maintain a monopoly in a trade mark it is essential that it is used for the registered goods or services. Failure to do so means that the trade mark registration will become vulnerable to cancellation for non-use – in most countries five years after registration – and therefore the right to future use of the trade mark will be lost. To avoid possible invalidity of a trade mark registration it is important that the trade mark is used in the form in which it is registered and that it is used for the goods or services covered by the registration. If a trade mark is updated (and this applies in particular to logos or labels) then advice should be sought as to whether any amendment of the mark covered by the existing registration is possible and, if not, then a new application for the updated version of the trade mark should be filed.

Similarly if it is proposed that the trade mark will be used on goods or services outside the scope of the existing registration, appropriate searches should be carried out and new applications filed.

■ Correct Use of Trade Marks

It is also important to ensure that the trade mark is used correctly to prevent it becoming the generic name for the goods or services, thereby leaving the registration vulnerable to cancellation on these grounds. The following are guidelines for the correct use of trade marks:

- Whenever they appear in text trade marks should be distinguished from the surrounding text by, for example, showing the trade mark in capitals, in italics, in bold type, in a different colour, or by placing it in quotation marks.
- Trade marks should always be followed by the generic name of the product or service, as in Xerox photocopiers.
- Trade marks should be used as adjectives and not as nouns or verbs.
- Trade marks should be used consistently in the same spelling and format.
- The trade mark owner should give notice to others that a trade mark is in fact being claimed as a trade mark, by use of the TM symbol (*TM*) if the trade mark is not registered or the R in a circle symbol (*R*) if it is. In addition it is a good idea to include a footnote in printed matter to the effect that 'X is a (registered) trade mark of Y company'.

■ Policing of Trade Marks

To maintain a monopoly in a trade mark it is important to act quickly when infringements come to light. Failure to do so will lead to a dilution and possibly the eventual loss of a trade mark owner's rights. As soon as an infringement comes to the trade mark owner's attention he or she should seek professional advice with a view to taking appropriate action. It is therefore important to monitor the activities of competitors and of the marketplace generally.

It is also possible to subscribe to a watching service whereby the trade mark owner is informed of the publication of any applications to register trade marks either the same or similar to theirs, so that they can raise objection if they wish.

■ The Effect of the UK Trade Marks Act 1994

The main effects of the Trade Marks Act 1994 may be summarised as follows:

- The definition of a trade mark is extended to include marks which would have been unregistrable under the old law such as shapes, sounds and smells and any mark established as being factually distinctive through prior use.
- The cost of obtaining registration of a trade mark has been reduced by allowing for applications covering any number of goods or services where previously separate applications would have been necessary.
- The infringement rights granted by registration have been extended to include in certain circumstances similar goods or services where before protection applied only to the precise goods or services covered by a registration.
- The Act provides protection for famous marks, even for dissimilar goods or services.
- Protection for trade marks in use but not registered has been limited making it more important than before to ensure that a mark is correctly registered.
- The licensing and assignment provisions have been simplified.

The 1994 Act replaced the Trade' Marks Act 1938, which was generally regarded as out of date, cumbersome and inappropriate for the current needs of trade mark owners. The changes brought about by the new Act are to the benefit of trade mark owners because they simplify the registration process and bring the UK more into line with its European counterparts.

■ Developments in Europe

■ The Community Trade Mark

The Community Trade Mark system has been in the pipeline since 1964 when it was first proposed by the European Commission, although an EU Regulation for the Community Trade Mark was not eventually finalised until 1993. The system is now operational and the Community Trade Marks Office, based in Alicante, Spain, started accepting applications on 1 January 1996 with the official commencement date being 1 April 1996. Applications filed during the period 1 January to 31 March 1996 have an effective filing date of 1 April 1996.

The purpose of the Community Trade Mark system is to establish a single trade mark registration covering all the member states of the EU. However, the Community Trade mark will not replace existing national registrations which will continue in parallel. ·

Applications to register a Community Trade Mark can be filed either direct at the Community Trade Marks Office in Alicante or at any one of the national

Trade Mark Registries. Applications can be filed in any of the official languages of the EU, although the working languages for the Community Trade Marks Office are English, French, German, Italian and Spanish. Applicants are also required to designate a second language, which must also be one of the five working languages of the Office.

The registration procedure involves official examination of the application to see whether the trade mark is registrable. The criteria which apply are effectively the same as under the UK Trade Marks Act 1994.

The Community Trade Marks Office also carries out an official search of the Community Trade Marks Register and draws the applicant's attention to any prior marks which appear to conflict. However, an application will not be refused on the basis of the results of the official search and the onus is therefore on the applicant to decide whether or not to proceed, bearing in mind that the owners of conflicting marks will be able to oppose the application. Similar searches will also be carried out in the national registers of those countries who wish to conduct official searches. Again, however, the application will not be rejected on the grounds of conflict with any prior marks found and those marks will merely be drawn to the applicant's attention.

Once accepted, a Community Trade Mark application is published for opposition purposes and there is a period of three months from the date of publication within which interested third parties may raise objections. In the absence of oppositions, the application proceeds to registration for an initial period of ten years, renewable indefinitely for further ten-year periods.

In the case of a trade mark available throughout the EU, the Community Trade Mark system is a simple and cost-effective way of obtaining a registration applicable in all member states. However, in practice, given that the registers in all member states are very crowded, many Community Trade Mark applications are likely to encounter third-party oppositions, apart from well-known trade marks already covered by existing national registrations. It is therefore worth noting that when a pending application is refused or successfully opposed, the applicant has the option of applying to convert the application to separate national applications, clearly an attractive feature of the system.

■ The Madrid Arrangement and the Madrid Protocol

The Madrid Arrangement for the International Registration of Trade Marks, known as the Madrid Arrangement, has provided an international registration system since 1891. An applicant, who should be a national of a member country or have a real and effective commercial establishment in a member country, first obtains registration in their home country and then applies to the World Intellectual Property Organisation (WIPO) in Geneva for an international registration by designating the members states in which protection is required. The application is then sent to the national office in each designated country, which examines and prosecutes the application according to its national laws.

The outcome is an international registration covering a number of countries, which is obtained more quickly and cost-effectively than by filing separate national applications in the countries concerned.

Although the Madrid Arrangement has worked very well over a considerable period of time, important countries such as the USA, Japan and the UK have not joined, for a number of reasons:

- The Madrid Agreement requires an international registration, to be based on a national registration which puts these countries at an immediate disadvantage because of the length of time normally taken to obtain registration.
- The Agreement includes provisions for 'central attack' whereby the international registration is dependent upon the national registration on which it is based for the first five years, during which time if the national registration is cancelled, the entire international registration is also cancelled.
- The national trade mark offices are required to notify WIPO of objections to international registrations within a period of twelve months, considered to be too short a time scale.
- The fees payable to national registries for handling Madrid Arrangement applications are considered too low.

The Madrid Protocol of 1989, technically a modification of the Madrid Agreement, is a parallel system which came into force on 1 April 1996, which will also provide for the international registration of trade marks and is intended to attract those countries for which the original Madrid Agreement was unacceptable. However, the Protocol is different from the original Madrid Agreement in several significant ways:

- Protocol applications can be based on national *applications* rather than national *registrations*.
- National trade mark registries will have up to eighteen months to examine applications and notify WIPO of objections.
- The fees will be higher and are expected to be equal to national application fees in the relevant countries.

A further advantage of the Protocol over the Madrid Agreement for English-speaking countries is that the official language of the original Agreement was French, whereas under the Protocol applications may be made in either English or French.

As a result of recent developments in Europe applicants in some countries will have the option of applying for registration of trade marks through their national trade marks office, via the Community Trade Mark system, the Madrid Arrangement or the Madrid Protocol. It will depend on the particular circumstances of each individual case as to which route is appropriate.

■ Conclusion

In order to maintain the value of your brand, it is vital to ensure that you protect its name, visual identity and other differentiating features of its getup as trade marks. The rights afforded to trade mark owners are substantial and it is important to protect your intellectual property as carefully as your tangible property; both are valuable assets.

In view of the complexities of trade mark registration and the number of different systems which operate around the world, it makes good sense for trade mark owners to obtain professional advice.

CHAPTER 9

Commercial Counterfeiting

Vincent Carratu

Carratu International

■ Introduction

> The nefarious but lucrative business of pirating or counterfeiting genuine trade mark goods has flourished too long unchecked to the incalculable injury of every consumer, of every honest merchant, manufacturer and trader, and has extensively multiplied costly and tedious litigation.

This statement is part of a petition which was presented to the United States Congress in 1876. It was signed by the principal manufacturers of New York, Boston and Philadelphia in their attempt to force the enactment of criminal sanctions against product counterfeiters: it could just as easily be included in a petition submitted today. Its message is as important and the problem even worse. The USA was not the only country to recognise this problem. In the United Kingdom, a draft Trade Mark Bill was drawn up in 1862 and actually became law in 1875. In France, the Union des Fabricants was established during the same period specifically to protect French industry against the counterfeiting of its products; the Union is still active today.

There is a great deal of confusion as to what is actually meant by product or commercial counterfeiting. Basically, it is where copies, usually inferior, are represented as being merchandise of the original producer with the deliberate intent to deceive consumers and 'steal' business from the trade mark owner. In true counterfeiting there must be an illegal use of the trade mark, but for the purpose of this chapter counterfeiting will include infringements of copyright, patents and the manufacture of 'near copies'.

Before the passing of the Trade Mark Act 1994, trade mark owners were obliged to use the common law against those manufacturers who produced articles so similar to the original, even though they did not carry the trade mark, that consumers were confused. Most countries handled these under their unfair competition, or similar, legislation but we have no such laws in the UK. We had to deal with these offences as 'passing off actions', which were expensive and very difficult to prove. Under the new Act, such common law actions are unnecessary, but one can still use the common law as a last resort.

■ Historical Background

Museums throughout the world have examples of early counterfeits. In the British Museum one can see imitation Roman pottery produced in Belgium in the early part of the first century BC, before the Roman Conquest of Britain, which was then exported to Britain. The imitators failed to appreciate the significance of the signs they used; they merely jumbled letters, but they still deceived the Britons to whom they were sold.

It is interesting to note that Belgium is still the home of counterfeit pottery – the majority of spurious Capo di Monte figurines seen today originated in that country! From these small beginnings, an entire industry has developed – an industry which, in recent years, has enjoyed phenomenal growth.

Product counterfeiters are frequently referred to as pirates and piracy is the generic term used to describe their activities, particularly within the entertainment industry where video and audio copying is almost endemic. Today's pirates are as devious and dangerous as those who sailed on the high seas. They resort to any number of subterfuges to confuse those trying to catch them. Recently they have employed private investigators to monitor the activities of those pursuing them and have engaged security consultants to advise them on how to counter investigations directed against them. With the direct involvement of organised crime, it is now quite common for them to resort to violence in protecting their operations. In the Far East and Latin America it is usual for the manufacture and shipment of counterfeit goods to be protected by armed guards. Even in Europe, counterfeiters are often armed.

It is this development which is the most alarming. The general view used to be that counterfeiters were mainly proprietors of small businesses, in urgent need of new markets, who succumbed to temptation. That may have been the case years ago, but not now. Today's pirate is usually a person who has deliberately set out to copy another's products, whatever they may be. Today he will produce fake designer perfumes, tomorrow he will switch to counterfeit sports shirts, then later he will import fake tennis rackets from Pakistan. Variety is his spice of life and the rewards make it all worth while.

Evidence of counterfeiting can be seen throughout the world. Inferior sports shirts bearing the Lacoste, Adidas or Fila logos are widely available on every continent. They may look the part, but after their first wash, the value of buying the genuine article is soon appreciated. There are fake Levi jeans which come apart within weeks; counterfeit tennis rackets and golf clubs that collapse during the first match; imitation Ferodo brake linings that need to be replaced within a few hundred miles; and fake Louis Vuitton luggage that falls apart during the first trip. Some counterfeit articles, however, are as good as the original, if not better. During one case in Spain, counterfeit leather goods were seized bearing an international famous brand name, Gucci. They were so good that even Gucci were confused. In Italy we were shown a counterfeit Rolex watch which has been keeping excellent time for more than twenty years, without having been serviced once.

MAISON FONDÉE EN 1854

Figure 9.1   Vuitton
Counterfeit products may look the part, but after use the
value of buying the genuine product is soon appreciated

■ Pseudo-Counterfeits

This may seem a contradiction in words, but not all counterfeits are fakes, in the literal sense of the word. It is not unknown for counterfeiters to obtain genuine reject products which they then alter so that they can be sold as first-quality merchandise. One case involved Royal Doulton porcelain. Royal Doulton only sell their 'seconds' to staff, but before doing so they remove their trade marks. The counterfeiters skilfully reinstated the marks using epoxy resin fillers and enamel. The new marks were virtually undetectable on first inspection and many expert dealers were deceived. Second-quality figurines, selling for less than ten pounds each, became approved products worth very much more.

One of the most alarming areas affected by this type of abuse is that of aircraft spares – unscrupulous dealers either sell inferior copy components, or sell parts obtained from scrap heaps which they have cleaned and retagged, with fresh identification labels and trade marks.

A well-publicised instance of this occurred following the Gulf War. A British Airways jet was badly damaged on the ground during fierce fighting to recapture Kuwait's international airport. It was officially written off by the insurers. They even arranged for their own loss adjuster to supervise its complete destruction and, although the insurers were presented with a selection of photographs showing a dismantled and burnt-out wreck, within weeks retagged parts started to appear on the market. They were confirmed as having come from the destroyed BA aircraft.

■ Overruns

A similar situation arises with overruns. Many companies use outside contractors to manufacture their goods; this is particularly so in the fashion industry. Fashion houses frequently have their silk scarves and ties produced in Italy; jeans are manufactured in Asia and South America; the leather industry has its handbags and luggage made in Italy, Spain or Morocco. The contracted manufacturers are instructed to produce their items with the owners' trade marks and designs, and the total production of these articles is the property of the trade mark owner, but the extra few thousand pieces produced at the end of the day, or even overnight – the overruns – are often considered by local management, and staff, as being a legitimate bonus.

Although they are produced by the appointed manufacturers, they are still false, as the use of the trade mark on these extra items was not authorised by the trade mark owner. Distinguishing such products from the genuine is an impossible task.

■ Economic Damage Caused by Commercial Counterfeiting

Unfortunately, there are no official figures as to the economic damage caused by counterfeiting. If it is successful, then no one, not even the trade mark owners, realises that copies are on sale. Counterfeiting has been likened to sex – it is widely practised, but no one knows how often, by whom and with whom!

Various government departments, and other organisations, periodically publish statistics, but none of these can be verified. The US Department of Trade many years ago stated that product counterfeiting was equal to 9 per cent of all world trade. We would not dispute this figure and would suggest that today it is even higher. There can be no doubt that it is one of the most underrated forms of fraud facing industry, and yet it is most damaging.

■ The Legal Situation

Almost every country in the world now has some form of trade mark legislation, but not all of it is effective. In many countries the laws are enacted, but then totally ignored. This is particularly the case in Latin America and India. Most of Latin America, where product counterfeiting is now endemic, is bound by the Inter-American Convention of 1929, which was based on French law, but signatories only grant protection to those overseas trade mark owners who can prove use of their marks in their countries within a specified period after registration and continual use thereafter. These provisions are familiar to infringers who have put them to wide use. In Mexico, for example, bogus Cartier stores and fake Gucci and Lacoste boutiques abounded until the trade mark owners realised what was happening and started exporting to that country.

In many Far Eastern countries the laws are just as weak. The Taiwan government, for example, has taken steps to combat counterfeiting but these have not been sufficiently aggressive, nor effectively pursued. In mainland China, counterfeiting is now a way of life; they have the legislation, but rarely enforce it. When they do, they do it with a vengeance. Some product counterfeiters in China have been executed for fraud!

■ The Current Situation

The last thirty years have seen an explosion in product counterfeiting. We have witnessed improved organisation on the part of the counterfeiters, a wider international scope and a massive increase in the size and diversity of their operations. These are no longer cottage industries but multinational businesses which, in organisation and know-how, can compete on equal terms with many of today's major corporations.

When Designer Sportswear Inc, a New-York-based counterfeiter of jeans, was raided, the authorities discovered that it had more than five hundred retailers distributing its merchandise. The proprietor and his associates, aided by a professional board, supervised the entire operation, including the bribing of bankers and others, and the obtaining of false credit references. In one of the largest international perfume cases ever cracked, we found that the counterfeiters had been financed by money supplied by one of New York's five Mafia families; money was used to set up operations in Italy, Spain, Mexico and the United Kingdom. Their raw materials came from various countries and their distribution networks were located in Luxembourg and the Middle East. The entire business was controlled from London in a highly professional manner and the quality of their merchandise was exceptional.

There are many reasons for this rapid growth in commercial counterfeiting. New computer technology has enabled counterfeiters to print duplicate product labels almost identical to the originals, without the expense of creating new artwork and printing plates. Sophisticated modern manufacturing techniques have allowed the low-cost production of fakes where formerly massive investment in plant and machinery was required.

Product counterfeiting has become an important part of the economies of a number of countries, not only in South East Asia, Latin America and India, but also in parts of Europe.

In Northern Italy, a well-known company was blatantly caught counterfeiting branded silk squares. They were prosecuted, but the case was dismissed by the local judge because the company employed more than three hundred people and, as such, was an important part of the community and its economy. So much for justice!

It must also be remembered that counterfeiting provides an attractive source of hard currency, which is of particular interest to all third-world countries, as well as those from eastern Europe. The former eastern bloc countries are now very active in counterfeit production.

■ The Counterfeiters' Products

Counterfeiters will copy every possible product that is manufactured and offered for sale. One always associates counterfeiting with luxury branded goods, such as perfumes, sports clothing and fashion accessories, rarely with products that can, and do, cause deaths. We try to classify counterfeit products as hazardous and non-hazardous, but this definition is never easy. For example, a number of cases of skin and eye infections have been reported as a result of the use of fake toiletries. These are serious, but not lethal, and are therefore classified as non-hazardous, as are counterfeit foods and drinks. In general the latter are safe, but we must never forget examples of mineral oils sold as vegetable oils that have been widely reported in Spain and the Middle East, and the sale of wood alcohol as branded alcoholic drinks, as these can, and have, resulted in blindness and even death.

■ Hazardous Products

In the hazardous category we include counterfeit pharmaceutical products, as well as fake aircraft and motor spares. Numerous reported deaths have been attributed to these fakes.

Fake medicines are to be found in hospitals and pharmacies throughout South East Asia, Latin America, Africa and the India subcontinent. They have even been found in Europe. Hundreds of heart pumps have been recalled because of dangerous fake components; these look like the real thing, but can be deadly.

Pharmaceutical companies spend billions of dollars developing new drugs for human and animal use. Selling prices must reflect these enormous investments and can therefore be extremely high when compared with production costs. This is appreciated by those unscrupulous individuals who are prepared to abuse the owner's patent and trade mark rights.

A few of the drugs that have been copied include: Zantac, the famous ulcer drug; Selokeen, a Swedish cardiac drug; Adriamicin, a treatment for leukaemia; and Fansidar, a treatment for malaria. These are bad enough, but the copying of over-the-counter drugs is even more serious. In Nigeria, 109 children died of kidney failure after being given a counterfeit painkilling syrup that was made in Holland: it contained industrial solvent. In Burma, villagers died after taking fake malarial drugs that had been given to them by a government agency. The list is endless.

The counterfeiting of pharmaceutical products not only infringes a company's trade mark rights, but invariably its patents as well. The enforcement of these rights can be complicated, time-consuming and expensive. Patents have on average a twenty-year life span and can either be concerned with the product in its entirety (that is, product patents) or with the process used to manufacture the active ingredient (that is, process patents). It is worth noting that at least twenty-eight countries have no patent laws whatsoever, and it is these countries that have the most problems.

Manufacturers in these patent-free countries produce and sell the active ingredient as a 'generic product'. It is left to their customers to blend this with other materials to produce the final capsule, tablet or other medicine, which is then offered to the retail market. In many cases, the counterfeits consist of glucose and chalk, without any active ingredient at all. These illegal manufacturers are not burdened with research, development or marketing costs and are therefore able to offer their products at a fraction of the price of the originals, something which even government agencies have not been slow to appreciate.

It is just a short step from here to true counterfeiting, for which the rewards are much greater. By printing packaging bearing another company's name and logo, the infringer can offer this product at a price closer to that of the original and very much more than the active ingredient alone. Product counterfeiting can ruin a company financially, but the possibility of a subsequent, unfounded product liability writ is of far greater concern to the pharmaceutical industry than simply the loss of revenue and subsequent profits.

As for aviation spares – fourteen aeroplane crashes, and at least two deaths, have been directly attributed to counterfeit spare parts. This problem is now so serious that the US Government has established a special investigation and prosecution task force to work with the Federal Aviation Authority to deal specifically with these issues.

Counterfeit motor spares are equally dangerous – fifteen people died in Canada in the late 1970s when a bus careered over a cliff because its fake brake linings failed. Counterfeit seatbelts, brake pads, clutch linings and alloy wheels abound. One set of fake brake pads seized in Nigeria were made from chicken manure and grass!

■ Non-Hazardous Products

Returning to non-hazardous fakes, the coffee crop of Kenya was ruined in 1978 when it was treated with useless, counterfeit fungicide. The list is endless! Dunlop, Hoffman La Roche, ICI, Adidas, Kodak, Chanel, Bell Helicopters, Rolex, Pfizer, Glaxo, Dior, Louis Vuitton, Gucci, Levi Strauss and Caterpillar are just a few of the companies that have had their products copied.

Counterfeiters do not waste time copying little-known products. They only choose products that the trade mark owner has spent millions in developing and marketing. They also favour products that are easy to copy, cheap to produce and simple to distribute, but of high value. Perfumes meet all these criteria. Every perfume house has display cabinets filled with counterfeits. Within the last few years there have been successful prosecutions against counterfeiters of Chanel, Estée Lauder, Elizabeth Arden, Helena Rubinstein, Dior, Jean Patou, Joop and just about every other fragrance producer.

Spirits, liqueurs, champagnes and wines are also favoured by the counterfeiter. It was during prohibition in the United States that organised crime made its first sortie into liquor counterfeiting. The Federal Authorities seized the contraband drinks smuggled into the country from Canada, Europe and elsewhere so the syndicates had to look elsewhere for their supplies. Illicit stills proliferated, but their 'moonshine' was not acceptable to sophisticated society. It was a logical step for the organisers to present their own 'moonshine', suitably flavoured and in containers and packaging that would confuse but satisfy their discerning customers. Counterfeit Johnnie Walker, Cutty Sark and other well-known brands became popular in the speakeasies.

When the National Prohibition Act (the Volstead Act) was finally repealed in December 1933, the need to counterfeit drinks vanished, but counterfeiters had tasted the rewards. Counterfeit branded drinks can still be found in many countries. The Italian police, for example, once seized large quantities of counterfeit Johnnie Walker whisky, both Red and Black Label, which had been produced at a state-owned distillery near Sophia, Bulgaria, and then shipped to the free port of Trieste for onward transmission to Africa.

The latest drink to be counterfeited is vodka. Apart from the well-reported trade mark dispute between the registered trade mark owners of the Smirnoff brand and the so-called Smirnoff family in the former Soviet Union, there are currently numerous imitation-brand vodkas on sale in the CIS. Most of these are poor-quality products, but their presentation is too close to the originals to be left on the market. The problem is finding officials who are not afraid to tackle the Russian mafia.

■ Video Piracy

The entertainment industry has always had to face the challenge of piracy, but in the late 1970s it experienced a phenomenal increase in the activities of those who chose to ignore its property rights – it was the advent of video piracy. Prior to the video age, reproducing celluloid film was expensive and technically difficult. Suddenly the home video enabled anyone to record films illegally, lend them to friends or rent them for a fee. It is impossible to calculate accurately the loss to the industry, but according to the Motion Picture Association of America it is believed to exceed a billion dollars per year. Though the industry has always been active in protecting its rights, its procedures proved totally inadequate to deal with the new problems.

The rewards of video piracy were such that organised crime quickly saw the potential and the industry was suddenly faced with pirates whose methods were reminiscent of the gangs of the thirties. In addition to the theft of master films from cinemas by armed gangs, it had also to face large-scale duplication and export networks. In 1978 the IFPI (International Federation for the Phonograph Industry) was expanded to include video, and their anti-piracy activities began to take shape. The problem was international, but in Europe it was particularly serious in the UK and the Netherlands. As a result, in 1982 they established their own anti-piracy groups – the Federation Against Copyright Theft (FACT) and the Stichting Video Veinig.

Unlike other forms of counterfeiting in the UK, video piracy has always been subject to criminal law. Apart from the trade mark offences connected with the copying of labels, and so on, the duplicating of film is an offence under the Copyright Act. Unfortunately, the police were never keen on prosecuting such cases; the penalties were so insignificant that they always suggested that companies pursue their own civil remedies. FACT lobbied Parliament and was instrumental in having the Copyright Act 1956 amended to cope with these specific problems. To be in possession of pirate video film and sound recordings for trade now carries severe penalties, with the police directly involved. These amendments are limited, however, as they relate only to the needs of the entertainment industry.

In the United States special sections were established within the FBI to liaise with the film and video companies, their regulatory and policing bodies, and in most European countries laws have been strengthened to enable the authorities to deal with this new criminal activity.

The lesson to be learned from the entertainment industry is that by working together, sharing one's resources and information and presenting a unified front, considerable progress can be made in the fight against the counterfeiter.

■ Computer Piracy

This was appreciated by the computer industry, which was riddled with counterfeits, both of its hardware (the actual computers) and its software. For years, dozens of companies in the Far East, particularly Taiwan, had thriving businesses copying computers. They not only copied the designs, but also the names. At one stage there were more than a dozen variations of the Apple computer – the counterfeiters used every imaginable fruit in their titles. Some of these computers were excellent copies and extremely difficult to distinguish from the original. The manufacturers fought back and, in time, they were able to reduce the numbers available. The counterfeiters then moved into the area of software piracy and this was much more difficult to control.

Software piracy became so serious that the industry decided to set up its own enforcement agency, along the lines of FACT. They called it the Federation Against Software Theft, or FAST. Even with the vast budgets given to this agency the problem still exists today. It is much easier to trace and prosecute the wholesale infringer, but impossible to find every computer user who runs off extra copies of his program for his colleagues at work. FAST, and the computer companies themselves, are monitoring users whenever they can, but currently they appear to be fighting a losing battle.

■ Legal Remedies

Years ago, the laws protecting intellectual property rights were inadequate, but the penalties were commendable. In the fourteenth century, an innkeeper found guilty of passing off an inferior wine as a Rudesheimer was ordered by the Elector Palatine to be hanged. In sixteenth century England and France the penalty for counterfeiting was death. In 1597, two goldsmiths in England who were found guilty of making and selling gold plate of less than the marked quality were sentenced to be nailed to the pillory by their ears.

As we have seen elsewhere in this book, the UK's weak Trade Mark Act 1938 has been superseded by a new Act passed in 1994. To quote the Department of Trade and Industry press release,

> The Act strengthens protection against counterfeiting, makes it simpler and cheaper for companies to protect their trade marks, ensures that trade marks have the same right and test for validity everywhere in the single market and introduces simpler procedures at the patent office.

The Act defines infringements as follows:

- Identical sign on identical goods.
- Identical sign on similar goods, or similar signs on identical or similar goods that are likely to cause confusion to consumers.
- Identical or similar signs on non-similar goods if the mark has a reputation in the UK and use, without due cause, would take unfair advantage of or be detrimental to the genuine mark.

This last section would have been useful when Taiwanese audio cassettes were sold in the UK under the name and trade dress of Seiko, a company that does not, and never has, produced audio tapes.

The common law offence of Conspiracy to Defraud can also be used by the police when dealing with these cases. It should be noted, however, that where the conspiracy is to be carried out abroad it is not indictable in England, even if it causes economic loss and damage to the proprietary interests of a British company.

The Trade Descriptions Act 1968 has also proved effective and has enabled trading standards officers to become very active in dealing with counterfeits sold in street markets and similar venues.

In the United States the Trade Mark Counterfeiting Act is proving invaluable for those engaged in prosecuting piracy; another useful weapon is their Organized Crime Control Act (the Racketeer Influenced and Corrupt Organization Act – RICO). For an action to succeed under the provisions of RICO, the plaintiffs must prove one of four specific activities:

- Mail fraud.
- Wire fraud.
- Interstate transportation of stolen property.
- Receiving stolen property transported interstate.

It would be impossible for a commercial counterfeiting conspiracy to function without committing either or both of the first two offences and therefore the provisions of RICO can frequently be invoked. Unfortunately, there appears to be a reluctance on the part of victims to make full use of this legislation. The idea that one is up against racketeers when dealing with counterfeiters has proved frightening to many complainants.

Frequently counterfeiters have been forewarned of a pending legal action, enabling them to deprive the plaintiffs of the evidence that had earlier been available and without which the case would be in jeopardy. It is therefore essential that the pirate's counterfeit stock, his machinery, if unique to the operation, and his books and records are seized to prevent their removal or destruction. This need has been acknowledged within the new Act and we now have a valuable addition to the armoury against counterfeiting – the ex-party Seizure Order. The actual number of such orders currently issued is not known, but within the United Kingdom and the United States their use has become routine.

Seizure Orders have their counterparts in Europe and elsewhere. The essential element of such an order is that one must first satisfy the courts that it is necessary to prevent the destruction or removal of essential evidence.

Apart from the provisions of the Trade Mark Act, trade mark owners in the UK can also apply for an Anton Pillar Order which not only enables them to seize documents, machinery and counterfeit merchandise, but also force the defendants to disclose their source of supply, their customers and any other information that is felt to be relevant to their action. These orders are now rarely used because of their expense and the restrictions placed on the applicant by the courts, but they still exist for those who need them.

The legal basis of the American Seizure Order is contained within their Trade Mark Counterfeiting Act, which authorises a court to direct seizure and confiscation of all infringing merchandise in a defendant's possession, custody or control. The need for such an order was typified in the notorious *Vuitton et Fils SA* versus *Crown Handbags* case which occurred in 1980. In that case Vuitton, after perusing the defendant's records, was unable to find any evidence demonstrating what portion, if any, of the revenues reflected in those records was derived from the sale of counterfeit Vuitton products.

As a result the courts awarded Vuitton costs based only on the offer for sale of six counterfeit bags by the defendants to Vuitton's own private investigator. This was a ridiculous state of affairs but, without direct evidence, there was no way of knowing whether the defendants had sold six, six hundred or six million counterfeit pieces.

In the UK and the US such seizure orders allow the plaintiff, or his agent, to be present during their execution, but in other countries orders are usually served by a court official. For example, in France a 'Saisie Contrefaçon' can officially only be executed by a *huissier*, or bailiff. This can present problems because the court official may not always be familiar with the ramifications of the case and consequently may fail to appreciate the significance of records seen but not seized. In Belgium the bailiff can be preselected by the plaintiff and briefed in advance, but mistakes can and do occur.

Seizure orders have proved invaluable in the fight against product counterfeiting and they have helped redress the balance in favour of the plaintiff.

■ Practical Steps

The first requirement is to be able to distinguish the genuine product from its copy. Secret codes on products, the addition of tracers in chemicals, deliberate flaws in stitching on clothing are all steps which manufacturers can take so that they can identify their own products quickly. But to be of value, knowledge of their existence must be restricted to only a few people, on a need-to-know basis. If they become common knowledge then the counterfeiters will duplicate them on their copies.

Having marked their merchandise, manufacturers must make frequent, but irregular, test purchases, particularly of products on the 'grey' market. This is extremely important in overseas markets where counterfeiting is tolerated. These surveys should be conducted by persons able to assess the size of the problem and, if necessary, conduct preliminary investigations. We do not recommend using the company's field staff: they are usually too well known and can easily drive the counterfeits underground.

Another essential task is to register your trade marks with the customs authority. Throughout Europe they are authorised to record these details and then hold up any unauthorised imports until they have been checked by the trade mark owner. If the owners know of an importation or suspect one, then they can have it seized.

Companies should have a product protection policy. This should define exactly what to do in the event of their products being counterfeited. Should the sales personnel be informed? Who should conduct the investigation? To whom should the investigator report? Consideration should be given to the use of public warnings, and the public should even be invited to assist the fight against piracy. Suitably worded notices can have a tremendous effect on a company's campaign, as demonstrated by Levi Strauss, United Features Syndicate (with Snoopy), Pfizer and many others.

■ Mutual-Aid Groups

Any firm must learn from the experiences of others. It should discuss its possible problems with companies whose products have actually been copied, since by sharing knowledge and information much can be achieved. This can be done by joining a mutual-aid group. The most active group is the International Anti-Counterfeiting Coalition (IACC), a voluntary body established in 1978 and based in Washington, DC, but with members throughout the world. It combats product counterfeiting by cooperation with law enforcement agencies and by mutual assistance. It also lobbies governments and regulatory authorities. It was this group that was instrumental in drawing up the International Anti-Counterfeiting Code. Within the United States its lobbying resulted in the enactment of the Trade Mark Counterfeiting Act 1984.

The British equivalent of the IACC is the Anti-Counterfeiting Group (ACG). Its basic objectives are the same as those of its international counterpart, but the ACG, for reasons best known to itself, cloaks its operations in secrecy; IACC, on the other hand, publicises its aims, its membership and its successes.

In Italy, the European home of counterfeiting, a group of Italian and Italian-based French companies have established their own intelligence operation, COLC. Exchange of information and the coordination of proceedings are high on their list of priorities.

■ Conclusions

Counterfeiting is a profitable and growing activity that poses a serious threat to manufacturers of branded products. It is frequently very well funded and organised and is prevalent throughout the world. Unfortunately, brand owners are frequently their own worst enemies. They fail to take even the most elementary precautions to protect their brands, and even where clear evidence of counterfeiting exists manufacturers often choose to ignore it, because of the costs. Fortunately that attitude is changing and brand owners are becoming more vigilant, but the battle has yet to be won.

CHAPTER 10

Brands as Financial Assets

Alex Batchelor

Interbrand

Introduction

A first lesson in economics at school will include the assertion that the primary purpose of business is the creation of wealth. 'Wealth', like 'business', is a word heavily encrusted with associations. The acquisition, ownership and distribution of wealth have for centuries excited controversy – often in a way that has little or nothing to do with the nature of wealth itself. If we can try and leave the joys of semantic and moral debate aside, for the purposes of this chapter let us consider 'wealth' as the value of all kinds of goods and services that people produce from the resources available to them.

Initially those resources revolved around individual labour, with its severe limitations (there is only so much one person can do alone – see the children's story of the elves and the shoemaker), and the ownership of land and property, which was confined to a tiny proportion of the population. With the advent of the Industrial Revolution those resources broadened to include machinery used in turning raw materials into finished goods. With the development of capital markets for lending and shareholding and their increasing sophistication, capital seeking rewards was matched with businesses seeking investment with the purpose of creating more wealth – the benefits of which would be shared between the business and those taking the risk of investing in it. This notion of risk is important, because the early definition of an asset was 'property available to meet debts' and this was only broadened in the second half of the twentieth century to mean 'any possession (person or thing) having any useful quality'.

Assets and Financial Statements

By this definition, then, any business is engaged in the activity of bringing together an array of resources, or 'assets', and adding value to them in some way. These assets are varied and include time, money, management, labour, land, plant, materials. Some are bought from suppliers and some are provided by the business itself. Some are tangible assets and some intangible. An entire industry has evolved that deals with what constitutes a tangible and intangible asset and how to separate investment in assets from simple operating expenses. All of this information is gathered about the business, checked by an independent body and then presented to the shareholders, and potential shareholders, in the form of accounts – which include a balance sheet, a profit and loss statement and a more recent innovation, a cashflow statement. Some of the key measures of business performance look at profit in relation to the tangible assets employed in the business and the amount of money that has been invested in the business by shareholders.

Tangible assets, be they plant, equipment, machinery or whatever, have tended to be seen as the basic, and in some cases only, components of wealth creation. Moreover, the assumption has been rightly that these assets have a finite life and that they lose value as they are 'used'. For the purposes of financial accounts, assets are therefore depreciated in value over a number of years that reflects their useful life – this can be as great as 20 years for a particularly long-lasting piece of machinery and as little as 2 years for some types of computer equipment and software.

These principles have a significant effect in the context of return on capital and its role as a key measure of business performance. Because the conventions that are followed for asset valuation and depreciation are stated in the accounts, and because any changes to these conventions have to be made clear, this should pose no real problems for shareholders. But there are two main things that can affect this. First, high inflation can rapidly make any historic cost evaluation of a business little more than an arbitrary assessment. Second, not all assets decline in value over a period that reflects their useful life; an example could be that stocks of a raw material can change in value dramatically, for example the diamond holdings of De Beers may not be so valuable if there is a sudden glut of diamonds from another source.

The major source of concern for this type of treatment for assets, depreciation in some form, tends to be property. In some countries the accounting profession has accepted the principle that not all classes of tangible asset automatically decline in value by allowing revaluations. In others the 'high church' belief that a balance sheet should represent only a historic record of transactions is followed. The main reasons for this difference are concerns about volatility and subjectivity in such valuations and revaluations. Financial journalists and analysts have commented on these potential anomalies many times:

Many fashionable techniques for judging corporate performance are variations on return on capital. While admirable in theory, all suffer from the weakness that, to calculate a return, one first needs to know the value of a company's assets and historic book values are often irrelevant. Hence one sees elaborate adjustments: goodwill write-offs and accumulated depreciation may be added back; the replacement cost of assets can be used or the price originally paid can be adjusted in line with inflation. All this wizardry is fair enough. But it can come at the expense of clear thinking about how to use return on capital in assessing performance . . . Such adjustments can simply divert attention from the fact that return on capital is not a useful measure for judging operating performance. (The Lex Column, *Financial Times*, 2 January 1997)

If the main aim of published financial statements is to provide information for existing shareholders and potential investors then these concerns can lead rapidly to a situation where most financial statements are precisely wrong as assessments of the business rather than roughly right. If revaluations of any kind are outlawed then all the information becomes increasingly unreliable as it gets older.

Thus it seems that simple asset ratios or even profit are not necessarily the best measures of business performance, and should certainly not be the only ones. But what kind of information would help? There is of course a clue to this in the title of the book.

We have called this book *Brands – The New Wealth Creators* because we recognised that against the economic and financial backdrop we have described, we need to broaden our understanding of what the assets of a business are. It would seem that in fact we can treat brands as wealth generating financial assets, albeit intangible ones, so that we can actually place a financial value on them.

■ Mergers and Brand Value

In the 1980s there was a considerable rise in the number of business mergers and acquisitions. What was even more interesting was the type of assets that were the focus of these mergers. A study of acquisitions in the 1980s showed that whereas in 1981 net tangible assets represented 82 per cent of the amount bid for companies, by 1987 this had fallen to just 30 per cent. It became clear that companies were being acquired less for their tangible assets and more for their intangible assets. This raised the whole issue of accounting for goodwill – the 'gap' left between the amount paid for a business and the value of its identifiable assets. Accounting practice left many companies, making what they believed to be good acquisitions, with two unpalatable alternatives. They could either suffer significant amortisation charges to their profit and loss account, or they had to write off the 'goodwill' to reserves and in many cases end up, irrationally, with a lower level of total assets than before the acquisition.

How does this affect brands? At the heart of any investment decision are assumptions made about the quality of earnings that a business delivers and about the security of those earnings into the future. One of the key attributes of brands has a direct impact on this – because brands represent an ongoing relationship between consumers and businesses and as such ensure both a level of demand and a security of demand that the business would not otherwise enjoy without the brand. Indeed as John Stuart, the former CEO of Quaker, put it: 'If this company were split up I would give you the property, plant and equipment and I would take the brands and trade marks and I would fare better than you'.

However, because branded-goods companies were many of those acquiring or being acquired in the 1980s and because the brands of these companies, though genuine intangible assets, were usually unrecognised, the impact of these acquisitions on their financial reporting as significant. Goodman Fielder Wattie made a bid for Rank Hovis McDougall in 1988. The RHM defence document stated that :

> RHM owns a number of strong brands, many of which are market leaders, which are valuable in their own right, but which the stock market tends consistently to undervalue. These valuable assets are not included in the balance sheet, but they have helped RHM to build profits in the past and will continue to provide a sound basis for future growth.

This assessment was reflected in the much higher final take-over price paid by the Tomkins Group.

The evidence of brand value could be seen in the huge gap between the tangible assets and the market capitalisation of many brand-based companies – the problem was how to assess and allocate what proportion of these intangible assets were brands. In 1988, in collaboration with the London Business School, Interbrand conducted the first 'whole portfolio' valuation for Rank Hovis McDougall. This established the principle that it was possible to value brands not only when they had been acquired, but also when they had been created by the company itself.

In 1989 the London Stock Exchange endorsed the concept of brand valuation as used by Rank Hovis McDougall, and there followed a number of other 'brand companies' that recognised the value of brands as intangible assets on their balance sheets. In the UK these included Cadbury Schweppes, Grand Metropolitan (when they acquired Pillsbury for $6 billion), Ladbrokes (when they acquired Hilton) and United Biscuits. In France brands were put on the balance sheet by, among others, Pernod Ricard and Danone, formerly BSN (which valued brands such as Bel Paese, Volvic, Lea & Perrins and Danone itself). In Australia and New Zealand balance sheet valuations have been carried out by companies as diverse as News International and Lion Nathan.

■ Brands and Wealth

It is already widely accepted that brands do create wealth. Maximising brand value is simply a part of maximising shareholder value – a goal that effective managers of all quoted companies recognise. Companies have increasingly come to be reorganised around brands and even in classic branded FMCG companies such as Unilever, their importance has been given a higher priority.

In their recent reorganisation the brands specifically were named as a key responsibility of the chairmen of the operating divisions – a far remove from the old model of brand manager control.

Balance sheet issues may have provided the impetus for the development of brand valuation, but its application does not stop there. There is certainly no doubt that more information on brands, brand performance and brand value should be disclosed in financial accounts. Companies are however wary of doing so and of disclosing the kind of information that they feel is competitively sensitive, and unless this is done their statements concerning brands end up looking like idle rhetoric and of little real use to investors.

Brand valuation can also be used in mergers and acquisition planning. A significant amount of explicit comment was made by both sides about brand value in the Rowntree/Nestlé and Granada/Forte take-overs – with all parties claiming to be able to maximise the value of the brands involved.

A similar role can also be seen in investor relations. Merrill Lynch issued a broker's circular in 1996 that argued that the share price of Burmah Castrol would have to increase by somewhere between 25 per cent and 50 per cent in order to cover the analyst's estimates of Castrol's 'brand value'. In a similar vein both P&G and Unilever annual reports would not be complete without the chief executive reiterating their commitment to building their portfolios of leading brands. The purpose of such communication can also be focused for an internal audience – and indeed can be used as explicit benchmarks for performance in rewarding management. Brand valuations of portfolios can also be used to help the crucial task of resource allocation and as a tool for evaluating the success of the decisions made!

Franchising and licensing deals, within corporations or with third parties, are increasingly popular and can also have implications for tax planning. Brand valuations have also been used in supporting negotiations with tax authorities, in supporting court claims for damages in cases of 'passing off' or in defending actions of unfair trading and even in the specific use of brands as a securitised asset to back specific borrowing.

Irrespective of its purpose, and recognising that it is only a single measure, it is no exaggeration to say that brand valuation has become an important technique for evaluating businesses. Its growing importance mirrors the growing importance of brands to the companies that own them.

■ How Much Wealth?

There is however one further question that any sensible observer will want answered too – *how much* wealth do brands create? The abstract notion that a brand represents a defensible legal property on which an incremental and future stream of revenue is based may be more widely accepted – but how to value that revenue stream is still the basis of some discussion.

When considering a valuation we first need to make sure that the revenue stream attributable to the brand is identifiable, that the legal title to the brand is unambiguous and that the brand could be sold separately from the business – however unlikely or even undesirable that may appear. Then we also need to consider the purpose of the valuation, because this will undoubtedly influence the assumptions that will be made. In valuing any asset there are a number of fundamentally different approaches, all with validity in certain circumstances. The three commonest are cost-based, market-based and income-based.

■ Cost-Based

Brands could theoretically be valued on the basis of what they cost to create or what they might theoretically cost to recreate. There are significant problems with both of these methods.

A historical aggregation of 'the costs of brand development' poses two major issues. Identifying those costs is a difficult enough task for relatively young brands. For brands over a hundred years old such as Coke or Kodak it would be both virtually impossible and irrelevant to identify what those costs of brand development were. This approach would also tend to focus on those brand-building costs that have a specific cost rather than on the value (or utility) that those costs have delivered. There are many brands on which a fortune has been spent and whose value is effectively nil. The principle that historical expenditure represents no guide to current value has to be accepted. The reality of brands is that they are hard to represent as a series of inputs because they are only really valuable as a series of outputs.

The valuation of brands on the basis of what they might theoretically cost to re-create is likely to pass through the realms of the acceptably subjective into the realms of the wildly fantastic. On what basis are we going to make assumptions about what those costs would be? Over how long are we going to assume that this investment should be made? Do we know whether the competitive situation is likely to remain static? By their very definition brands are unique assets and as such cannot simply be re-created – this tends to make the appealingly attractive siren call of replacement cost as a valuation method an ultimately futile quest.

■ Market-Based

Market value is another beguilingly attractive valuation method. For a stock or share there are a number of identical products and their price is set in a simple fashion by the laws of supply and demand. When there are sufficient products, sufficient buyers and sellers, and not too much regulation in the conduct of such business, then markets can be termed 'efficient', and this is a topic that has been the subject of vast amounts of academic and business-related study.

So what is the problem for brands? Well, many of the tests that we apply to determine whether there is a market for something would appear to be invalid.

The brands are by their very nature unique and therefore hard to compare. It is also unlikely that there will be adequate publicly available information about comparable market transactions on which to base a valuation. Few companies have a single brand, and if they do then it is unlikely to be for sale as a separate entity. Given the paucity of relevant information it would be wrong to use 'market value' as a primary method of valuation when it is clear that there is no open, comparable market in brands. It can however have a useful role as a 'reality check' for other methods of brand valuation.

■ Income-Based

□ *Royalties*

The principle that brands generate a level of demand (and therefore of income) and have a security of demand (and therefore of income) makes the logical progression to an income-based valuation method an easy one.

The simplest type of income-based valuation is the 'royalty relief' method. This approach values the brand by reference to the amount of royalty that a brand owner has been relieved from paying to a third party. By owning the brand the company is 'relieved' from paying a license fee ('royalty') for the use of the intangible asset – hence 'royalty relief'. This royalty is often calculated as a percentage of sales over a given period. The main problem with this approach is that there is little comparable data on what royalty rates are being paid. Where royalty rates are available they are often skewed because patent rights, copyrights and other forms of intellectual property are also incorporated. Frequently the royalty rate will have been arrived at as part of a larger complex transaction which adds further confusion. More importantly the rate charged for a brand in one sector or geography will vary when that brand is being licensed into new market sectors or new territories. It can therefore be extremely difficult, if not impossible, to identify an appropriate royalty rate for a particular brand valuation.

□ *Economic Use*

The best income-based approach is an 'economic use' valuation which seeks to determine the economic value of a brand to the current owner in its current use. This is the type of approach pioneered and championed by Interbrand.

Historical earnings valuations, which were the first type of brand valuations, tended to focus on a multiple of earnings – which offered a pleasing symmetry with the basis on which many companies were valued. The problem with such multiples is twofold. The first is which multiple to use. In the case of companies this is often done on the basis of comparable transactions – price/earning (p/e) ratios for the sector will be used as a benchmark. The second problem is posed by the issue of past performance as a guide to future performance and the volatility that is inherent because of the use of just one or two years in the calculation.

A better alternative is based on the discounted value of future brand earnings – stemming from the relationship the brand has with its consumers. By using 'fully absorbed' profits and identifying the excess net earnings that are attributable to ownership of the brand this revenue stream can be projected into the future.

The value today of a brand's future earnings is a function of how high these earnings are and of how likely it is that they will be achieved. It should thus take into consideration three things about the brand: its *financial* performance (in order to identify its true net earnings); its *marketing* strength and its competitive advantage over other brands (to establish the security of demand) and its *legal* position (to prove that it is a separable property).

It is not enough to look at brand value simply in terms of financial numbers. The discount rate applied to the earnings of the brand should reflect the security they enjoy. If there were two brands each producing the same earnings in a given market but one was Coke and the other a new, less well-established brand, then they would of course have different values. Interbrand has developed a model of brand strength that examines the various marketing and legal factors that affect the risk of a brand and uses it to derive the risk rate. Strong brands will have a higher brand strength score and therefore a commensurately lower discount rate.

■ **Conclusion**

Brands are financial assets and their importance in relation to the tangible assets of most businesses continues to grow. The management of brand value is simply another aspect of managing shareholder value. As such it is a key task of all management. If more companies were committed to demonstrating, on a consistent and clear basis, the extent to which they were doing this, then the need for platitudes about branding in annual reports would become a thing of the past. A number of companies such as Skandia and Dow Chemicals are beginning to publish statements of value alongside their statutory reports, and an EC think tank is currently actively proposing this route. As balance sheets and profit and loss statements came to be augmented by cashflow statements, so this triumvirate may need a further addition.

Companies would be able to make factual statements of the sort they do about financial performance about all aspects of corporate value, and shareholders would be able to evaluate brand and ultimately corporate health with more reliability than they do now. Whether this is done through the mechanism of the balance sheet is ultimately a diversionary issue and has not affected the trend towards environmental and even ethical reporting by many companies.

The pioneering work that Interbrand did in assessing the value of brands for inclusion in balance sheets was highly controversial at the time. It forced companies to reconsider what balance sheets were for and how the true value of assets should be represented on them. Interestingly, such debate took place against a background of much wider debate about balance sheets, their purpose and their preparation. As can be seen, there is debate about the tangible items on balance sheets as well as the intangibles.

But what is more interesting is that the balance sheet debate has raised awareness of the key point that brands are assets of companies and that they are a key part of the 'wealth creation' basis of the business. This then has important implications for the way in which businesses manage their brands. They can no longer take brands for granted; they need to monitor brand value over time; they need to invest behind their brands to ensure that value is maintained; and they need to give brands proper senior responsibility. In short they need to treat brands (and their other intangible assets) in the same way as they have traditionally created their tangible assets. A move like this is required if companies are to enter the twenty-first century armed with a concept of wealth creators that is a bit more advanced than the one devised in the nineteenth!

CHAPTER 11

Brand Licensing

Raymond Perrier
Interbrand

◼ The Commercial Reality of Brand Value

As we have seen from the previous chapter, regardless of the accounting debate about balance sheets, the fact remains that the amount being paid to acquire branded-goods companies such as Rowntree MacIntosh, Pillsbury, Bond Brewing and Nabisco has focused attention on the value of brands and their importance in the net worth of businesses.

Brands do comprise a significant element of business value and this is now recognised by analysts, by shareholders, by company boards, by bankers and by key regulatory authorities (not least the London Stock Exchange and the Monopolies and Mergers Commission). What is more, for many businesses the brand element is often more important than the tangible assets that traditionally have been regarded as the core value of a company.

◼ Licensing of Intellectual Property

One field in which brand valuation and the concept of brand value is beginning to have an impact is the area of trade mark licensing. In recent years there has been a marked increase in the attention given to the licensing of trade marks as well as of other intellectual property such as copyrights, patents and designs.

The notion of a licence is a simple one: the owner of a piece of property allows another party to make use of the property and in return can expect to receive some form of compensation. The party (individual or company) issuing the licence is called the licensor; the party receiving the licence is called the licensee. Licences need to define a number of elements, especially the following:

- The piece of property being licensed (for example, the right to use the trade mark Gucci).
- The entity to whom the property is being licensed (for example, by John Smith and Sons Pty Ltd).
- The geographic extent of the licence (for example, only in Australia).
- The commercial extent of the licence (for example, only for the manufacture and distribution of polystyrene beer can holders).
- The duration (for example, for a period of five years from the date of the licence).

Because of the desire by the owner of the property to safeguard what is being licensed and ensure that the licensee does not undermine its value, licences usually include strict provisions covering quality control for both production and marketing, reporting of performance, collaboration with the licensor and other licensees and conditions for termination.

Licences will also define in one of one or more of a variety of ways the manner of calculating and remitting compensation. The list below gives some examples.

Examples of royalty charges
- 5 per cent of the value of all remittances received (net sales) in relation to products carrying the licensed properties.
- 5 per cent of the value of all remittances received (net sales) in relation to products carrying the licensed properties or a minimum of $100 000 per annum, whichever is the lower.
- 20 per cent of the value of the gross contribution received in relation to products carrying the licensed properties, defined as net sales *less* cost of goods *less* marketing expenditure.
- 50 per cent of the value of audited earnings before interest and tax received in relation to products carrying the licensed properties.
- 50 per cent of the value of audited earnings before interest and tax received in relation to products carrying the licensed properties or $1 million, whichever is the higher.
- $500 000 per annum either in the form of cash or in the form of advertising expenditure of a manner and type to be agreed with the licensor.
- $10 for every gross of product sold.
- $15 per hectolitre for the first 10 000 hectolitres of branded product sold; $10 per hectolitre for every hectolitre thereafter.
- $2 million of branded product to be bought from the licensor every year in equal amounts per quarter at the licensor's annual published price list.

As can be seen, sometimes the 'royalty' is assessed as a percentage of sales, sometimes as a percentage of gross profit or net profit, sometimes as an amount per litre or per unit or per kilo, sometimes as a fixed amount. Often maximum and minimum amounts are stipulated, and also the rate may decrease or increase with volume on a sliding scale.

It is also important to recognise that the amount of a pure royalty may be reduced or eliminated by the use of other means of gaining compensation for the use of the brand: a management fee, an extra contribution to advertising and promotional expenses, the rent on a retail site or the price of a raw material that the licensee is obliged to purchase. For example, agreements between Coca-Cola Corporation and its third-party bottlers or between Body Shop International and its franchisees do not tend to require an explicit payment for the use of the Coke or Body Shop brands. Instead the licensee will be required to purchase the essential sticky brown concentrate for making a Coke-branded cola or the finished products for sale in a Body Shop-branded outlet and will have to buy these at a given price and in certain minimum quantities.

But though the payment for these products may appear to be for a tangible transfer, it is clear that the amount that can be demanded is influenced as much by the trade mark rights that go with the product as by the qualities of the products themselves. It is only by buying these ingredients or these products that the licensee can make use of the brand, and so the charge for the use of the brand is hidden within the charge for buying the tangible elements.

■ Trade Mark Licensing

The licensing of technological know-how and patents has long been established and it is accepted that often significant royalties should be paid by licensees for the use of such assets. Moreover, the agreements governing such licences are often very complex and recognise that the maintenance of the value of the intangible asset is an important task and is the duty of both the licensor and the licensee.

Until recently, however, trade mark licences were not treated seriously and indeed sometimes were just added in as the 'icing on the cake' of patent/technology licences. For example, when the Japan Victor Company (JVC) was licensing its home video recorder technology to other Japanese and American companies in the 1970s, they included in the licence (but without charge) the right to use the trade mark VHS. This was indeed a shrewd move, because it meant that as JVC's format for video technology became established as the norm (over that of Philips or Sony), their trade mark VHS became the standard descriptor for the format. In this case, JVC's strategy enabled them to create value in their trade mark as well as in their patented technology. But in many other cases, allowing a patent licensee to use a trade mark as well amounts to giving it away.

But the increasing awareness of the value of brands has prompted brand owners to wake up to the notion that, although intangible, such properties *do* have significant value and that their licensing cannot be regarded as a mere formality.

One of the first effects of this is that licence agreements with third parties now pay much more attention to the fact that the property being licensed is valuable. Higher royalty rates are being demanded (and justified) and stricter conditions are put in place to ensure that proper use and maintenance of trade marks – both in legal terms and in marketing terms.

For example, it has long been established in the area of luxury goods that the licensor (say, Dunhill) has the right to set very strict rules about the design, manufacture and distribution of its licensed goods and may even stipulate specific suppliers of key raw materials. Regular audits, site inspections and blind trials are all part of this approach. But it is also now common to find licensees of brands in which 'quality' is less of an issue being subjected to the same strict quality inspections.

However, at the same time as the duty of licensees is becoming more onerous, their contribution to and participation in the brand is seen as greater. For example, licensees will often now participate with the brand owner in the development of global advertising campaigns and the design of a visual identity programme. In some organisations, for example, the Body Shop, little distinction is made between the operations that are wholly owned and those that are franchised or licensed. It is only in this way that the integrity, and thus the value, of a brand can be safeguarded.

■ Internal Licensing

The growth in the awareness and importance of licensing to third parties has made more and more companies aware of the role that internal licensing might play. An internal licence is one in which the licensee is a subsidiary company or an associate company of the licensor. In such a situation – where the interest in and control of the two parties is common – it might be thought that a trade mark licence was redundant. After all, if I am a wholly owned subsidiary of Texaco Inc, not only will I probably be using the Texaco trade mark but I may well expect to have the *right* to use it.

But it should not be forgotten that a trade mark, in common with other forms of property, has a defined owner – and within a group of companies the user may not always be the owner. Thus, the trade mark Texaco is owned in most countries by Texaco Inc, but is used in the UK by Texaco Ltd. Though the UK company is a wholly owned subsidiary of the American corporation, it is a separate legal entity and its use of the mark can be only with the permission (explicit or implicit) of the trade mark owner.

In many cases, the external licensing of trade marks (to third parties) is what has made companies more aware of the need for internal licences. For example, for many years Castlemaine Perkins Pty Limited (an Australian brewer) has licensed its main brand Castlemaine XXXX to a UK brewer (first Allied Breweries Ltd, now Carlsberg Tetley Ltd) who brews and distributes XXXX-branded lager in the UK market. Since its amalgamation into the Lion Nathan group of breweries, Castlemaine Perkins has also seen its brand being brewed by associate companies within the group (for example the Swan Brewery Company Pty Ltd in Western Australia). Because both breweries are wholly owned by the same parent company, Lion Nathan Limited, a licence between the two breweries might seem excessive, but in fact one has been put in place to formalise the relationship between the two and to ensure that the rights and duties of both trade mark owner and licensee are well understood.

Ironically, the UK licensee of XXXX is also itself a good example of internal licensing. Carlsberg Tetley is (at the point of writing) a 50 : 50 joint venture between Allied Domecq of the UK and Carlsberg of Denmark. It brews a number of brands but it owns none of them. Rather (as with XXXX) they are licensed from a third party, or (as with Tetley) they are licensed from the UK partner company, or (as with Carlsberg) they are licensed from the Danish partner company. Though one of the top five brewers in the UK, in a market which is dominated by strong, well-established brands, Carlsberg Tetley is in the unique position of not actually owning any brands itself!

■ Centralising Trade Marks

These internal licences – sometimes developed *ad hoc* between associated companies within the same group – are now being further systematised by the use of central trade mark holding companies. In such a situation, trade mark registrations are transferred from the operating companies that created or acquired them to the parent company itself or to a legal entity that reports directly to the parent and has been given charge of owning the trade marks. Nestlé is one of the famous examples of this policy of owning most intellectual property centrally (trade marks but also patents and copyrights), licensing the right to use it back to subsidiaries and then charging subsidiaries for its use. Thus, for example, even though many of the brands acquired by Nestlé as part of Rowntree were purely British brands (Quality Street, After Eight, and so on), they are all now owned by the Swiss company and licensed back to the English company.

■ Role of Internal Licensing

Internal licences and especially centrally controlled internal licences have a number of implications for the good management of trade marks and brands. A few examples are given below.

● Centralised internal licences ensure that development of brands is controlled centrally and directed to the benefit of the whole group and not just of a subsidiary.
  For example, a European biscuit company owns subsidiaries in both Poland and Finland. The Polish company is very keen to add to its portfolio a brand created by the Finnish company – it has the capacity to make the product itself, but realises that even though it is part of the same group it has no right to use the Finnish company's brand and needs permission to do so. The Finnish company would be reluctant to grant permission because it feels rationally that such use will undermine its own international strategy, but also because it feels irrationally that the brand is so much a part of its heritage that it does not want to see another company producing it.
  However, the trade mark now belongs to the parent company, which can therefore consider more objectively the cases put by each of the operating

companies. It concludes that the overall value of the brand would be maximised if the brand were extended into Poland and is prepared to put in place covenants to protect the Finnish interest. However, there is also a wider group issue unknown to either the Finnish or Polish companies: the question of the long-term position of the Polish company within the group. Serious consideration is being given to the possibility of divesting of the Polish company in the next eighteen months and with that in view it seems safer to delay any possible licensing of the brand until the position is clearer.

- The maintenance of brand rights – such as the registering and renewing of trade mark registrations, policing, prosecuting infringement and passing-off actions – is coordinated and carried out consistently across the world rather than being left to the interests or abilities of local management.

  Some multinationals have found to their embarrassment that protection of seemingly international trade marks varies markedly from one country to another. In some cases, local management has been too fastidious and has spent an excessive amount registering the mark and pursuing the most unlikely infringement actions. In other cases, local management, keen to be seen to be reducing overheads, has been too lax and cut corners in terms of registrations and failed to pursue some winnable actions. A centralised trade mark department is the best way of ensuring that such problems are avoided and that, with advice from local management, an appropriate and consistent policy of trade mark protection is pursued worldwide for international brands.

- The licensing of brands, and the charging of brand royalties, rescues brands from the closed world of the marketing department and makes their value the responsibility also of financial and legal departments. Their position as an asset of the company – rather than a toy given to amuse a junior brand manager for a few years – is crystallised.

- International brands, whose marketing may be shared by more than one company within a group or even by more than one division, are centrally coordinated to ensure maximum coherence in terms of brand image, product development, advertising, and so on. For example, for a long time now Philip Morris has recognised that management of its Marlboro brand cannot be left to the individual companies within the PMI group but needs to be centrally coordinated. The success of PMI in creating an international franchise for the Marlboro brand has now prompted other tobacco companies (for example BAT) to follow this approach and to ensure that autonomy for local companies does not become an obstacle for good international brand management. Centralising ownership of brands – as BAT is doing through its BatMark subsidiary – is one way of ensuring that this happens.

- Brands can more easily be extended into new areas and licensed to other subsidiaries while firm control is still kept on the integrity of brand equity. For example, after its acquisition from Rowntree, Nestlé recognised that the Aero brand had a franchise in the UK market that was potentially wider than the just the aerated chocolate product that Rowntree has used to carry the brand. Recognising developments in the dairy desserts market in which another Nestlé subsidiary, Chambourcy, operated, Nestlé has now licensed the Aero brand across to Chambourcy and is making a success of this extension that will benefit both subsidiaries and ultimately the parent group. Thus, operating companies are made aware that the brands they use are as much a shared resource, and a property of common value as, say, research laboratories, recipes and patents.

- Country managers can be made responsible for the local maintenance and development of a global brand. Their contribution to brand value is after all a contribution to shareholder value and should be rewarded accordingly.
- Internal licences, whether within the home country or overseas, increasingly incorporate the payment of a royalty that reflects the true value of the asset being used rather than just being a nominal amount to 'cover administration'. Making a financial charge for the use of a trade mark (or other intellectual property) focuses the user on the value of the asset and the need both to protect and exploit that value.
- The royalties received from licences to overseas subsidiaries can be used to repatriate funds in return for the use of a genuine piece of property. This can have major fiscal implications.
- New licences negotiated within the group, with joint venture partners and outside the group, can be placed in a context of genuine brand licensing and realistic royalty rates, giving the opportunity to negotiate much higher returns for the use of brands than has been the case commonly in the past.

Brand valuation has made a critical contribution in all of these areas both in raising awareness of the concept of 'brand value' and in putting a monetary value to a brand. Insisting that a brand has value is one thing; being able to state what that value *is* is the best way to make the maintenance and development of that value part of company strategy. It also helps to communicate to the world that the company takes its brands seriously.

■ The Fiscal Advantages of Internal Licensing

One aspect mentioned above is the fiscal implication of charging overseas subsidiaries and third-party licensees a proper rental for the use of brands. At Interbrand our experience is that many companies have yet to realise that the royalty rates they demand are far too small for the value of the trade mark asset being licensed. Increasing the royalty rate demanded has not only managerial benefits but also transfer pricing advantages.

An example illustrates this. Brand A is being used by FoodCo Japan and FoodCo UK. It was actually developed by FoodCo UK and is used under licence by the Japanese company. However, the Japanese company now makes and distributes all its own A-branded product and relies on FoodCo UK only for rights to use the brand. FoodCo UK charges a royalty to FoodCo Japan and there is a subsequent tax saving to the group (Table 11.1). By setting up a trade mark owning company (FoodMark) the group is able to benefit from legitimate transfer pricing to improve its tax position. Where the subsidiary is paying tax at 50 per cent and the parent company at 33 per cent, the tax benefit is a net gain of £17 in every £100 of allowed brand royalties.

With such clear commercial benefits companies are keen to ensure that their licensing of brands in reflecting their management structure also provides a fiscal benefit where possible. But when arguments are put forward to tax authorities to justify increasing royalty rates they lack the financial robustness of a valuation of the asset. Instead, tax authorities bring the argument back to comparability with other royalty rates and, of course, it is the tax authorities themselves who have the best information on what comparable rates are being charged.

This imbalance of power could, we believe, be greatly improved in two ways:

- If companies took a more scientific approach to the setting of royalty rates rather than relying on what has been done in the past.
- If companies pooled their royalty rate information so that they were as well informed as the tax authorities with whom they were arguing.

Table 11.1 Example of Internal Licensing

With licence	FoodCo UK	FoodCo Japan	FoodMark	FoodCo Group
Sales	1000	1000	0	2000
Pre-tax profit	100	150	0	250
Royalty rate for use of brand	10%	10%		
Royalty charged	−100	−100	200	0
Profit after royalty	0	50	200	250
Tax rate	33%	50%	33%	
Tax payable	0	−25	−66	−91
Post-tax profit	0	25	134	159

Without licence	FoodCo UK	FoodCo Japan	FoodMark	FoodCo Group
Sales	1000	1000	0	2000
Pre-tax profit	100	150	0	250
Royalty rate for use of brand	0%	0%		
Royalty charged	0	0	0	0
Profit after royalty	100	150	0	250
Tax rate	33%	50%	33%	
Tax payable	−33	−75	0	−108
Post-tax profit	67	75	0	142

■ Comparable Transaction Methods

It is sometimes argued that it is possible to determine royalty rates in controlled transactions by the use of comparisons with other transactions. However, we do not believe that such an approach would be appropriate in many cases. For such a method to work it is necessary to have one or a number of comparable transactions that can be used as a base for comparison. These should be transactions in similar circumstances between similar parties and should not have been influenced themselves by any control that one party had over the other. When the transaction is not directly compatible then an understanding of it is required so that appropriate adjustments can be made to achieve a genuine comparable.

The problem is that is it rare to find situations in which there are comparable transactions that would be suitable for use in such an approach. For the transaction to be comparable it would have to:

- Deal with the licensing of a brand to be used in the same or similar product market and in the same or similar territory.
- Involve the licensing of a brand that has been in existence for the same period of time as the one with which it is being compared.
- Involve the licensing of the brand to entities that already have well-established brand names themselves.
- Involve the licensing of a brand with similar general and specific consumer values.
- Involve a licence of similar duration, with similar terms of renewal, similar restrictions and similar obligations.
- Be competing in an environment with rival brands that cover a similar spread of weakness or strength.

From our experience it is rare to find such comparables, and royalty rates based on so-called comparables often provide a false basis for comparison; for example:

- We might know that there is a food manufacturer who has agreed to pay a licence rate of 2 per cent to put the Mickey Mouse brand on a biscuit product (in a low margin, competitive market). But to put the same brand on a T-shirt selling in the same market we could certainly expect a higher royalty.
- Also, the royalty that should be charged to put the Mickey Mouse brand on a theme park in no way is reflected in the royalties that may be charged for the use of the brand on food items or on character merchandising.
- Similarly, though we may have a comparable of a brand being licensed in a new territory (say, China) we would expect that a royalty for the same brand in a territory where it has been established for many years to be much higher, all else being equal, since its value is more proven and better understood in the latter country.

Brand extension: Virgin has successfully and profitably applied its name to products completely outside its mainstream business. Its product range now encompasses airlines, vodka, cola, financial services and jeans

By simplifying pricing and providing an amount of call time in the monthly charge, Orange attracted a substantial share of the market very quickly

The 'intangible' brand values of Marks & Spencer allow it to extend into new and different product areas, the most recent attempt being financial services

MARKS & SPENCER

 # DAEWOO

Competition may not always come from the obvious competitors, an example being Daewoo, which has circumvented the traditional dealerships

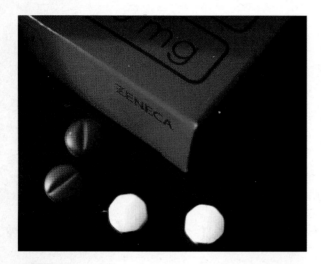

The name Zeneca was loosely derived from the word 'zenith', meaning 'highest point'. The active sounding 'z' invests the name with connotations of technology and modernity

'I knew a trade name must be short, vigorous, incapable of being misspelled to an extent that will destroy its identity and, in order to satisfy trademark laws, it must mean nothing. The letter K had been a favourite with me – it seemed a nice strong, incisive sort of letter. Therefore, the word I wanted had to start with K. Then it became a question of trying out a great number of combinations of letters that made words starting with K. The word "Kodak" is the result.' (George Eastman on creating the Kodak name)

The Kit Kat and Bass brands have similar packaging designs to their originals. They are examples of classic brands that have stood the test of time

When the classic barbell-shaped glass Listerine bottle was redesigned, a hard-edged rectangular barbell shape was used which echoed the shape of the old bottle, yet said 'strong', 'hard-working' and 'effective' to the consumer

When Jhirmack reformulated its product to include the addition of Vitamin E, a new graphic device representing an abstract of hair in the process of mending was added to the packaging, thus attracting new buyers

The Dark & Lovely logo
was modified to make it
more colourful, graphically
impactful and feminine

Companies such as Sony
have a global brand
umbrella which acts as
the 'corporate glue' when
entering new geographic
markets or product areas

As one of the most focused
and well-managed corporate
brands, The Body Shop is
inextricably linked to the
personality and vision of its
founder Anita Roddick

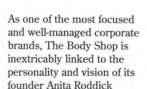

Castlemaine XXXX is an example of internal licensing of the brand name between two brewers owned by the same parent company, ensuring that the rights and duties of the trademark owner and licensee are well understood

The success of PMI in creating an international franchise for the Marlboro brand highlights the importance of centrally coordinated brand management

Operating for more than four decades in a fiercely competitive marketplace, McDonald's has established a reputation as one of the world's most successful franchising organisations

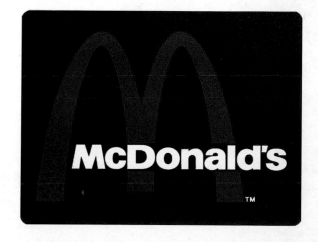

HONDA

Coca-Cola is an excellent example of a powerful international brand which has been with us for generations and which continues to be enormously successful

MIGROS

Over the last seventy years the huge global sales and profit that have been generated by the Mars bar have been underpinned by only a few factors documented in a short brand strategy statement that lives by the brand manager's bedside. To change any one of these attributes would take several years of discussion and would probably have to be agreed by the CEO

For retailers such as Sainsbury's who stock around 50 per cent private label, the retail brand has probably become the dominant brand in the consumer's mind

Tesco has 17,000 product lines, 435 stores and 120,000 front-of-store checkout operators, counter-staff and shelf-fillers. The Tesco customer's experience of the brand is a combination of all the products he/she buys there, the shopping environment and the level of service

Imigran is an example of a brand name which clearly indicates the use of the drug in treating migraines

Apple is
dedicated to the
empowerment of
man – to making
personal
computing
accessible to each
and every
individual so as to
help change the
way we think,
work, learn and
communicate

Bic extended its
brand inline with its
perception of special
expertise: BiC
disposable pens to
BiC disposable
lighters and razors

Red Tribe, recently
launched by
Manchester United,
is a first attempt away
from more traditional
licensing into the
launch of sub-brands

The problem with setting royalty rates by recourse to comparables is that often the so-called comparables are based on peripheral uses of the brand rather than the core of the brand itself, and thus give only marginal help in determining an appropriate royalty rate.

■ Conclusion

We believe that the managerial and fiscal implication of trade mark licensing are profound, and that brand valuation has a key role to play in adding method and objectivity to an area that in the past has been plagued by doubt and misunderstanding. As companies become increasingly aware of the importance of brands and trade marks they will begin to focus on the better management of these assets, and one of the ways of improving such management is the creation of appropriate structures for the internal and external licensing of the brand.

CHAPTER 12

Brand Franchising

Andrew Taylor
Executive Vice President and Chief Operating Officer
McDonald's UK

■ Introduction

The success of McDonald's as a leading brand on the international stage owes much of its momentum to the company's unique approach to franchising. Operating for the past forty years in a fiercely competitive marketplace, McDonald's has established a reputation as one of the world's most successful franchising organisations. At the heart of this success lies a unique interdependence between franchiser and franchisee that few other companies have been able to emulate. The purpose of this chapter is to examine the historical roots of McDonald's approach to franchising and to show how this approach has been instrumental in building one of the strongest and commercially most successful brands of the nineties. First, however, must come an introduction to franchising.

■ The Franchise Industry

The franchise industry is now a huge and mature one and is global in scope. It continues to expand, and in the last twenty years or so there has been tremendous growth in the areas of catering, retailing and the provision of services. Statistics on the growth of franchising have been hard to find, but the European Franchise Federation has published the figures for 1993 given in Table 12.1. France leads the field in Europe, followed by Germany.

■ What is Franchising?

Franchising is a partnership between, on the one hand, the owner of a business system offering a branded product or service and, on the other, a network of individuals each selling that branded product or service in accordance with the system through an operating unit that they own and run. In addition to access to the system the owner grants rights in the intellectual property of the business. This includes trade marks and logos and can often cover the look and design of the business, the uniforms of employees, promotional materials and so forth.

Table 12.1   European Franchise Federation statistics 1993

Country	Number of franchisers	Number of franchisees	Annual turnover, ECU bn	People employed
Austria	170	2 700		
Belgium	135	2 495		
Czech Republic	7	27	0.83	760
Denmark*	42	500		
France	500	30 000	31	310 000
Germany	420	18 000	10	
Hungary	150	1 000		10 000
Italy	361	17 500	7 5	50 000
Netherlands	340	12 120	6.8	69 750
Norway*	125	3 500	3	
Portugal	70			
Spain	250	20 000	2.3	
Sweden	200	9 000	3.6	
UK	396	24 900	6.4	188 500

*Figures at 31 December 1992.

The system owner, the franchiser, will have invested in developing and testing the brand and system, and continues to support the network with business development, promotion, training and administrative services. The owners of the operating units, the franchisees, will each have invested in setting up the business within the network, and they pay a regular fee to the franchiser. This is to compensate the franchiser for the continuing benefits they receive from remaining in the system and for the franchiser's support services.

Both parties build, to their mutual advantage, the brand and its reputation, and their sales and profitability. Interflora 'flower relay', Dyno-Rod drain and pipe clearing, Prontaprint printing and copying shops and McDonald's fast food restaurants are all examples of highly successful franchised businesses.

■ The McDonald's Approach – How It All Began

Fundamental to any insight into McDonald's approach to franchising is an understanding of what is expected of a would-be franchisee. An applicant for a McDonald's franchise is expected not only to understand the functional requirements of their role as a franchisee, but also to assimilate themselves and their staff enthusiastically into a deep-rooted and all-pervasive corporate vision. The willingness and ability of a prospective franchisee to share a commitment to this vision is valued as highly as any amount of theoretical knowledge or commercial experience gained outside the company. The qualities required are best exemplified by reference to Ray Kroc, McDonald's founder, whose single-minded strength of vision, character and determination embodied a spirit that still pervades many aspects of the company's operations today.

In 1954, Ray Kroc approached two Californian brothers, Dick and Mac McDonald, seeking his own franchise to trade under the McDonald's name, a name already synonymous in California with good value-food and fast, friendly and efficient service. Kroc was a salesman, supplying five spindle milkshake multi-mixers to the McDonald brothers' drive-in restaurant in San Bernadino. He had calculated from his own sales figures that the restaurant must be selling over 20 000 milkshakes a month. Intrigued, Kroc made a personal visit to the restaurant and spent several hours watching passing trade from his parked car. What he witnessed filled him with a sense of exciting potential. From a small octagonal building located in a suburban parking lot, the restaurant was filling orders for fifteen-cent hamburgers with fries and shakes every fifteen seconds. One hundred and fifty customers were on the lot by mid-day. When he learned that this continuous demand was unlikely to let up until late evening, Kroc knew he had to get involved and the rest, as they say, is history.

Forty years on, a prospective franchisee is, like Kroc, expected to demonstrate a similarly entrepreneurial spirit, displaying an instinctive desire to build business for both themselves and McDonald's. In *Behind the Arches*, his definitive book on McDonald's, John F. Love notes the importance of Kroc's legacy:

> From the outside, it is easy to assume that McDonald's is run by clones.
> Those on the inside know differently. Franchising's most talented service
> organisation was built not by dictating to managers but by giving them
> enormous decision-making authority. From the beginning, the team consisted
> of extremely diverse individuals, not the type of managers who typically
> survive in corporate bureaucracies. These were not organisation people; they
> were corporate entrepreneurs.

Ray Kroc was not alone in recognising the opportunity when he opened his first restaurant at Des Plaines, Illinois, on 15 April 1955. The willingness of the American public – especially families – to leave their homes and their TV sets for an inexpensive meal out had been noticed by others. By the time Des Plaines opened, competitors such as Burger King and Kentucky Fried Chicken were already established and beginning to grant their own franchises. On the face of it, Ray Kroc was just another entrepreneurial player joining a very hard game. Nothing was guaranteed. With every step there lay new challenges ahead. Today, every new McDonald's franchisee is expected to show the same pioneering spirit displayed by Ray Kroc forty years ago.

■ 'Enthusiasm and Commitment'

Success is something that McDonald's never takes for granted. We grant franchises for a variety of reasons which can be financial, operational or geographical in nature. One constant factor in the franchising process is our desire to recruit operators who are prepared to work harmoniously with the corporation without dampening their entrepreneurial spirit and personal determination to succeed. It is no coincidence that franchisees have been directly responsible for a number of successful innovations in the area of new product development. Our flagship product, the Big Mac, was invented in 1968 by Pittsburgh franchisee Jim Deligatti. Nine years later, the same franchisee was responsible for the creation of the Big Breakfast, a product which was to help change the breakfast habits of millions of Americans in the years that followed. Another much documented example of franchisee-driven menu innovation took place in a Cincinnati in 1963. Lou Groen, a local McDonald's franchisee in the predominantly Catholic area of the city had noted a marked decline in the restaurant's Friday trade. The result was the Filet O' Fish, which went on to become one of McDonald's most successful products worldwide.

The transmission of the enthusiasm and commitment from franchisee to staff and, ultimately, customers has played a key role in the development of the McDonald's brand. From the earliest days of Des Plaines, operational efficiency has always been a central issue. Relying on a strong sense of shared purpose from staff working in a safe and spotlessly clean environment, Kroc set out his vision for the McDonald's brand. McDonald's restaurants, insisted Kroc, would offer a better value experience than any of his competitors. This single-minded vision of the McDonald's 'difference' was quickly short-handed to QSC&V, an acronym for 'quality, service, cleanliness and value' which remains the system's credo to this day.

Ray Kroc's personal application and ambition to make Des Plaines a success is legendary. Fred Turner, McDonald's current Senior Chairman and one of the original staff at Des Plaines, recalls in a subtle but revealing anecdote, the Saturday morning when he discovered Kroc cleaning out the tiny holes in the restaurant's mop wringer, armed only with a toothbrush. This anecdote demonstrates more than one aspect of the dedication McDonald's expects from all of its staff. It shows, of course, that Ray Kroc was a man willing to roll up his sleeves and do a dirty job himself, displaying an egalitarianism which characterises McDonald's management structure to this day. The story also serves as a colourful illustration of the 'extra mile' franchisees are expected to travel in order to ensure that standards of cleanliness are maintained. The story is cited by Turner as an example of his boss's dedication to operations efficiency. The operating principles of QSC&V were developed through the kind of energy and dedication exemplified by Turner's story. As a company, we have not slackened in our adherence to these principles with the passing of years and our franchisees have been instrumental in maintaining the standards that have made McDonald's a byword for quality in the popular catering sector.

Empowerment is key to the success of McDonald's franchising system. Ray Kroc's pledge to nervous new franchisee recruits was that if they maintained high standards of QSC&V then the money would take care of itself. He recognised that, however assiduous the monitoring of operational standards by the franchiser, the ultimate responsibility lay with the franchisee and his restaurant staff. Should standards in any way fall, the special bond of trust between brand and customer would be irreparably damaged. Kroc's unique vision was to see this bond of trust operating across cultural, geographical and class divides. Our long-term mission, as a corporation, is to achieve a truly ubiquitous brand positioning as the world's favourite quick-service restaurant.

The establishment of a shared vision and commitment between franchiser and franchisee to develop the principles of QSC&V – and, by extension, the strength and character of the McDonald's brand – remains one of Ray Kroc's greatest legacies. He believed that if something could be improved, right down to the efficiency of a mop wringer, it was the shared responsibility of everyone in the restaurant – regardless of position – to see it through. As Kroc himself famously put it, 'None of us is as good as all of us.' A McDonald's franchisee is buying into a shared vision and that vision is broad and ambitious in its scope.

■ Developing a Global Franchising Business

Ray Kroc's vision was to establish in the consciousness of all McDonald's customers a brand image whose essential characteristics and appeal never wavered. As the first restaurant succeeded, with the granting of further franchises, the need to maintain the consistency of both product and operational standards became central to the development of McDonald's brand character. Kroc believed that the key to global dominance of the food service industry lay in establishing the belief in customers that wherever they travelled in the world they could expect, under the sign of the famous golden arches, an experience every bit as familiar and enjoyable as that to which they were accustomed in their local McDonald's restaurant. That vision has truly realised: a Big Mac served in our largest restaurant in Beijing, China, is the same product in all respects as a Big Mac Served in Eureka, California. McDonald's is something you can rely on.

Early operators in the popular catering boom of the 1950s were often quick to lose sight of important long-term objectives in favour of short-term profit motives. Such companies would grant franchises to individuals only too happy to adapt the product while cutting operational corners and costs. Without the kind of rigorous controls imposed by companies like McDonald's, a short-term gain could perhaps be made by less scrupulous operators with little regard for the long-term reputation of the brand. Individual restaurants would respond to local tastes and quality control and reputation would suffer accordingly. McDonald's, as we shall see, has succeeded in building local customer loyalty through franchising while ensuring consistent product delivery through QSC&V in every restaurant. Ray Kroc saw the shortcomings of the short-term-profit ethic. He believed that the bond of customer trust was paramount and deliberately resisted any tampering with the product that, while providing short-term gain, might ultimately compromise that bond of trust.

The development of McDonald's as a successful global franchising business has always been based on careful screening of individual franchise applicants.

We have never granted territorial franchises and look for every franchisee to prove themselves with their first restaurant before any consideration is given to expanding into a second site. We provide every franchisee with business support, assessment and advice in accordance with rigorously laid-down standards. Of course, a prospective franchisee needs to be reassured that their investment will ultimately yield a profit. In order to discourage franchisees from compromising operational standards when faced with the temptation of short-term profits, we encourage a relationship based at all times on mutually shared expectations. We believe that our franchisees should neither be placed under an overpowering financial burden nor develop the feeling that we, as franchiser, have no interest in developing their business.

■ Working Together

A guiding principle of our approach to franchising is the treatment of all franchisees as equal partners. This principle of interdependence is critical to success. Operating a franchise is not a self-regulating business. McDonald's has an absolute commitment to making every one of its restaurants successful, regardless of franchise status. We lend our expertise and experience to the franchisee, in the expectation that they will share the financial risks in equal measure. Although a prospective McDonald's franchisee is expected to fulfil certain basic financial entry requirements, we ensure that these requirements are neither burdensome nor excessive. If, for example, an individual does not have the necessary capital outlay to purchase a franchise outright, provision is available through the McDonald's Business Facility Lease (BFL) to facilitate funding in another way. Through this scheme, the restaurant may be leased for a period until such time as the franchisee, having made the business a success, is able to buy it outright. Of course, like every franchising organisation, we carefully review the business record of potential applicants. However, while a proven record of commercial acumen may be advantageous, other qualities, as already noted, rank equally in importance. When a new franchisee opens their first restaurant, our aim is to provide ongoing support, advice and encouragement in a managerial style that is based on the spirit of partnership. As Ray Kroc put it, as a McDonald's franchisee, you are 'in business for yourself, but not by yourself'.

The screening process begins with a two-to-three-hour interview, after which the prospective franchisee will spend a week undergoing on-the-job experience. This hands-on experience is a vital part of the process. We have always attached great importance to the restaurant interface with our customers. If a prospective candidate is not comfortable in the dynamic, busy and sometimes stressful environment of the restaurant, then they are unlikely to succeed as a McDonald's franchisee. The strength of the connection between the business ideal and the reality of customer service has been and remains central to McDonald's success.

Once a prospective franchisee has passed through the initial screening, training begins in earnest. We are proud of our educational and training programme. Candidates are given a thorough grounding in operating principles and all aspects of food preparation, cooking and presentation. When Ray Kroc opened our first 'Hamburger University', many were sceptical, believing the idea to be ridiculous and unnecessary.

Today, recognising the grass roots dedication of McDonald's franchisees, many rival businesses acknowledge the quality of our training programmes. The founder of one rival hamburger chain in the US went as far as to concede publicly that 'Anyone who says they have operations as good as McDonald's is lying.' More importantly, this dedication is recognised by our customers around the world.

■ 'Acting Local'

Franchising has enabled us to bring another important dimension to the continued expansion of our international restaurant base. We have always placed great importance on local knowledge and community involvement. In what is, essentially, a people business, a franchisee's knowledge and understanding of local culture is particularly important in forging a strong link between a restaurant and its local clientele. When we open a new restaurant, such local knowledge is critical in ensuring that we establish early momentum in the marketplace. This is especially important in new international markets where cultural differences can be considerable. In developing such markets, we eschew a traditional multinational approach, relying rather on local talent and expertise, supported by the buying power that we, as a global corporation, are uniquely placed to leverage.

The establishment of a strong and loyal customer base is the immediate priority in all new markets we enter. In this respect, families play a key role. While at a corporate level Ronald McDonald is the image most readily associated with our special affinity with young children, franchisees have always been encouraged to develop family business through their own local marketing and promotional activities. Franchisees are ideally placed to establish links with local schools and youth organisations and we, as the franchiser, are fully supportive of such local initiatives. Through our franchisees, we aim to develop a comfortable, trusting relationship between an individual restaurant and its regular customers. The franchisee and his staff – most of whom are also drawn from the local community – represent the friendly, human face of McDonald's each time a customer walks through the door.

■ Shared Understanding

The difference that continues to give us an edge over our competitors is rooted in a shared understanding between corporate management and franchisees that restaurant control should be neither too tight nor too generous. Quite simply, McDonald's combines all the benefits of a large corporation with all the benefits of a small business. Once a franchised restaurant has been successfully established, the franchisee is actively encouraged to develop ways of building business and motivating staff. As the franchiser, we see ourselves in the role of business consultants, grading and assessing restaurant performance and providing ongoing advice on all aspects of restaurant management, ranging from equipment to marketing and human resources. Not surprisingly, the personal financial stake in a McDonald's franchise invariably tends to add an extra dimension to the vigour and efficiency with which a franchisee runs their own restaurant. Given their financial stake in the business, it is no coincidence that, historically, franchised restaurants have outperformed company-owned outlets.

The success of McDonald's as one of the world's leading international brands owes much to the role of franchising in perpetuating the entrepreneurial spirit fostered by Ray Kroc. Maintaining that spirit through the dedication and commitment of our growing number of franchisees remains our mission. In spite of increasingly hostile competitive pressures, we have consolidated our dominant position in the quick-service restaurant business by building a reputation based on consistent delivery of excellence in all aspects of our operations. Franchising has enabled us to ensure that, with every new restaurant opening – be it in Moscow, Canberra, Bogota or Birmingham – the principles of quality, service, cleanliness and value are consistently executed with due sensitivity to local needs and customs.

A McDonald's franchisee's ability to assimilate corporate philosophy involves more than mere implementation of a tried and tested 'system'. It requires a like-minded passion for the business of selling hamburgers that remains unmatched by any of our competitors. The interactive nature of our relationship with our franchisees is one of our competitive advantages. It is a relationship that is based on mutual trust and genuine partnership. We offer our franchisees encouragement and support in building profitable businesses that reflect our corporate values and principles. A franchisee is not left to 'sink or swim', nor kept so firmly controlled that he or she loses the freedom to build business in their own way. We have few secrets in our business; the relationship is an open, mutually supportive arrangement, working to the ultimate benefit of both parties.

■ Franchising and the Future

The quick-service restaurant business in most of the markets in which we operate is faced by increased competition and rising consumer expectations. As we enter our fifth decade in business, we, as a corporation, are faced with considerable challenges. Franchising will continue to play a vital role as we seek to expand our global presence and raise our standards higher still. We face the future with confidence. We expect self-discipline, ambition and business acumen in our franchisees, but, above all, we look for the inherent strength of character necessary to adapt to a system that was itself built on individuality and innovation. One of our most important achievements has been in knowing how to integrate the individuality of our franchisees within that system. It is never very long before a franchisee comes to realise that being part of the McDonald's family can be both fulfilling and rewarding.

CHAPTER 13

International Branding

William G. Tragos

Chairman and CEO, TBWA International

International branding on a truly global scale was once a rosy futuristic scenario to all but the most well-heeled or adventurous marketers. Now, brand marketers face a vast frontier of international branding opportunities. Any company that considers itself a major player is shooting itself in the foot if it is not thinking globally. What brought on this new era? What changed a pipe dream into a strategic imperative?

First and most obviously, the fall of communism brought political and economic liberalisations to previously untouchable territories – Russia, the eastern bloc, China. For populations whose most luxurious choice was formerly between a Trabant and a Lada, the lid has been blown off their long-simmering demand for western products. Equally crucial factors – economic, cultural and media globalisation – have been predicted for decades, and are now achieving their fullest realisation to date.

The realities of mature, oversaturated domestic markets, of share battles for fractions of points, have forced US brand marketers to begin to try to catch up in the international game. Western European branded-goods companies, having enjoyed established Common Market traditions, have for years looked beyond the limits of their own borders for the necessary mass to maximise return from economies of scale. Japanese marketers, facing similar pressures, share the 'Export or Die' attitude.

US businesses, by contrast, long enjoyed the luxury of concentrating on their own vast consumer audience. Foreign markets proved tough nuts to crack, capital-intensive financial crapshoots, to be explored only by super-conglomerates. Today, many US-based multinational businesses – Hollywood film studios, most conspicuously – rely on overseas markets for their overall corporate profitability. If anything, the blinding speed of change on the economic landscape, coupled with the insatiable appetite worldwide for western pop-culture, has helped level the global playing field.

The need for new markets, for massive pools of fresh new consumers, is a hard fact of life for major branded goods businesses everywhere. Thus, a modern gold rush mentality is turning international branding into an new strategic imperative – plant your flag or risk being shut out. This competitive environment is driving the surge of international brands.

■ The Growth of International and Regional Brands

To brand internationally is to identify and differentiate products or services consistently across varying cultural, linguistic and geographic markets. This consistency applies not only to the name and visual identity or packaging design, but also to communications tactics or programmes. Two main types of international branding are addressed in this chapter: global branding, which (if regarded in its most widely used, and not its literal, sense) refers to maintaining consistent brand image and character across a wide range of disparate geographic locations; and regional branding, practised in many proximate nations – South America, the former eastern bloc, Southeast Asia and so forth.

In daily life, we frequently come across examples of one of the main forces driving international branding: converging worldwide demographics. A perfect example often visits TBWA's New York headquarters: he's a young messenger in his mid-twenties from Ancona, an Italian town on the Adriatic Sea. His flowing brown hair reaches his shoulder blades. If he's not wearing Levi's jeans, he's wearing black leather trousers and bright red cowboy boots sported by his favourite rock and roll musician. His devotion to Marlboro cigarettes began back home in Italy, as did his love for McDonald's and Coca-Cola, and though his English is broken, he can say 'I want my MTV!' with barely a trace of accent. In short, he probably has more in common with his contemporaries in Manhattan's East Village than with some of his old schoolmates back home in Ancona. He's a walking, breathing example of converging worldwide demographics.

The theory of consumer convergence proposes that the advance of communications technology and the narrowing gap in international living standards is creating global markets of consumers who crave similar products and services they have heard about, seen, or experienced. TBWA itself has discovered, and based much of its advertising strategy upon, the fact that ABSOLUT Vodka drinkers in Prague more frequently resemble counterparts in Milan or Sydney, in lifestyle and in purchase patterns, than their own next-door neighbours. Now more than ever, target marketing on a global stage is less a question of geography than of intersecting psychographics.

This convergence is most evident in younger generations, whereas the forty-plus age segment in emerging markets, in general, has stronger ties to their established consumption patterns, resisting the advancing influence of western culture. But as countries open their doors to global companies and establish new patterns of consumer behaviour, growing domestic economies inflate the ranks of the middle class, whose new entrants of all age groups are flexing the muscle of their new disposable income.

MTV Europe, in particular, has made a strong impact. Most significantly, by featuring a large number of English-speaking musical performers, MTV Europe has established English as the lingua franca of an entire generation of what are now twenty- and thirty-somethings across the continent.

MTV as a worldwide phenomenon is a perfect expression of the globalisation of media. Depending on who you ask, media globalisation is either a result of the worldwide economic liberalisation that followed the fall of the Berlin wall, or was a major factor in that earth-shattering chain of events. Either way, it's a prime component driving global demographic convergence. Customised versions of western publications such as *Elle*, *Cosmopolitan* and *Newsweek*, sponsored by powerful international publishers, are making inroads in eastern Europe by delivering mainstream appeal to broad target audiences. Pan-European and pan-Asian satellites are broadcasting CNN and ESPN right across Japan down to Indonesia and bringing opera from German television and French documentaries to screens in Brussels and Madrid.

This media overlap exposes viewers to the diverse products of other countries, as well as to familiar brands advertised under a different name in a different language. Properly leveraged, this overlap can beam a single brand positioning to a host of markets. But if mishandled it has the potential to confuse potential consumers by broadcasting unrelated brand messages.

Broadcast advertising has been especially instrumental in the development of international brands. In countries where there is a proliferation of television channels, broadcast advertising generally precedes the actual arrival of the product. Broadcast advertising then assumes responsibility for driving consumer attitudes, especially when the resources for supporting public relations, direct marketing and sales promotion are embryonic at best.

Procter & Gamble's recent domination of the Chinese shampoo category, as described in the *Wall Street Journal*, offers a good example: using broadcast as 'air cover' in their initial advertising bombardment, the company's monthly media buys equalled the annual media outlay of its strongest Chinese competitors. As a result of the television campaigns, combined with ground-level sampling and sales follow-up, P&G's three shampoo brands in China, Head & Shoulders, Pantene and Rejoice (Pert in the US), now command a 57 per cent market share, according to research done in three major cities. This effort shattered the myth that China, with its fragmented provinces and populace, is not a national market.

Recent economic liberalisations in themselves have energised international branding, much as the seafaring ages of Columbus and Magellan opened new worlds to commerce centuries ago. In the last five years both China and India have scrapped decades-old barriers to foreign investment, slowly opening their fortress-like walls to joint ventures and a subsequent stream of western products. The market potentials of these two countries, with combined populations of nearly three billion, are vast; although further analysis suggests that true middle-class incomes number only 200 million out of China's 2 billion people, and only something over 20 million among India's population of 910 million, it is still a fact that reaching a possible 220 million new consumers is the equivalent of discovering a new United States on the planet, and it is hardly surprising that the list of western companies entering these markets grows daily.

In the western hemisphere, the NAFTA and GATT agreements promise the possibility of a pole-to-pole free-trade zone, encouraging economic build-ups in Mexico and throughout Latin America. The political reconfiguration of South Africa has stabilised a once tense, uncertain economy. Greece, Turkey, Israel and the southeast Asian 'tigers' – Hong Kong, Thailand, Malaysia and Singapore – have all been identified as booming global hotspots.

The former USSR and its former eastern satellites, where this latest revolution all started, has proven an economic mixed bag, an oil gusher in some countries, a question mark in others. While it's been rough going for many western brands, marketing giants such as McDonald's, Coca-Cola, and Pepsi have established footholds, armed with both a long-haul perspective and ample capital investment.

■ Advantages of International Branding

'One product, one message' is the nirvana to which international brands aspire. The rugged image of the Marlboro cowboy is a brand character recognised the world over. Coca-Cola, with few exceptions, positions itself and runs advertising almost unaltered internationally. The ABSOLUT bottle and the ubiquitous two-word headlines that accompany it everywhere symbolise taste and style in 45 countries.

Tobacco, soft drinks, alcoholic drinks – 'badge' products that consumers buy in part because of their expressive values, what they say about them – blazed the early trail of international branding. But producers of household products are catching on. Colgate-Palmolive's Total toothpaste, for example, uses virtually the same positioning, advertising, and packaging across the 75 countries in which it markets.

The prize for successful international branding is potentially enormous bottom-line profitability. From an operational perspective, consolidating manufacturing, packaging, and marketing functions represents tremendous savings. From a competitive viewpoint, the cost savings and efficiencies ideally enable a brand marketer to achieve low-cost producer status in its category – key to dominating the marketplace.

From a marketing operations standpoint, 'one product, one message' reduces the need for large ground-level operations in many different regions, reducing the tendency to 'reinvent the wheel' in each market. This structure demands the collection of an organisation's best strategic minds with their different cultural perspectives and the application of that brainpower to research, marketing and advertising. In this way, companies leverage the best talent their organisation has to offer.

It is just as crucial for brands that wish to become successful on a multinational scale to pump up their distribution muscle. A 1995 Nielsen report on the top 100 European grocery brands observed, 'As the European Union continues to lower trade barriers, brands within the single market European nations will increase their share of fixture space in European supermarkets. . . The age of the Eurobrand is truly upon us.' There is no reason to think this self-generating cycle – international brand strength generates greater distribution power, which generates greater brand strength – will not be equally applicable on a world stage.

■ Advantages of Regional Branding

While nothing could be more straightforward than 'one product, one message', many marketers prefer a regional version of international branding. This could be referred to as the 'think global – act local' strategy, where the brand's 'master' platform is adapted to specific market conditions. The alterations, either minor or substantial, are coordinated through a regional office that makes certain that any modifications are consistent with the overall brand strategy.

Why should this more complicated approach be so much more prevalent? Because while worldwide markets have moved a lot closer to demographic convergence over the last generation, domestic cultural influences still have a powerful influence on consumers' desires and purchase behaviour. This is where an international company will find it important to have grass-roots expertise in a region; it can make the crucial difference between successful branding and irrelevance.

Food is a category where domestic differences are particularly marked. TBWA developed and executed a pan-European strategy for their client Barilla Pasta, but modifications were made by country, based on pasta's role in diets across the continent. Pasta is a staple in Italy, but a question mark in France. It is not prominent on German menus, but is considered an emerging product in Spain. With such diverse considerations, adjustments in marketing tactics to suit the region can prove more effective than a universal approach that relies on communicating brand attributes in broad strokes.

A number of other case histories illustrate how regional structures can be crucial in gauging and modifying an international brand platform for maximum local effect.

Gatorade, the world's leading sports drink, is positioned in the United States as nutritional replenishment for active, athletic consumers, but elsewhere, where the market for athletic consumers is much smaller, Gatorade is marketed as a sports drink to be consumed following strenuous activity specifically associated with each country, like a traditional drum ceremony in Korea.

Evian, positioned around the world as the original premium mineral water, stresses health and fitness associations in the US, but in markets like Europe and the Middle East, where the populations are generally more sedentary, Evian is marketed as a non-alcoholic alternative drink to the 'cafe set'.

The American market supports a host of low-calorie products domestically, but the low-calorie concept does not carry the same weight universally. Miller Lite originated and popularised low-calorie beer in the US, but in the UK, the word 'lite' in conjunction with alcohol is interpreted as low-alcohol, not low-calorie. A name change necessitated adjustments to global marketing strategy.

Cultural variations often require changes in the product themselves. Cigarettes manufactured for northern Asia, for instance, compete in a much lower-tar environment than that of Indonesia, where a heavier-tar recipe is critical to provide the fuller flavour the market demands. Shampoos positioned as dandruff fighters have been huge successes in China, where the universal dark hair makes dandruff an especially visible problem, but anti-dandruff formulas mean less in countries where oily hair is a far greater concern.

Corporations find regional branding makes the most sense when it plays to their organisational strengths – especially if those strengths include an established international network or even one foreign-based division that has proved its marketing acumen in a specific territory. Some companies incentivise foreign offices by granting them the autonomy and budget control to shape their own destiny – and their own profits. Companies that acknowledge that their best decisions for South America or northern Asia do not always come from New York or London often find regional branding strategies more comfortable.

Proponents of international branding long for an age when products can easily leap over national and cultural demarcations, but the age of the 'one-world' consumer, free from notions of nationalistic pride, is not here quite yet. It is still far too easy to be offensive if you are not respectful of a culture.

In anticipation of the 'Euro-consumer', the majority of western European marketers have entered the former Eastern bloc countries with adaptations of Western European advertising campaigns; however, by doing so, they have risked alienating entire marketplaces. *Campaign* magazine recently noted how Hungarian consumers are openly resentful of advertising that they clearly sense was developed with German consumers in mind. Xenophobic reactions against Pepsi, Coca-Cola and McDonald's have threatened, at the time of writing, India's budding economic liberalisation.

In short, it is simply bad business to impose western values without considering fundamental national differences. A regional structure and strategy that recognises and responds to these ingrained cultural variations can be critical to implementing an international brand platform.

■ The Secret of International Branding: ABSOLUT Success

The key to international branding can be summed up in an elementary mathematical concept: common denominators. The more commonalities that can be individually leveraged or collectively aligned – for example: a focused,

ABSOLUT®
Country of Sweden
VODKA

Figure 13.1   ABSOLUT

ABSOLUT's advertising has created brand personality attributes that, in themselves, constitute the brand's point-of-difference, and appeal to a specific psychographic audience throughout the world

limited range of product usage; a narrowly defined target market; unified marketing strategy and operations; universal interpretations of brand character attributes – the greater the chances of successfully implementing an international strategy.

ABSOLUT VODKA represents an extremely successful example of a global branding programme; the approach maximised common denominators in positioning, packaging, product usage, target market, marketing operations and the communication of brand personality. The ABSOLUT name and bottle are symbols of quality, sophistication, and cutting-edge style wherever the brand is marketed. ABSOLUT's advertising has created brand personality attributes that, in themselves, constitute the brand's point of difference, and appeal to a specific psychographic audience throughout the world.

In 1980 ABSOLUT had little working in its favour. It was (and remains) a colourless, nearly tasteless and odourless product. ABSOLUT – a brand owned by Vin & Sprit of Stockholm and distributed worldwide by Seagram – is from Sweden, a country, unlike Russia, lacking in perceived vodka heritage. The name was regarded as odd, the bottle unwieldy. The advertising campaign began by turning these negatives into positives, repositioning the odd-shaped bottle from a quirk to a symbol of unique quality. The first adverts, led by the famous 'ABSOLUT PERFECTION', featuring a halo over the bottle, concentrated on messages of product quality. In all executions, the graphic, layout and copy concepts remained consistent. The advertising generated brand personality attributes – intellect, humour, sophistication, an overall image that established the brand's added value. That sophistication and intellect designated the ABSOLUT drinker as a member of a somewhat exclusive club.

The next generation of ABSOLUT advertising extended this élite status, associating ABSOLUT with vanguard symbols of contemporary culture. Maintaining the familiar layout, the next advertisements featured depictions of the ABSOLUT bottle by cutting-edge art world figures, from 'ABSOLUT WARHOL' to 'ABSOLUT HARING' and so on. Next was the 'ABSOLUT FASHION' campaign, featuring parts or the whole bottle woven into dresses or stockings conceived by the world's most stylish designers.

It was found that the target community that ABSOLUT reached was not confined to the USA, but was international in nature. More importantly, people who wanted to be seen as part of this fashionable, sophisticated community existed in large numbers throughout the west.

Focusing on this niche, defined more by mindset than by geography or economics, ABSOLUT was able to extend its brand platform internationally – and the campaign eventually reflected the 'borderless' nature of this community in the 'Cities' campaign. In these advertisements, the ABSOLUT Bottle became Central Park in ABSOLUT MANHATTAN, a swimming pool in ABSOLUT LA, sheet music in ABSOLUT VIENNA, an Ionic column in ABSOLUT ATHENS.

Currently, the campaign runs unaltered in nearly eighty countries. Only two offices – TWBA New York and TWBA Paris – develop creative work, in order to maintain creative quality and consistency. Depending on the market development in each region, some of the early, quality-focused messages are rotated among newer executions. All in all, ABSOLUT is a paradigm of successful international advertising-driven branding. It was one of the inaugural three brands, along with Coca-Cola and Nike, to be included in the American Marketing Association's Hall of Fame.

■ Managing a Diversified Portfolio

When developing truly international brands, if comprehensive decisions are made centrally then it is much easier to focus on developing a clearer and more consistent brand equity. The greater the influence exerted by foreign operating units, the more brand equity tends to become diffused, even if in some cases it can become more relevant to individual markets. The fundamental question that each company needs to answer for itself is: how much power will be held centrally and how much will be distributed among foreign operations? Whether a company is more successful with a global or regional marketing approach depends on how influence is allocated. Will decision-making be primarily a function of a central office, will there be a balance between centralised decision-making and regional input, or will local operations lead the way using the advantage of their closer relationship with individual markets?

Selecting one of these approaches as an overall policy can make international marketing operations more efficient. This is not to say that corporations that market a portfolio of brands cannot enjoy the luxury of choosing a level of centralisation that best suits each individual brand.

■ Seagram: A Case History

Marketing a host of premium spirit brands worldwide, Seagram Spirits and Wine Group offers a perfect example of coordinating different strategies that work for different brands.

As we have seen, ABSOLUT VODKA is positioned, marketed, and advertised consistently around the globe. All major marketing and advertising decisions for ABSOLUT are coordinated from one central office. Strict rules are enforced as to which advertisements run in which market. Depending on the state of local category development, foreign divisions choose from a certain set of advertisements mandated centrally. Budget control makes the most effective form of centralising marketing decisions – he who holds the purse strings calls the shots. The media budget for ABSOLUT is controlled centrally.

However, for some other Seagram brands a less centralised approach has been adopted. Brand strategy for Chivas Regal is also coordinated centrally, but regional variations in category development require greater input from local operations. In Latin America, for example, Chivas retains much the same cachet as it did in North America two decades ago, when scotch was positioned as the drink for mature palates, for those who had 'arrived' at the higher echelons of success. But while scotch in the US has been fighting a long decline, refuting the image of a 'grey-haired' beverage, the traditional associations with success are very effective in Latin American Chivas advertising.

Chivas uses a pan-European branding strategy and ad campaign, but different advertisements are used in different countries, respecting the mixed bag of category development across Europe. As is done for ABSOLUT, a menu of ads is offered from central marketing operations, but greater flexibility is granted to foreign subsidiaries, allowing them either to use existing executions or to develop programmes that conform to their particular market.

The plan for Glenlivet, a super premium scotch brand, is further down the liberal end of the continuum. Glenlivet is a single-malt scotch, marketed to and purchased by a predominantly connoisseur audience. The market for such a brand consists of evolved palates, and is therefore much smaller than Chivas or most other brands of spirits. Seagram feels a market of that size requires less of an international brand strategy than it does increased ground level expertise in the demographics of super-premium scotch drinkers.

Market-specific approaches are also used for products like Godiva Liqueur, which is only advertised in the US, or Captain Morgan Spiced Rum, which is simply called Morgan Spiced Rum in the UK. These are examples of very particular tastes, and opportunities for these products do not exist in some markets as much as in others.

■ Nissan: A Case History

The example of automobile manufacturer Nissan typifies challenges faced by marketers of divergent brands and product lines. Automobiles, of course, represent a highly considered purchase, and Nissan's branding efforts focus on specific products rather than its corporate label.

Corporate branding works best, again, by leveraging common brand character attributes across a range of products – see revered soupmaker Campbell's in North America or Nike throughout the western world. But obstacles occur when distinct brand personalities have been cultivated country by country – Heinz means ketchup to Americans, but Heinz in the UK says beans.

A few car manufacturers have so effectively branded themselves at a corporate level that the corporate brand takes precedence over the individual sub-branding of their model lines. These companies – Mercedes, BMW, Volvo, Range Rover, Porsche – offer a limited range of product lines targeting a narrow audience niche, and consistently promote the same product attributes – top-of-the-line engineering, durability, safety, and so on – across their entire product line.

Car manufacturers who, like Nissan, market broader ranges of product offerings must decide whether their customers are buying a model or buying a brand. When a brand image map resembles a checkerboard, as it does for Nissan, model lines become the central focus.

Each of Nissan's three autonomous business units – Asia, Europe, and North America – pursue different strategies and there are few links between the three. The European operation alone is made up of 20 different licensed distributors, each with a different heritage. Nissan has had distribution in the UK for 28 years, but the Nissan tradition is less established in Italy, where long-time import quotas have recently fallen. Nissan had cultivated an image of cost-efficient reliability in UK, almost a 'discount' positioning; in different parts of northern Europe the Nissan is seen as a sporty second car; in southern Europe it is often the family car. In Asia, Nissan competes by communicating its mix of Japanese technology with European luxury. Multiply those contrasts twenty times over and the impediments to unified international branding are evident.

The pan-European launch of the Nissan Almera in the autumn of 1995 was a major demonstration of how a new car can be launched into such diverse markets. The strategic platform positioned this hatchback model as the car that delivered to the mass market quality and features previously reserved for the élite – 'the car they don't want you to drive.' A pool of four broadcast executions is used across Europe, with dialogue modified to reflect cultural advertising tastes: in the UK, the ads are humorously ambiguous, but the modified soundtrack for the same ad in Germany employs a direct call to action, leaving nothing to interpretation. Although this proved very successful, it is much easier to brand a new product internationally than to standardise an existing product previously known in different markets by different names, positionings and ad campaigns.

The Almera launch nevertheless makes a significant point about international branding: consistency of marketing operations and communications must produce consistent impressions upon consumers. The goal is to combine the greatest possible commonality in execution while maximising local cultural appeal. If such an approach means using four advertising executions internationally instead of 10 or 20 then the marketer is gaining ground. Companies cannot afford to wait until total integration is accomplished.

■ Which Approach Is Right for You?

Coca-Cola, Marlboro, McDonald's – it is no coincidence that many of the world's greatest global brands all share deep pockets. But resources alone are not a guarantee of international branding success. A David can go up against a Goliath in the international branding arena as long as the company has the right combination of structure and market know-how. To determine the most suitable international branding strategy, a company needs to ask itself tough questions about its own structure, its products and its adaptability.

It is not enough to determine whether a market exists internationally for a company's products and services. The potential for developing a robust brand personality has to be evaluated. Does that personality translate easily across the markets that present opportunity? If so, it must form the basis of competitive advantage within each market, not just an excuse to achieve cost efficiencies. It is futile to achieve operational efficiencies at the cost of missed opportunities and ineffective communications.

A company's own international structure is a prime consideration. It is crucial that a company evaluates the intellectual capital contained in each foreign division. Imposing a centralised international strategy could squander this critical resource. The possibility of internal backlash should not be underestimated either: the 'not invented here' syndrome, and subsequent drops in motivation, can result when an office is a mere caretaker of a strategy developed elsewhere.

International branding demands flexibility. Adjusting to a multitude of differing regulatory environments can turn the most cohesive of international brand strategies into a patchwork quilt, particularly in advertising. Oddly enough, tobacco and alcohol products, though among the trailblazers in international marketing, are subject to more advertising regulation than just about any category. In the US, cigarettes are not allowed to be advertised on television; in other countries, cigarettes are not only seen on TV but in cinema advertising. Marketing restrictions vary from country to country. Navigating between the more liberal environments, where television ads regularly feature exposed women's breasts, to the most restrictive, where naming competing products is forbidden, can demand greater levels of local marketing expertise.

Sometimes, local conditions become effectively prohibitive – take the example of Gatorade, whose pan-European strategy was interrupted when it ran into a French ordinance requiring a certain ingredient to be present in all sports drinks. Added to the Gatorade recipe, it rendered the beverage undrinkable, so Gatorade, needless to say, is not on sale in France.

■ Conclusions

The two most sage pieces of advice which can be offered to international brand marketers are related: expect the unexpected and be persistent. The unexpected awaits in every corner of the globe: from India, where, despite strong currents of backlash against western fast food and snack food, American cereal marketer Kellogg's has established a solid niche in a country that has no strong tradition of having cereal for breakfast; to Venezuela, where in a country mired in recession, 'even a family living in the tiniest shack,' *Campaign* reports, 'will have two television sets.'

In every market, there are discoveries like these that fly in the face of conventional wisdom, and that open the door to opportunities for those who persist. Making the most of international branding requires the persistence of the ancient Greeks who, in the translated words of Theocritus in 353 BC, 'took Troy because they never gave up trying.'

CHAPTER 14

Branding in the European Union

John Murray

Mars

Strategic branding and the building of loyal brand franchises have become primary concerns of manufacturers of consumer goods today. Effective branding helps achieve the enduring, predictable and profitable growth sought by all manufacturers. In the 1990s regional, and ideally global, brand franchises with consumers are increasingly feasible with the rapid recent liberalisation of the world's economies. Major manufacturers are spreading their brands as quickly as possible from developed markets such as the USA, France or the UK throughout the Americas, the former communist bloc and the Asian-Pacific region as local market restrictions are broken down and regional market arrangements emerge.

The European single market has been an early leader in regional liberalisation, although other regions can be expected to catch up very rapidly. In order for consumers and manufacturers in Europe to enjoy the benefits of more efficiently marketed, regionwide brands it is crucial to see further rapid progress towards uniformity of legislation and codes of practice within the European Union. For the moment the extent of the single market is still limited, not only by the natural differences faced by marketers in component countries and their heritages but also by different legislation and restrictions. Branding in the European Union increasingly aims to be Europe-wide (and to have global potential) but the branding framework is still quite variable in its applicability. Nevertheless, the opportunity is increasingly present to create brands with 'one look, one sound, one feel, across the EU'.

The Extent and Limitation of the Single Market

What Does It Mean in Concept?

The concept of the European single market emerged during the early 1980s. A number of forces drove the concept. They included the difficulty being experienced by the Community in agreeing harmonising legislation between the member states, the glaring inefficiencies created by historically different national legislation, politically motivated, and the obvious comparison with the USA, where interstate regulatory variations were minor, and did not impede trade flows. It is often forgotten that in 1979 most European countries had exchange and capital controls, and that the documentation required for one consignment of goods across a European border could extend to more than fifty pages.

These inefficiencies had an enormous cost. In a report on the cost of non-Europe, Paolo Cecchini estimated that this cost amounted to 200 billion ECU (approximately $240 billion or £160 billion). The cost arose for many reasons, both tangible and intangible; for example the long delays at border crossings, and the burden of the accompanying paperwork; and the opportunity cost incurred by firms who could not invest time and money to make their goods so that they conformed to other country's regulations.

So the concept of the single market was born. In 1987, the Commission proposed that, in principle, within the European Community there should be free movement of people, services, goods and capital. It would mean that the Community's external borders would have to be secure, but that once goods were inside the Community then they could move freely. The Commission argued that not only would companies save money, but European industry would be more competitive with the American and Asian equivalents, which had none of these burdens.

■ **What Does It Mean in Law?**

From this original vision, some very important legal principles emerged. The first is the principle of mutual recognition; if a product is legal in any one country of the European Union, then it may legally be exported to any other member state and sold there. This concept, written into EU law by the European Court of Justice in a landmark case known as 'Cassis de Dijon', did away at a stroke (at least in theory) with the old requirement to harmonise national regulations. It has since provoked fierce argument that at bottom stems from national protectionism, but it has prevailed every time (even in the case of the German beer purity laws).

A second concept of equal significance is that of subsidiarity, which was borne of the Maastricht Treaty. Essentially it says that the EU should not take action if the desired result can be equally or better achieved at member state level; that, in short, regulation should occur at the lowest institutional level and as close to the need as possible. Obviously the EU should not determine where a pedestrian crossing should be placed in a busy main street, but the EU might determine the safety principles that should govern the crossing, so that common standards prevailed across Europe.

When Europe agreed the principles of the single market, and enacted the necessary basic legislation, one further important step was also taken, namely the setting of a deadline, 1992. This concentrated minds, and meant that by 1 January 1993 most of the implementing legislation was in place, and beginning to be effective. Since that date goods have crossed the borders more easily, capital flows have been largely liberalised, and EU citizens have experienced few formalities at EU internal borders (and none at all between countries that are members of the Schengen agreement).

■ What Does It Mean in Practice for Branding?

Although the European single market is substantially in place, the environment for European branding is not uniform. There are in practice fifteen different markets within the single market that the European brand must recognise. The consumer, the competitor and the customer (the retail and wholesale trade) differ markedly across the countries of Europe. There are also important differences within a country, for example between Paris and Marseilles, in terms of taste, attitude and income, but the differences at the national level are much more marked. This section examines the nature of differences and similarities that exist between the countries of Europe with respect to consumers, competitors and customers.

□ Consumers

Taste

Surprise, surprise: national tastes differ! In the UK consumers take milk in their tea; in the south of Europe, tea is taken with lemon. The popularity of different tea blends varies accordingly. High pasta consumption in Italy compares with high potato consumption in Sweden. These differences derive largely from differences in climate and patterns of agriculture. Modern distribution systems have made many more ethnic foods available but patterns of consumption and taste derive from history. This is illustrated in Table 14.1. Southern Europe likes spicy flavours; blander food is preferred in the North. The implications for

Table 14.1 Annual per capita sweetener consumption in Europe (kg)

UK	54.6
Netherlands	54.3
Ireland	52.8
Switzerland	52.0
Belgium	50.6
Denmark	50.6
Sweden	46.8
Finland	45.2
Germany	44.3
France	41.5
Norway	39.8
Spain	37.4
Greece	34.7
Italy	30.8

European food brands are significant. Uncle Ben's stir-fry sauces are sold throughout Europe, but the varieties available, and the recipes of the individual varieties, vary from country to country. Branding and packaging design are uniform; the recipe varies.

Attitude

Consumer attitudes vary significantly across Europe. These attitudes have many drivers; for example family values influence the number of single-person households, which comprise as many as 40 per cent of all households in Denmark (Table 14.2).

Table 14.2   Changing households, 1960–90

| | % Single-person households | | | |
	1960	1970	1980	1990
W. Germany	21	26	32	35
Netherlands	12	17	21	29
France	20	22	25	27
UK	11	18	22	26
Italy	11	13	18	19

Changing households

Different attitudes are also reflected in different patterns of frugality, permissibility and humour, all of which must in turn influence branding and advertising. Differences also show in the frequency of shopping, the type of stores, and pack sizes. The large, out-of-town food store is more popular in Spain and Portugal, where the traditional family household is more prevalent, than in Sweden or Norway, where shopping frequency is high and family size low.

Usage occasions

Usage occasions vary across Europe, influenced by taste and attitude, climate and culture. In southern Europe chocolate products are perceived as sweets and are eaten primarily for pleasure, whereas in northern Europe chocolate is also seen as a nourishing food, used to complement the meal occasion and as a satisfying snack. This is shown in the level of chocolate consumption in Europe (Table 14.3).

Table 14.3 Annual per capita chocolate confectionery consumption in Europe (kg)

UK	8.94
Belgium	8.85
Norway	8.24
Switzerland	8.20
Austria	7.98
Germany	7.81
Ireland	7.42
Denmark	6.65
Sweden	5.40
Netherlands	4.40
France	4.35
Finland	3.66
Greece	2.87
Italy	2.24
Spain	1.55
Portugal	1.44

Source: ERC.

Differences in usage have a profound effect on market size, the number of competitors in the market and the allocation of selling space by the retail trade. They influence the type of products sold and portion size. The Italian confectionery market is characterisea by low-weight, high-volume products, while in the UK the average weight of products sold is much higher.

Language

Different languages affect European branding in two ways. Comprehensible pack labelling is essential; separate labelling for each of fifteen countries in the desired language is inefficient and costly; but multilingual labels are very unpopular with the consumer. Second, differences in language affect both the execution of the advertising and the richness of a brand's USP (unique selling proposition). The concepts of nourishment associated with the Mars Bar have both physiological and psychological connotations in English, but they are more difficult to capture in other languages.

Income Levels

Income levels shape the market composition and determine the branding priorities. Differences in income levels in Europe are significant and affect per capita expenditure, as Table 14.4 shows. The income gap is also widening, as Table 14.5 shows.

Table 14.4   Per capita expenditure (ECU) – 1992

Switzerland	11 463
France	10 914
Denmark	10 863
Belgium	10 545
Germany	10 078
Netherlands	9 714
Austria	8 771
UK	8 697
Sweden	8 326
Norway	7 875
Ireland	6 540
Greece	4 347
Portugal	4 323

Source: Eurostat.

Table 14.5   The consumer, affluent and poor

	Incomes ratio: richest 20% to poorest 20%		
Netherlands	4.0 (1981)	6.9 (1986)	7.7 (1988)
UK	5.8 (1981)	7.2 (1986)	8.6 (1990)
France	8.0 (1979)	7.8 (1984)	8.3 (1989)
Italy	4.9 (1983)	4.9 (1985)	5.4 (1988)

☐ *The Age of the Average is Dead*

National averages no longer provide useful information. There will be pockets of affluence in countries where the national average is relatively low (such as the Milan region or the southeast of England). Thus market opportunities exist despite the national average income. The challenge for manufacturers is to achieve effective distribution and awareness for their brand in these regions. This is made difficult by national retail chains with common policies on range and space (see 'Customers', p. 141). Affluence grows over time. When Portugal entered the EU in 1986, consumers were unfamiliar with prepared pet foods, but as income levels have risen so patterns of food purchase and consumption have changed, and so has the need for prepared pet food to meet the feeding requirements of dogs and cats.

These different levels create different marketing objectives for the same brand across Europe. In some countries the primary goal is achieving product awareness; in others the goal is to achieve increased usage or retain loyal users. In each situation the role of advertising, pricing and portion or pack size will clearly be different.

Conclusion

There are today very large differences in consumer attitude, lifestyle and spending power across Europe which lead to differing brand strategies. Some of these differences occur at a national level, some at a regional level. But there is a convergence that, over time, will reduce but perhaps never eliminate the differences. This convergence in attitudes and lifestyle is driven by forces that are often extraneous to the EU but present in each EU member state. These forces include the universal effect of popular music, the deployment of satellite and cable television, the growth in home computing and access to the Internet, and the growing use of English as the common language of Europe. These trends percolate faster through the younger generations, and as the young become middle-aged, so they extend through the population structure.

☐ *Competitors*

A key factor in the development of a brand is the nature of competition. Competition was once purely national; manufacturing was local and met local needs. In chocolate a national pattern of traditional but different leading producers developed, as Table 14.6 shows. In each area, the nature of the products varied; thus block chocolate dominates in Germany, by contrast with filled bars in Britain. Product range, the chocolate taste, pricing and patterns of distribution and so on, vary with region. The challenge for the manufacturer is whether to extend into new regions with his traditional product form, or imitate the market leader. Different solutions have been chosen by different manufacturers.

Table 14.6 Market leaders in chocolate confectionery

Market/Region	Market Leader
Iberia	Nestlé
Italy	Ferrero
UK/Ireland	Cadbury
Germany	Kraft Jacobs-Suchard
Nordic countries	Marabou*

* Now owned by Kraft Jacobs-Suchard/Philip Morris.

☐ *Customers*

Consumers remain largely local; manufacturers are transforming themselves from national to regional players; retail structures and trade practices remain substantially national. Channels of distribution vary substantially from country to country. Thus, for example, the CTN (Confectioner, Tobacconist and Newsagent) is important in the UK, Ireland, the Nordic Countries and Benelux, but does not exist in the Mediterranean markets. Other factors that lead to unique national solutions are local planning policies, legislation and licensing. In Italy a store requires a licence to operate and a separate licence for each category sold. In Sweden, grocery shops are not allowed to sell spirits because of the state monopoly, and in the UK pharmacies are less regulated than in most continental countries. Consumers have similar shopping requirements, but these are met in different ways across the European Union.

Similarly the patterns of retail concentration vary greatly. Table 14.7 illustrates the differences. Although trade power is concentrated in most countries, retail operators remain predominantly national. There is no pan European retailer. It is therefore difficult for any manufacturer to secure a European-wide supply agreement for other than a minority of his sales. Different trade structures also lead to differences in range and margin policies across Europe.

Table 14.7   Store concentration in Europe

People per store			
Switzerland	925	Sweden	503
France	844	Austria	427
Finland	830	Norway	417
Netherlands	822	Ireland	391
UK	700	Italy	269
Belgium	689	Spain	253
Denmark	515	Portugal	202
Germany	511	Greece	194

Source: Nielsen Europa.

The importance of this to branding in the European Union is twofold. First, it is impossible to develop consistent trade marketing policies and second, the national retailer has an increasing influence on the national consumer purchasing decision. The reduction in store numbers, the development of outlets out of town and decreasing shopping frequencies all combine to make it increasingly improbable that the consumer will switch stores in search of a favourite brand.

Furthermore, most consumer decisions to purchase a particular brand (as opposed to the category) are made at the point of sale, giving the retailer the opportunity to influence the decision through allocation of shelf space and the presence of private-label products. *Store Wars* describes this phenomenon succinctly: 'As they (the retailers) begin to manipulate these marketing variables to further their own objectives, they construct an obstacle between the manufacturer and the end consumer' (Corstjens and Corstjens, 1995). The retailers now control the in-store marketing-mix variables – shelf position, price, promotions, merchandising and sampling – as well as having access to detailed information on shopping and brand choice behaviour via scanning data and loyalty cards.

There is no single market in retailing, but there is a common force which dramatically affects branding; a force driven by information technology and consumer choice of retail outlet.

■ **No Single Market in Branding**

The single market is incomplete; for example, value added tax, VAT, is a major revenue source for the member states as well as by far the largest provider of funds for the European Union itself. In 1987 it was levied at many different rates across Europe, and still is today. Moreover, to help eliminate border delays, internal exports are zero-rated, which both perpetuates the concept of 'export', and is an invitation to fraud. Another example of an unresolved issue is the group of directives known as vertical directives; they harmonise recipes for certain foodstuffs such as chocolate, honey and coffee. As a result there is still no single market in these foodstuffs. Chocolate may not yet be made legally in France to the same recipe as chocolate made in Britain.

Another unresolved area significantly affects marketing. Marketing communications are regulated differently between the member states. It is therefore impossible to plan one consistent, common programme across all fifteen European Union member states in any type of marketing communication. Some specific examples are:

- Certain products may not be advertised in some countries but are permitted in others (pharmaceuticals, sanitary products, contraceptives).
- Advertising to some audiences is restricted (no advertising to children under twelve in Sweden, no advertising of toys to children in Greece).
- Sponsorship restriction; some countries restrict, or even ban, types of sponsorship that are not regulated at all in other countries (events sponsorship is in effect banned in the Netherlands).

□ *The Commercial Communication Green Paper*

The Commission has recognised this, and has taken action. A major Green Paper was published in 1996, covering all aspects of commercial communications. Its key findings are:

- There are significant differences between Member States in the way in which they regulate commercial communication.
- These differences already affect the smooth functioning of the single market. Because of the advances in technology, and the increasing ease of cross border communication, regulatory differences may seriously hamper future commercial communication.
- Therefore there is a need for community action.

The Commission goes on to propose what action may be appropriate, and to invite comments. The results of this process will certainly affect the way in which marketing programmes are designed and implemented in the future; because the Commission's clear intent is to liberalise, not increase the regulatory burden, it is widely hoped that European campaigns will become more efficient, more helpful to the consumer and less burdensome to create.

■ Other EU Marketing Initiatives

Other aspects of European legislation directly affect branding in the single market. The 'Television without Frontiers' Directive of 1989 affects both the amount of advertising that can be carried, and the types of products that may be advertised. It is currently being revised. There are also extensive legal provisions affecting trade marks, direct mail and distance selling, and labelling and packaging. One of the earliest Community acts was the misleading Advertising Directive of 1984, which *inter alia* provided for specific means of consumer redress. Marketing in Europe has for long been conditioned by its European regulatory environment and this seems certain to continue to be the case.

■ The Branding Framework and Its Applicability Across the EU

Mars, Incorporated believes that European brands can best meet the needs of European consumers. The question is how to create European brands, given the differences that exist between consumers, competitors and the customer base. The challenge is how to optimise the brand proposition with the local consumer and meet the national requirements of different trade channels, while achieving the necessary economies of scale. The answer is in recognising that there is no one correct approach for all brands in all markets.

Each brand and each form of the brand (for example Mars Ice Cream) must be examined against a common framework that recognises the key elements of branding, and matches these with the variations in consumer, competitive set and structure of distribution. The key elements of branding have been defined and redefined many times in marketing textbooks, and we believe that there are six marketing basics, namely:

- Positioning.
- Product Design.
- Value.
- Availability (including product conformance).
- Advertising.
- Promotion.

■ Positioning

The brand is more than the product's physical characteristics and trade mark. It is a combination of the perceptions, sensations and satisfactions derived from the brand's consumption and from the consumer's beliefs about the brand. The brand promise must be supported by the product concept and not mislead the consumer. The positioning of the brand is the promise of what it offers to the consumer in both functional and psychological benefits. The positioning is thus based on the essence of the brand, which is the relevant and distinctive and inviolate substance of the brand. At Mars we see it as being composed of the following elements:

- Product attributes: the distinctive tangible characteristics.
- Product benefits: the relevant reasons for usage.
- Brand relationship: how the consumer relates to the brand.
- Brand personality: the personification of the brand.
- Essential message: the core promise of the brand
- USP: the unique selling proposition and reason why.

■ Product Design

The product design is a basic description of the physical product that defines its distinguishing characteristics. Product design descriptions may differ depending on varieties, line extensions and packaging formats, and in response to local market conditions. Product design decisions have to be market-driven (especially in Europe given the consumer diversity). Consumers are always changing. Different consumers have different wants, and the same consumer will have different wants in different situations. Chocolate confectionery provides a good example of the need to vary the product design to fulfil the brand positioning. Thus in Italy, for example, the consumption of chocolate is less for hunger satisfaction and more for taste and the psychological benefits associated with reward and 'uplift'. Importantly, the climate in Italy influences when, where and how much chocolate is consumed, so a Mars Bar will be smaller in size (shorter) than in Northern Europe but will retain the same features in its recipe. Nevertheless, the product must fulfil the brand positioning, so there are lower limits on bar size, even in a warm climate such as Italy, if product design and positioning are to be in harmony.

Product design also embraces the primary packaging such as the label on a can or jar, the wrapper on a confectionery product, or the box. Packaging is the immediate and tangible presentation of the brand to the consumer, particularly important at the point of sale. The essence of a European brand is that it should have the same look, touch and feel. Thus quite apart from seeking to harmonise the brand logo and appearance, it is desirable to have a common set of guidelines so that the label can be made locally relevant, for example, with local language instructions.

■ Value

Value in the context of a brand is much more than price. It is also more than value for money where value is measured in how much is obtained for a particular price. While this is a significant advance on price as a measure of value, it is still a functional measure and at its most basic is seen in measures of price per kilo or litre. Value is what the consumer assesses to be the value to them of the brand's benefits. The principal reflection of this value is their willingness to repurchase. Competitor pricing within a market is a crucial secondary consideration but becomes more important the smaller is the difference in benefits between competing brands. So value is the consumer's perception based on price, product quality, relevance, uniqueness and the psychological values associated with the brand as conveyed by advertising.

The achievement of similar perceptions of a brand's value across Europe is a complex exercise given differences in units of currency, in exchange rate volatility, in income levels, in the cost and availability of advertising, and the regional nature of competition. For the moment, value can only be assessed at the national level.

■ Availability

Availability is a key consumer benefit. The European brand must maximise availability subject to a satisfactory profit return. Availability must be measured in terms of quantity of distribution points and the quality of display at each of those points, including the freshness of the product on sale.

Distribution of European brands is best handled at the national level. Guidelines for the availability of each brand can apply to all markets, for example the impulse nature of buying and consuming confectionery requires this to be widely available through a range of channels from vending machines to convenience outlets. The challenge of achieving distribution in Europe depends not least on recognising the pervading influence of multiple grocers, who through their pricing strategy and continuous introduction of new categories undermine the commercial viability of traditional specialist outlets.

■ Advertising

The purpose of advertising is to communicate convincingly the unique benefits of brands and to convey the reasons for usage. The content of the advertising will be based on the brand's unique selling proposition, and since this is tied to the brand positioning, which is constant, it follows that, in principle at least, advertising should also be consistent across Europe. While this is undoubtedly the goal for any European brand there are a number of practical reasons why it may not be achieved.

Advertising must be convincing and it must capture the attention of the consumers. Given differences in culture, there is frequently a need to adapt the content of the advertising. This is particularly true with food products where there are significant differences between north and the south. For these reasons the content of the Uncle Ben's advertising varies between countries. On the other hand, there are some simple messages that transcend these differences and the Bounty advertising is the same across Europe. Only the language of the voice-over changes.

Harmonised advertising reduces the cost of production and is totally compatible with the brand essence, but not at the expense of relevance. Advertising must relate to the brand-building objectives and these will vary across Europe. Where the goal is to build usage, advertising will focus heavily on the product benefits. Where the usage is extensive and the brand is well known the objective of advertising will be to remind the consumer of the psychological values of the brand and so the balance of the advertising content will vary. The core element of the commercial will be common, providing production economies, but there will be local variations.

Advertising for European brands must therefore be developed within a European framework to support the brand essence, but needs to be adapted to each national environment. Achieving the right balance will be difficult, but as a simple rule of thumb I suggest that the onus of proof of the need to differ from a European norm will normally reside with the national market.

■ Promotion

Promotional activity is designed to generate additional sales by stimulating top-of-mind interest in the brand. The characteristic of successful promotions is to provide an additional incentive to the consumer to try the brand, or to repurchase it. Experience suggests that promotional activity will be most effective if consumer and trade interest are combined. A consumer promotion will be linked directly to the essence of the brand, and it is conceivable that these are organised at a European level such as the Snickers promotions linked to the sponsorship of the European Football Championships. However there are many events that are uniquely local that can be used as a basis of promotional activity, and these will have at least as much impact with the local consumer (and all consumers are local) as the European event. Consumer promotions will have different mechanics, and not all countries are capable of implementing the same one. The legality of promotions varies greatly from country to country (Germany being one of the most restrictive countries). If promotions are not to be reduced to the lowest common factor then it follows that there must be freedom to determine and implement consumer promotions nationally and even at a regional level.

Trade promotions are increasingly organised with the customer, and have to be managed and implemented at a local level. Even where there are international retailers, the experience of efficient implementation of European promotions is very rare, largely because retailers have yet to achieve store control from a European level, and most are struggling to achieve it at a national level, with some notable exceptions such as Belgium or the UK.

Promotions remain an important tool in building brand equity. However, to capture consumers' attention in each member state they have to be initiated and implemented locally while ideally creating European benefits as well.

■ Case Studies

The following, contrasting case studies of branding in the EU have been chosen to illustrate a number of the points made above.

■ The Uncle Ben's Brand – Case Study 1

Throughout Europe, the Uncle Ben's brand – originally rice and now increasingly sauces – is firmly positioned in consumers' minds as standing for high quality, consistency and convenience. To ensure the continuing success of Uncle Ben's as a brand leader it has been crucial to adjust elements within the marketing mix to allow for country-by-country differences. This has been particularly important for sauces which were launched in 1990 – these cover a variety of tastes to match different eating habits and palates. When we look at each of the elements in the marketing mix these variations can be clearly illustrated.

□ *Product and Positioning*

A key driver in most European markets on ethnic dishes has been the growth of 'foreign' restaurants and experiences of different tastes through travel abroad. In the UK this has led to Uncle Ben's important sauce sales being Chinese Sweet & Sour and Indian Curry. Virtually every English town has both a Chinese and Indian restaurant – what's more, Sweet & Sour is a dish which most food preparers would not know how to make themselves.

Sweet & Sour sauces have met with similar success in other markets such as France and Benelux, which also have a high number of oriental restaurants. Curry sauce sales are, however, lower because this is not a taste which many French, Belgian and Dutch consumers have experienced. In France a most popular sauce product is Basquaise, a style very popular in the South of France.

The product positioning of Uncle Ben's – enabling one to successfully create great-tasting different dishes – is common to all markets. It is the product offer which varies to ensure the maximum acceptance in each market.

□ *Value*

Throughout Europe, Uncle Ben's must be seen to offer value for money but still deserve an affordable premium. Packaging plays a major part in the value equation, particularly at point of purchase. On sauces this has led to some variations on jar sizes and shapes to remain competitive on shelf and, in the rice sector, to the recent introduction in some markets of resealable 'coffee bag' packs instead of boxes.

☐ *Availability*

The brand enjoys high levels of distribution in all EU markets, although the number of varieties available in larger stores is obviously greater than smaller outlets. The pattern of store sizes varies by country and Uncle Ben's range availability therefore matches this. Some small variations occur according to retailers' policies on own label. Moreover in France the high cost of entry demanded by the larger buying groups influences the number of brands and varieties stocked.

☐ *Advertising*

Although the core Uncle Ben's positioning is the same in each market the advertising executions vary to achieve maximum effectiveness locally. Variants such as the brand's history, competitive campaigns, consumer knowledge and attitudes must all be taken into account. UK advertising recognises Uncle Ben's as a brand leader and focuses on the high quality of ingredients and processing – the reasons why Uncle Ben's is better.

France has a long history of Uncle Ben's advertising. Uncle Ben himself is seen as a person and the USP of *'il ne colle jamais'* ('it never sticks') is part of the French vocabulary. In the latest advertising for both rice and sauces he is again seen in person.

Benelux advertising emphasises how rice and sauces fulfil the consumer's wants for exotic tastes. The advertising therefore taps into this with symbols and images of countries of origin.

Less developed markets, where stir-fry is not a widespread cooking method, are covered through a more explanatory advertising approach.

Despite these necessary variances the core of all Uncle Ben's advertising is the offer of perfect results when using Uncle Ben's rice and sauces.

☐ *Promotion*

There are still major national differences on the legality of various promotional methods. As with all brands the activity for Uncle Ben's must take account of these. Tactics must also be varied according to local needs such as encouraging trial and remaining price-competitive.

Uncle Ben's strategy in Europe can be summarised as 'freedom within a framework'. While some items of the mix remain the same, others have to be optimised to match local market conditions and needs.

■ **Lee Jeans – Case Study 2**

☐ *Product Positioning*

Unlike many other markets, the core jeans target of 15-to-24-year-olds exhibits broad homogeneity across Europe. The youth culture that influences jeans purchase is united by electronic technology. This culture sees the same brands, the same films and even the same television programmes – MTV, *Baywatch*, *Beverley Hills 90210*, *Friends*, *The Simpsons* – acting as icons for the youth market. The key task for Lee is to try to become an icon itself and to break Levi's stranglehold over the consumer. If one brand defines youth culture it would be Levi's (apologies to Nike!): it has a rebellious past, it has a fashionable present, and, one would think, an assured future.

The similarity of geographically separate youth cultures is shown by Lee's pan-European strategy, which is as relevant to a twenty-year-old in London as it is to an eighteen-year-old in Prague.

Lee's strategy – 'Real jeans with sex appeal' – is intended to differentiate Lee's from Levi's, which today has moved on from a rustic heritage to more of a fashion garment positioning. The 'sex appeal' is a vital ingredient given the whole category concerned with youth 'display'. Lee's sex appeal has suffered from its tough, no-nonsense workwear heritage.

☐ *Value*

Given Levi's pre-eminence in all countries, it is no surprise that pricing is relatively consistent across Europe. Levi's is consistently the price leader, with a level of premium according to its market share.

Figure 14.1   Lee
The key task for Lee is to try to become an icon in itself
and to break Levi's stranglehold over the customer

☐ *Distribution Channels*

Distribution channels exhibit similar trends with a decline in independents and the growth of specialist chains. This is in line with the worldwide trend towards the concentration of retailing power.

☐ *Advertising*

A pan-European strategy leads to a pan-European television and cinema campaign. Within this are some separate media such as local press executions in Germany, where the marketing strategy is slightly different, and some local radio in Belgium and Ireland. These local campaigns push specific national styles.

☐ *Promotion*

Promotional activity is regional, for example the sponsorship of the European music awards; and national, with national trade partners.

■ Conclusion

As can be seen from these case studies, it is possible to create successful brands Europe-wide. However, while some similarities exist between the different national markets, particularly for products that are targeting defined age groups, such as clothing, there are still many local differences in other product areas such as food. It is vital to understand that there is no one right strategy that will work for all brands. Successful pan-European branding requires the brand owner to take into account both local differences and international similarities and then put into place a strategy that allows the balancing of central controls with local input and implementation.

■ Reference

Corstjens, Judith and Corstjens, Marcel, *Store Wars* (Chichester: Wiley, 1995).

CHAPTER 15

Managing Retail Brands

Michael Jary and Andrew Wileman

OC&C Strategy Consultants

■ 'The Real Thing'? – Are Retail Businesses Really 'Brands'?

CEOs and senior managers in retail businesses can find the concept of a 'retail brand' frustrating, particularly if their background is with a branded fast-moving consumer goods (fmcg) producer. If their businesses or fascias are really brands, why does it seem so difficult to run them like Coca-Cola or Levi's? Why can't they seem to agree on a clear, effective statement of brand positioning that is concrete and actionable, and that doesn't change from month to month? Should they create a position of brand manager, like any consumer goods company, to impose sustained and consistent brand positioning on the functions of buying, merchandising and retail operations? And how is it possible to build a brand when a single failure such as the bad attitude of a lone checkout operator can wreck carefully built customer loyalty? In short, are retail businesses really 'brands', and can they be managed as such?

The situation is made even more frustrating now that 'retail brands' account for the majority of the top advertising expenditures in the UK – a very different picture from twenty years ago, when producer product brands still ruled the roost (Table 15.1).

Table 15.1 Top ten advertised UK grocery brands

Brand	1995 spend (£m)	Change on 1994 (%)
Kellogg's	69	0
Sainsbury	40	59
Boots	39	23
Safeway	39	119
Persil	30	5
Coca-Cola	29	104
Tesco	27	−11
Birds Eye	23	−11
Cadbury's	22	−27
Wall's	20	34

Source: Register – MEAL, OC&C.

Much energy is wasted on the question of what is a brand and what is merely a fascia or a label. All products and services are 'brands' to some extent; a more important question is whether the brand franchise is strong, sustainable and valuable.

A 'strong brand' is a product or service that, relative to competing brands, commands from consumers a price premium and/or volume preference at price parity. Graphically this can be represented as in Figure 15.1, Relative Volume and Price, Strong vs. Weak Brands:

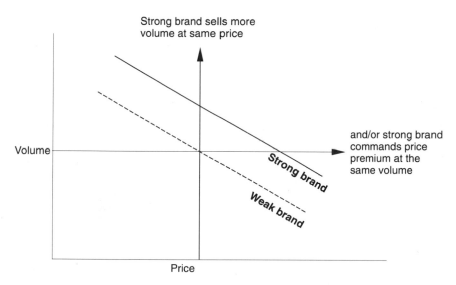

Figure 15.1   Relative volume and price, strong vs weak brands

From a brand owner's point of view, this effect is achieved by investing in all or some of the following:

- Marketing/advertising.
- Product quality and features.
- Service.

Consistent investment in product/service performance over time is crucial to building a strong, resilient brand franchise. The brand owner hopes to benefit, in the long run, from 'super-profits' deriving from a mix of higher market share and higher margins versus competitors. If the right balance is struck between cashing in and reinvesting these super-profits, brand profitability and growth should be more robust and sustainable against periodic competitive attacks.

From the consumer's point of view, loyalty to a strong brand is often – though not always – an aspirational act, enhancing self-image or self-esteem or at least reinforcing peer group membership (actual or aspirational); reducing worry and uncertainty (providing reassurance); or simplifying choice and saving time (what we might call 'editing'). The first of these is the most glamorous, and it is often brands in this category that attract most attention – Smirnoff, BMW, American Express, Harvey Nichols, Fortnum & Mason, to name but a few. However, many very strong mass brands primarily fulfil the other, more utilitarian functions; for example, Heinz, Persil, Marks & Spencer and McDonald's all primarily provide reassurance and/or aid decision-making.

Retail brands naturally appear in the above lists from the consumer's point of view, alongside the heavyweight global producer brands. From the brand owner's point of view, Marks & Spencer is a classic example of a highly robust, sustainable and profitable retail brand.

However, there are very important and significant differences between retail and producer brands – differences both of an essential nature and of degree. We can discuss them under four headings.

■ The Development of Private Label

Until recently, outside fashion categories, retailers were primarily 'stores' of producer brands. As such, they were weak as brands in their own right, and had little interest in either 'marketing' or 'branding' in the classic senses of those words. In many sectors where global manufacturers are dominant (for example, electrical goods, toys, sporting goods) this is still the case and the consumer therefore mainly selects retailers on price and breadth of range. However, in other sectors (most notably, grocery), the consolidation of retailers into large chains has made possible the growth of private labels, which has enabled differentiation of the retailer's product offer.

The greater the penetration of private label, the more the retailer has the opportunity to develop a true brand with attributes such as value, quality and innovation. For retailers such as Sainsbury and Boots, who stock around 50 per cent private label, the retail brand has probably become the dominant brand in the consumer's mind. With a retailer like Marks & Spencer, where the own brand has achieved complete penetration, the retail brand is the producer brand and owns consumer loyalty.

■ Brand Name Visibility

Producer brands reinvest in advertising partly to keep their name visible to the public, as well as to define and reinforce brand positioning; otherwise the brand name risks being out of sight on the top shelf in the kitchen.

High street retailers have historically used their prime high street frontage and fascias to achieve the same effect. The importance of 'location, location, location' in traditional high street retailing was that it not only maximised passing traffic but also gave brand visibility. As a result, advertising-to-sales ratios for high street retailers were until recently close to zero – premium rents for prime space performed the same function in the cost structure as above-the-line advertising spending did for producer brands. (As an interesting cross-reference, part of Coca-Cola's economic justification for the enormous investment in its worldwide vending machine programme was the advertising value of the brand logo on the machines.)

This is changing with the development of out-of-town, large-store destination retailing. Category killers like Toys 'R' Us and Ikea need to draw customers rather than rely on capturing passing traffic. They use advertising as part of the marketing mix to do this, with advertising-to-sales ratios at up to 2 per cent of sales, although still a long way from the 10 per cent-plus of producer brands. In response, high street retailers with enough overall scale are having to start spending on advertising as well, to fight for the high street's survival versus such out-of-town destination stores – a new and disconcerting experience for them just when their overall margins are under severe pressure.

■ Price-Based Competition

A strong producer brand, particularly a category leader (for example, Nestlé in coffee, Pedigree in petfood), will expect and need to achieve over the long run a consumer price premium. Superior benefits including quality and brand image are offered to support this, although there will be periodic bouts of price competition to keep the number two brand in its place or to see off a new entrant.

For most large scale retail brands, even strong ones, price is more important in the overall marketing mix than it is for strong producer brands. This is partly due to the high fixed costs characteristic of retailing and therefore the tendency for repeated price skirmishes. It is magnified further in sectors with perishable or limited shelf-life products such as fashion, where there is a great temptation in the inevitable periods of underperformance to clear product by heavy markdown or promotion. Often price becomes the key element of brand positioning – for example, KwikSave (which, unlike Sainsbury or Tesco, has only very weak private label strength), Toys 'R' Us and C&A.

With price so much more important for retail brands, the ability to extract and sustain a price premium from a strong brand is much more constrained. However it can be done with strong brands, if it is supported by a high private-label penetration that precludes direct price comparison with competition. Marks & Spencer, for example, sustains an estimated 10 per cent to 30 per cent 'premium' over other retailers on broadly comparable basic non-fashion clothing.

The brand premium for strong mass-market retail brands is more likely to result in greater volume and market share (number of customers and visits, or share of customer spend), either at price parity or at a discount versus competition. The strong retail brand will win economically via superior overall margin and profit, even though percentage margins may well be lower than weaker competitors. Out-of-town category killers provide the most striking examples of this, with low gross and net margins, supported by higher throughputs and lower operating costs (Figure 15.2).

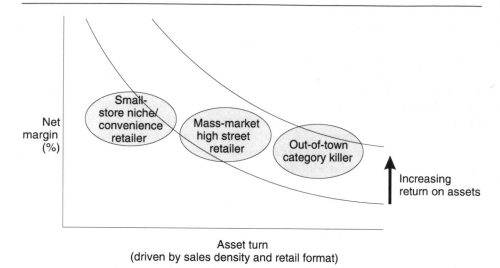

Figure 15.2   Retail brand premium: volume more than price

Retailers forget this characteristic of retail brands at their peril. In the boom days of 1986–9, many UK retailers believed their own hype and concluded that their brands could extract large and sustainable price premiums from consumers. They ratcheted up selling prices and gross margins, and ignored for as long as they could the subsequent rapid decline in traffic, sales volume and (later) overall return on assets – until the inevitable collapse in their net margins. Next was a classic example before its near-bankruptcy.

These first three differences between retailer brands and producer brands – the role of private label, brand name visibility, and price-based competition – are structural and evident. The fourth and last is in many ways the most interesting, and the most likely to drive to distraction a manager coming from an fmcg brand background – it is the complexity of the brand.

■ **Brand Complexity**

A Mars Bar has sixteen ingredients (chocolate, sugar, and so on); a few key eating characteristics (taste, texture, and so on); a wrapper, with a strong visual identity and logo, material feel, and so forth; and a few key brand positioning themes ('work, rest and play', etc.), documented in a short brand strategy statement that lives by the brand manager's bedside. These two dozen or so tangible and intangible attributes, and the brand strategy statement, constitute the Mars Bar brand and have underpinned its huge global sales and profit generation for the Mars corporation over the last seventy years. Changing any one of these attributes would take several years of discussion and would probably have to be agreed by the CEO.

The decision to extend the Mars brand to ice cream took over five years of debate, research, NPD and trialling – and was a gut-wrenching process for an organisation that for over half a century had kept sacred the notion that each brand name had to have one and only one clear 'slot' in the consumer's mind.

Tesco, in contrast, has 17 000 product lines, 435 stores, and 120 000 front-of-store checkout operators, counter staff and shelf-fillers interacting directly and daily with customers. Simply multiplying out these numbers produces millions of brand attributes – since the Tesco customer's experience of the brand is a combination of all the products he or she buys there (range, price, quality, and so on), the shopping environment and the service level.

Not only that, but 30 per cent of the product lines, or 5000 lines, change every year. Within the key value-added area of private label ready meals, there are 20 new product introductions per quarter. In-store staff turnover runs at around 30 per cent a year. Tesco's chief executive would get a hard time from his family if he tried personally to review, however briefly, a significant proportion of these changes to the brand.

The core day-to-day problems and frustrations involved in managing a retail brand stem primarily from this difference – the enormous multiplicity of brand attributes (product range, store environment, store service) and their constant high rate of change. This is the primary reason why retail CEOs or senior managers find it so difficult to achieve simple statements of brand strategy and positioning that are also enduring, concrete and actionable; clear, effective decision-making centred on an fmcg-type brand manager, or at least a workable organisational home for the brand management function that doesn't cause war to break out with buying or operations; and a sound night's sleep without worrying that the bad attitude of a £4 per hour checkout operator has just wiped out fifteen years of careful loyalty-building with a hundred customers in Leeds.

The careful, centralised decision-making and control processes of an fmcg brand simply don't work in retail. The role and supremacy of the brand manager can't be replicated. Somehow the CEO and senior manager have to find a different day-to-day organisational and operational way of managing the business, in order to preserve the integrity of a brand's intended core values through the chaos of thousands of daily decentralised decision and customer interactions.

■ 'Just Do It' – Organising for Brand Management

■ Should There Be a Marketing Function?

The first three aspects of retail brands described above – private label, brand visibility, and price-based competition – involve tough strategic decisions and good operational management. In this respect, retail brands are 'The Real

Thing', and retail marketing is becoming more like classic fmcg marketing. Clear decisions can be made in an orderly and centralised way that do not require fundamental reappraisal every quarter, and steady progress can be made. This argues strongly that there is a requirement to create or reinforce a 'brand management' or marketing function that will champion the development and integrity of the brand.

The retail marketing function should take on the management of the classic fmcg marketing activities: advertising and media; image communications and PR; promotions; and non-product-specific consumer or competitive research. It should also manage all activities relating to the development of direct customer relationships, including store cards, loyalty schemes and customer sales and service databases.

In the case of fashion retailers with strong style point of view, marketing should take on responsibility for 'store look': front store design, window display and visual merchandising.

It is however more important to define what the retail marketing function should not take on – or what it should not be. It should not be a back-room planning function. It should not take on the responsibility of category and space planning, nor should it carry out product- or category-specific consumer research. These areas must remain clearly within the remit of the buying and merchandising functions (B&M), or, in the modern retail management structure, more precisely within the 'product and supplier selection' side within B&M. If these capabilities and inclinations are not adequately present today in the B&M area, they should be built into the B&M organisation, rather than into the marketing function.

The marketing function warrants (with few exceptions such as discount retailers with little private label, such as KwikSave) a direct-reporting relationship to the CEO, on a level with the other key line and support functions.

■ Who Then Will Be The 'Brand Manager'?

In fmcg, the answer to this central question is usually straightforward. The marketing function is dominant in the organisation. Within marketing, the brand manager is king or queen.

The answer in retail is more complex, as a result of the brand complexity and the inevitable chaos of decentralised decision-making. On a day-to-day basis, retail management must be a complex team effort, requiring constant integration between marketing, product and supplier selection, and store operations.

The ultimate strategist for the brand, determining long-term direction, positioning and top-level policy, must be the CEO. The CEO is also the arbiter of last resort when major differences of opinion arise among his functional heads as to how to interpret and apply the long-term brand strategy.

For the business to run well, and for the brand to develop consistently in the right direction, the CEO's long-term brand strategy must be as concrete as possible and clearly articulated; the functional heads must have a deep, shared understanding – almost a set of reflexes – as to how that strategy converts into individual tactical decisions; and they must be able to push that understanding down into their own functional organisations. OC&C has seen several retailers experiment with making the marketing head also the 'brand manager' – to get closer to an fmcg-type structure. Our experience has been that this doesn't work. Other functions, particularly product and supplier selection, are too strong in retail (and rightly so) to be dominated by the marketing function. The only workable solution is a team effort, given clear leadership and focus by the CEO.

How can the CEO (supported by their top team) find a way of managing the enormous complexity inherent in the retail brand, and what should they focus on as their core working practices? How can they 'Just Do It'? It is time here to state four fundamental experience-based beliefs:

- Communicate the brand strategy clearly and persistently through the organisation.

The goal is to create a set of reflexes throughout the organisation, down to the trainee buyer and check-out operator, that manifest a consistent interpretation of the brand strategy agreed at a senior management level.

- Get into the details, frequently.

There is no substitute for this in retail. The retail CEO who believes his job is to set policy and direction and to delegate details and execution to his staff will most likely fail, as will the B&M director, and so on down the organisation. The CEO and the senior team must be involved deeply and frequently in item-level range reviews, in-store visits and in both formal and informal consumer research.

The process is one of detailed quality control and constant feedback. The involvement must, however, be structured rigorously to be productive, since random and incoherent reviews are almost as dangerous as total delegation. Senior management must have a clear agenda and checklist for the range reviews and store visits. Sam Walton probably epitomised this necessary characteristic of successful top-level retail management. Right up to his death he was still involved in extensive range reviews at Wal-Mart; he visited several stores every week, where he showed detailed knowledge of sales performance down to item level. While this still allowed direct involvement in only a tiny proportion of the multitude of decisions, it set the tone for his top team, and was thus carried on down throughout the organisation.

> • Develop effective head office decision support systems.

Given the mountain of detail involved in retail management, and the obligation to work at a detailed level, effective decision support systems (particularly in B&M/product and supplier selection) are an absolute necessity for top management. In practice this area still represents a massive opportunity and imperative, even in large and sophisticated retailers.

> • Get commitment from the front-line in-store staff, with performance-related pay and a positive employee culture.

It's hard to think of a long-term successful retailer that doesn't have some kind of pay scheme that ties the fortunes of its store staff to those of the company, or that doesn't go to great lengths to create a positive shared culture among its thousands of store-level staff. Sainsbury, Marks & Spencer and John Lewis all adopt this approach. How else can the CEO have a chance of relying on a faithful execution of the brand strategy by the checkout operator in Leeds?

These four working practices are of course basic common sense – but they reflect a difference in emphasis and priority when compared with the more centralised and controllable environments of fmcg brands and organisations.

■ In Summary

Retail brands *are* 'The Real Thing', although they are in several important ways very different from fmcg brands, not least because of the difficulty of managing the multiplicity of attributes of a retail brand.

Senior retail management can organise and operate in such a way as to make it possible to 'Just Do It' with a retail brand, but this does require the development of a dedicated professional marketing function and the tireless pursuit of processes and practices that deliver brand quality and integrity across the whole range of products and stores.

CHAPTER 16

Commodity Branding

Joe Pope
ENZA

David Cullwick
Ernst & Young

Jo Kennelly
Ernst & Young

■ Introduction

In marketing the term commodity is synonymous with primary products and raw materials. A commodity undergoes minor processing before being sold or traded in the marketplace. A commodity can either be a primary product that is used in the manufacture of processed products, such as oil, which is used to make plastic, or it can be sold as a sourced product, such as drinking water, which is packaged and marketed in bottles.

In a commodity market, nearly identical products can be bought from different producers. Traditionally, there tends to be limited customer loyalty to any producer as customers readily purchase entirely on the basis of comparative pricing. This leads to cut-throat competition for customers and hence to a relatively low profit margin.[1] Thus, companies competing in a commodity market have minimum advantages in terms of differentiation and cost.

In more conventional packaged-goods markets it is relatively easy to differentiate products by adding value to the packaging, in terms of convenience by means of a better delivery system. However, for some commodity products, such as metals, crude petroleum products and agricultural products like grain, this is not always possible.[2] Moreover, the commodity mindset is so powerful that, even when companies do have products that can be differentiated, many of them do very little to distinguish their products effectively from those of competitors.[3]

Commodities differ from manufactured products in that their perceived value reflects the fundamental attributes of the product, while the perceived value of manufactured products reflects the costs incurred and the benefits contributed via the processing of the original raw materials.

Faced with such obstacles, one might wonder whether commodity producers have anything to gain by attempting to brand their products. It can be done, however, and this chapter aims to describe how producers can brand commodities and what benefits a branded approach can bring.

The second part of this chapter demonstrates that branding may be an integral part of selling a commodity. Next the chapter outlines the main elements of branding and details global examples of commodity branding for each element. A short section focuses on the success of the New Zealand Apple and Pear Marketing Board's apple brand ENZA, and finally the question of whether commodity branding is worth it is addressed briefly.

■ Can Commodities Be Branded?

There are two ways of approaching the issue of branding commodity products. The first is to develop a brand for the commodity itself, the second to develop a brand to embrace not only an appropriate commodity specification and quality but also the add-ons.

In the first instance, a commodity brand will focus upon the following:

- Product form.
- Product quality marks and/or standards (including consistency).
- Performance relative to customer expectations.
- Texture, flavour (in the case of foodstuffs).
- Distinctive origin, for example California grapes.

The following article from *Supermarket News* illustrates how such an approach can be pursued by a producer:

Dole Sets Out to Brand Nearly All its Vegetables[4]
Dole Fresh Vegetables Co. here is poised to brand nearly 100% of the commodities it ships. 'Our goal is to make all our vegetables – as much as we can – easily identifiable to consumers as Dole products' said Bill Heintz, president, Dole Fresh Vegetables Co.

. . . It [Dole] is exploring ways to brand unwrapped lettuce, as well as its bunch stalks of broccoli, he said, adding that an asparagus branding program has also been budgeted for next year. Dole is also attempting to encourage retailers to accept more of its celery and leaf lettuce packed in sleeves. On another front, Dole is seeking ways to pack strawberries. . .

. . . Dole and other major suppliers are making such efforts because of the rewards branding offers, such as demonstrating quality, bolstering consumer confidence and pulling in higher retail margins.

. . . But while Dole officials are greatly aware of the emerging growth opportunities of branded produce, they also recognise the limitations certain fruits and vegetables pose. Some commodities 'do not naturally lend themselves to branding.'. . .

In the second instance, when branding embraces not only the products themselves but also the add-ons level, key elements of the branded offering might include:

- Packaging.
- Non-product appeals.
- Security and continuity of delivery.
- Technical support.
- Value perception of right product, right place, right price, right time.

Again, an article from *Food Business* serves to illustrate this approach:

Turning a Commodity into an Upscale Brand[5]
Stella Cheese, a Brookfield Wisconsin based food marketer, focuses on a core product of Italian cheeses in a wheel form. Consumers of Italian cheeses are most familiar with non-branded wedges which they purchase in the deli section which has not been an arena for strong brands. The Stella label has emphasised a range of wedges (rather than wheels) with upscale packaging and graphics. This approach has been complemented by a line of fresh shredded cheeses in five ounce deli cups including Romano, Parmesan and Asiago. Further developments are expected in blended, shredded and grated cheeses. The product initiatives are supported by in-store campaigns and television advertising which is expected to grow significantly. *Food Business*, August 1992.

Often, in commodity markets, the brand name and the enterprise name are the same; this provides an umbrella for developing and promoting other products under a specific brand. Well-known international examples include Dole, Del Monte and ENZA.

■ Converting a Commodity into a Brand

The inherent nature of commodities means that, as far as consumers are concerned, minimal differentiation is perceived between competing products. In order to change this situation, a very clear understanding of the purpose and role of branding is required. Next, a clear brand development programme must be agreed. Almost certainly, such a programme will need to include a detailed analysis of expected returns that will justify the additional product and marketing costs.

Essentially the basic rules of marketing commodities are no different from the basic rules of marketing manufactured goods, as this case history about Robinson Brick Co. illustrates:

How to Convert a Commodity into a Brand Name[6]

Since the mid 1970s Robinson Brick Co., founded by George Robinson's grandfather in 1880, had been tooling along as the largest maker of residential brick in Colorado. 'We were sitting on top of the world' Robinson recalls, until a series of recessions hit Colorado starting in 1984.

George's challenge was to make Robinson bricks more than just a commodity. Here's his strategy:

You need a better product. The people who buy what you're selling may be many things, but they're not stupid. If your product is no good, advertising won't help.

Tell people why they are better. Advertising types refer to this as the 'unique selling proposition.' With every communication you make – letters, brochures, advertisements – you must get the message across. Does your product last longer or work faster, or is it simply a better buy? Tell people why they should pick you.

Word of mouth. Try to influence the people who influence others. Robinson Brick tries to spread the word through distributors, since they interact with builders, architects and consumers.

Endorsements. Forget high priced pitch-men. Better to find an independent, objective authority who will say you really do have a better product.

■ Why Brand Commodities?

The fundamental reasons why commodity producers wish to pursue a branded approach are in order to achieve a stronger consumer and trade franchise, better retailer support and overall profitability. 'Attaching an established brand name to a previously unbranded product can add 30 per cent or 40 per cent or even 50 per cent, or more to what consumers are willing to pay for it.'[7]

Thus, branding of commodities has two key objectives:

- First, the creation of a 'package' of attributes that will appeal to the consumer more than other similar products, and hence will be able to achieve a price premium
- Second, the creation of a customer franchise within the market that will be a catalyst for increased consumer preference and loyalty

Companies who successfully brand commodity products can thus hope to gain many of the advantages afforded by any strong brand. These include:

- Greater consumer recognition.
- Greater focus for differentiation.
- Increased competitiveness.
- Increased consumer loyalty.

These advantages over time lead to:

- Higher and more consistent pricing.
- Maintained or improved market share.
- A more focused marketing programme.
- A brand value which is a realisable asset.

Although the benefits of a well-thought-out brand development are clear, the lack of differentiation inherent in commodity products means that it can be extremely difficult for such brands to achieve success. For example, an attempt to brand New Zealand lamb in British supermarkets failed because consumers could not see enough branded benefit. Equally, the dominance of own-label branding by retailers in some commodity sectors represents a further barrier to entry for commodity producers.

■ Elements of Commodity Branding

In order effectively to brand a commodity a producer must therefore ensure that as many as possible of the following principles are used as a guide:[8]

- Establishment of a unique consumer benefit.
- Immediate visual recognition of the brand by all target consumers.
- Quality consistency.
- Good distribution coverage to ensure accessibility to all target consumers.
- Sufficient promotional support to create awareness of brand benefits and build loyalty.
- Appropriate commodity bundling.
- R&D to achieve innovative processes and products.

The emphasis on the different elements presented above will differ from commodity to commodity and may differ from context to context. Further explanation of each of these elements is given below.

■ Unique Consumer Benefit

Most really successful brands have built their success upon basic product differentiation – usually one or more features or benefits that are unique to that product. In the case of commodities – nearly identical products – this is often difficult to achieve. Producers, thus, often rely upon external features, such as country of origin and delivery, or less tangible benefits such as imagery and packaging.

■ **Country of Origin**

Producers wishing to market their commodities on the global market have
sometimes opted for country of origin labelling – Norwegian salmon, New
Zealand lamb, Californian grapes, Australian wool, Welsh leeks and French
onions. In recent years such labelling has been reinforced with the development
of country-of-origin trade marks. A country can be a strong symbol,
particularly at home and internally, as it has close connections with products,
materials and capabilities.[9] To some consumers it can also indicate quality and
consistency in delivery.

However, people's perceptions of a country and the symbolism associated
with it may differ from one country to another and may alter over time as
economic, political, social and environmental circumstances change. Thus there
was a temporary decrease in demand for primary products from the northern
hemisphere following the Chernobyl disaster in 1987 and a collapse in demand
for Chilean grapes following Pinochet's removal of Allende.

■ **Bottled Water**

Bottled water is an excellent example of how a commodity product can be
branded in such a way as to appeal to the consumer and demonstrate
apparently unique benefits. Despite the commodity nature of the product,
consumers of bottled water are highly image-conscious and branding in this
market is vital for success.[10] Over the last ten years the world's markets have
been awash with waters from France, Italy, Germany, Belgium and many
southern hemisphere countries. French mineral waters, such as Perrier and
Evian, dominate the European markets and are making a significant impact on
the bottled water market in the United States.

Bottled water has been branded at both the product level and the add-on
level. At the product level, purity, flavour, effervescence, and source have been
used to brand water; some waters are sought after because they come from
springs, spas or icebergs. At the add-on level distinctive bottles, including
colour and shape, have been used to reinforce the brand messages.

■ **Chicken: Value-Enhanced Products**

Some of the best examples of branding the add-ons associated with a
commodity are found in the USA chicken industry. Despite low profit margins
and variable feed prices and distribution problems in this industry, several
companies have successfully differentiated their product from other products in
the market place – Perdue, ConAgra, Holly Farms, Tyson. Through the further
processing of its products – deboning, cutting and prepackaging – Tyson, for
example, offers both the retailer and customer greater convenience. Added to
this, one of the key elements driving Tyson's success has been effective product
innovation, such as new flavours.

■ Visual Brand Imagery

Designing a visual identity that is immediately recognisable is a further significant way of helping to identify for the customer the unique benefits of a commodity. A strong visual identity will over time become associated with a particular standard, specifications and an image. The challenge is of course to create a value perception for which consumers are prepared to pay more and that will then give the producers an appreciably better return.

■ New Zealand Wool

Traditionally, commodity selling has placed considerable emphasis on extensive advertising and promotion programmes. The aim of these has generally been to build generic demand for a particular product. International commodity producers would often group together in order to fight off competition from alternative products or to revive flagging consumer demand. A notable example of this is the successful promotion by the International Wool Secretariat (IWS) of the Woolmark symbol.

However, the economic advantages of IWS's generic marketing approach have been questioned by some of its member countries. In the case of New Zealand this has led to the belief that a greater value positioning for New Zealand wool could be achieved outside the partnership. In 1995 the New Zealand Wool Board began to promote its own wool to processors and consumers under the Fernmark brand.

**WOOLS
OF
NEW ZEALAND**™

Figure 16.1   New Zealand Wool

In 1995 the New Zealand Wool Board began to promote its own wool under the Fernmark brand, in the belief that a greater value positioning could be achieved outside the marketing programme of the International Wool Secretariat whose aim was to build generic demand for the product

■ **Farmed Venison**

Another recent example of the application of branding techniques to commodity products is the brand development programme for farmed venison undertaken by the New Zealand Game Industry Board (NZGIB).[11] In order to break out of the 'commodity trap' the NZGIB has developed a dual marketing strategy for its product. In markets where venison is well known and an established meat product, such as Europe and Asia, New Zealand farmed venison is sold using the quality product mark ZEAL, and in markets where it is a relatively new product, such as New Zealand, North America and Australia, it is sold as the branded product Cervena. The objectives of this branding strategy are to build awareness of New Zealand quality venison and to develop customer preference for it. NZGIB's decision to brand venison as Cervena for sale in some markets is aimed not only at building awareness and quality perceptions, but also at repositioning the product by removing the traditional associations of venison with Walt Disney's *Bambi*.

Figure 16.2   Cervena
Cervena, the brand for New Zealand farm-raised venison, is an example of the application of branding techniques to commodity products

■ **Quality Consistency**

The importance of delivering consistent quality in order to fulfil a branded promise cannot be underestimated. Perceived quality provides a reason to buy, a point of differentiation, an opportunity for premium pricing, channel interest and a basis for brand extensions. The keys to delivering quality are to identify those quality dimensions that are important to the consumer and to communicate those messages in a credible manner.[12]

Perdue chickens and Chiquita bananas illustrate that a commodity product can be successfully branded. Each has developed a formidable awareness level and quality reputation for a product that was thought not so long ago to be a pure commodity.[13]

■ Effective Distribution

If a branded commodity is to succeed, effective distribution must be achieved on both an international and a local basis. In the traditional commodity trading situation a product often passes through a range of wholesalers and/or traders before reaching the consumer, meaning that the original manufacturer has little control over the channels.

It is obvious that it is essential for the branded commodity producer to retain as much control over the channels as possible. For 'fresh' commodities, such as chicken, lettuce and fish, traditional packing procedures sometimes require that the production plant be within a reasonable distance of the market. For example the chicken industry in the United States is characterised by the regional domination of branded products: the West Coast is dominated by Foster Farms and Zachy Farms, Perdue is well known in the Northwest and Tyson predominates in the Midwest.

However, the development of effective distribution channels and packaging can provide a producer with a competitive distribution advantage and, thus, opportunities for establishing a premium product. An example of this is the distribution and sale of live lobster by the Canadian firm Clear Water Lobsters in Europe, especially around Christmas time. Their branded product Clear Water Hardshell Fresh Brand is flown to Europe and kept alive in especially designed cooling containers.

■ Sufficient Promotion

Long-term advertising and promotion is vital in order to build a successful brand. Sales promotions can provide short-term incentives to make a purchase decision, although they should not be relied upon as primary brand building tools. For long-term brand building, advertising is required that strengthens brand associations and improves brand awareness. Promotion can be used to improve consumer loyalty, enhance perceived quality, and notify customers of additional value, properties or uses for a particular product.

The promotion of flax by the Canadian company Randoff and James Flax Mills Ltd is a good example of how the message of added value and diversity of use can be communicated. Flax was traditionally a non-food crop, used among other things for making dollar notes. But Randoff and James found, after a series of tests on the chemical and physical properties of flax, that it contained many health-related benefits and was a suitable cereal substitute. The promotion of the benefits associated with flax as a food product and the innovative packaging of the product, branded as Northern Edge, in brass coloured aluminium foil by Randoff and James were so effective that the product began to appear in processed foods, such as bread and muffins. Consequently, Randoff and James became both an ingredient (commodity) and product (branded) supplier of flax.

■ Commodity Bundling

Commodity bundling involves grouping related products together in a unified market offering. The objective is to develop a competitive position that produces value for customers and differentiates the bundling from its rivals. The potential advantages of this approach include lower promotional costs, enhanced competitive advantage and the improvement of customer orientation. An important objective of commodity bundling is to lock in customers and thus deny them to competitors. An example of this was presented by Lawless (1991):[14]

> IBM offers a line of non-impact printers that rely on IBM mainframes for most information processing needed for printing jobs. This linkage acts as an important incentive for customers – particularly those committed to IBM mainframes – to buy the complete line of office equipment. Other suppliers (for example Siemens) must offer much greater value to induce customers to add their equipment to an IBM-based system.

This strategy has the potential to be used increasingly by commodity marketers to differentiate products. For example, the New Zealand Dairy Board offers strong technical support, pilot scale facilities and training with sales of milk proteins in the USA. It also tailors commodity production to meet tight customer specifications.[15]

■ New Products and Innovation

Research and development activities undertaken by producers vary considerably in character and cost. A good example of R&D working for producers in the commodity market is the development of highly effective extraction technologies by Export Packers (Canada) for extracting the protein con-albumin from egg whites. Con-albumin is used as an ingredient in nutraceutical food bars throughout North America. Research and development moved Export Packers from being a producer of a commodity product – egg whites – to being one of a high-value protein product.

■ The ENZA Experience

The recent initiative in commodity branding undertaken by the New Zealand Apple and Pear Board illustrates many of the principles that have been outlined above.

The ENZA brand came about as a result of a coordinated activity embarked upon by a cooperative of small apple and pear growers, situated in the South Pacific and isolated from the major northern hemisphere markets – the risky business of launching a global brand for one of the most traditional of all commodities, namely apples.

The international market for apples is extremely fragmented with no dominant player evident. Apples are produced in most countries of the world and, as they are a bulky, low value-product that requires expensive refrigerated transport, the percentage of internationally traded product is less than 10 per cent of the total world production of 36.5 million tonnes.[16] Yet despite this, there exists an over-supply of apples in the world markets, as evidenced by the volumes that have been withdrawn through 'intervention' in the markets by the European Commission under their Common Agricultural Policy.

Southern hemisphere producers account for approximately 35 per cent of the world apple trade. Due to the seasonal variation in apple production, they have a market window for fresh out-of-season produce in the affluent northern hemisphere markets between the months of April and August.

The country that exports the highest percentage of its total apple crop is New Zealand. With a small domestic market (3.5 million people) and access to its nearest neighbour, Australia, denied, New Zealand exports 82 per cent of its apple crop to mainly northern hemisphere countries. Of the total apple crop 58 per cent is exported as 'fresh' product and 24 per cent as processed product.

Compared with its traditional competitors, Chile and South Africa, New Zealand is a high-cost producer of apples. Growers do not receive agricultural subsidies from the New Zealand government and high freight costs are incurred in shipping apples to northern hemisphere markets. New Zealand, therefore, has no cost advantages and relies on developing and maintaining other forms of competitive advantage to market its apples overseas. This it does by differentiating its product with new varieties, maintaining consistently high quality, controlling distribution by establishing in-market distribution and selling capacity and, last but by no means least, by branding.

■ ENZA Brand Development

The cooperative that exports New Zealand apples, the New Zealand Apple and Pear Marketing Board (APMB), is a statutory cooperative and is obliged to purchase all apples and pears offered to it that are fit for export. It is controlled, financed and in effect owned by the apple and pear growers.

Given the fragmented and highly competitive environment in which it operates internationally, the APMB believed it was not enough to differentiate in the traditional commodity areas of adding value by packaging, convenience, or delivery systems. In the mid-1970s, when the industry faced a collapse of exports and the APMB was insolvent, a commitment was made to develop real and sustainable competitive advantage.

Until the early-1990s the 'brand' applied by the APMB was 'New Zealand'. International consumer research showed that New Zealand was seen as a credible source of top-quality food, and as the APMB was the sole exporter, the New Zealand brand was felt by many to be not only appropriate but sufficient.

However, the increasing realisation that the APMB could not own, and therefore control, the brand name, and that many other food products sold through the same retail outlets could use the same brand name, led to the decision to develop and introduce a true brand strategy. This was implemented in a systematic manner.

■ The Strategy

APMB apples were targeted at the premium segment, with the objective of obtaining a 10 per cent premium against like products. Consumers in this segment were known to be more interested in quality, trying new products and looking for the excitement of the taste of new apples.

APMB aimed to outperform the world apple industry by developing an integrated quality system in orchard transport and storage activities to achieve a consistently high quality of product. This was supported by stringent grading standards and control of the produce through the distribution channel to retailer.

Control of distribution for the produce had been a feature of APMB's strategy since the late 1980s, with the establishment of a sales company in London (previously a sales representative office), the purchasing of its master agent in continental Europe and the taking of a shareholding in the master agent used in North America. These changes in distribution structure were supported by the appointment of qualified brand marketers into these companies to lead the branding programme down to the trade and to the retailer.

A critical first step in the development of a new brand was the choice of a suitable name and visual identity to replace the old 'brand': a red and green apple symbol containing the words 'New Zealand' in very small letters. As the original symbol was deemed to have some value associated with it, it was retained although the width of the symbol was increased slightly. A new four-letter brand name was to be prominently displayed across the symbol.

A team of two top creative staff from the APMB's agency, Colenso, a patent attorney and two APMB marketing executives were charged with developing the name. The name needed to be available as a trade mark internationally and, ideally, a link to New Zealand was sought The chosen name was ENZA. The name tested well internationally, with the only consumer concern being a vague association with chemicals.

The product positioning was clear: fresh, quality, taste excitement, healthy. Overlying this was the perception of New Zealand as young, innovative and able to take on the world and win.

But how did APMB gain trade confidence in their new brand of apples? In the late 1980s and early 1990s there was still considerable opposition to even placing stickers on apples, which is fundamental to any branding programme. There was also doubt among staff and growers that branding was the correct strategy.

The development of an innovative approach to promotion was seen as an important element of the brand development strategy. Priority objectives to be met were:

- To engender pride of ownership in the brand among staff and growers.
- To show the trade that the APMB was seriously committed to branding as a key marketing strategy.
- To lift the new brand out of the morass of new brands and products by giving it a 'kick start'.
- To build a consumer franchise for the brand.

Consequently, APMB entered into a series of international yachting sponsorships that involved both extensive world-wide television and other media coverage, and also gave the opportunity for considerable in-market promotional activity. The positioning of ENZA and yachting was deemed to be a close fit, for in both cases a combination of human endeavour against the elements and technology is important.

The yachting sponsorship included the following events:

- 1992 America's Cup, San Diego.
- 1993 Whitbread Round the World Race.
- 1994 Jules Verne Trophy – Non-stop Round the World Challenge.
- 1995 America's Cup, San Diego.

Winning the Whitbread Trophy with *New Zealand Endeavour*, the Jules Verne Trophy with *ENZA New Zealand* and the America's Cup – Team New Zealand and *Black Magic* – in three successive years in a yachting-crazy country such as New Zealand certainly engendered pride of ownership of the distinctive ENZA logo, which was prominent on all three yachts.

The apparent scale of the yachting sponsorships, which in effect were quite modest and funded within normal promotional spend, helped convince the trade of APMB's commitment to the new brand. This commitment was also reinforced by the yachting greats, Sir Peter Blake, Sir Robin Knox-Johnston and Grant Dalton, taking an active role as part of their own campaign in trade promotions and staff functions throughout Europe and the United States.

The yachting brand programme, together with APMB's involvement in key trade fairs, the placing of stickers on individual fruit pieces and the recent move into consumer television, radio and print campaigns, have all helped to support the new brand. Surprisingly, spending on total promotion has remained below 3 per cent of sales.

The ENZA branding programme has been supported through APMB's long-term commitment to product development and research, which has provided an array of new products, such as Braeburn, Gala, Royal Gala, Pacific Rose and Southern Snap, and enabled the first production of Fuji outside Japan. Moreover, New Zealand is the only southern hemisphere country successfully to produce and export Cox. This diverse product portfolio accounts for 80 per cent of revenue and has firmly established the APMB as the world leaders in new apple variety marketing. It has also become evident that the cool climate in New Zealand, credited for the success of its wine exports, also produces apples of superior taste.

After four years the ENZA brand appears on two billion pieces of fruit sold in nearly sixty countries. All the objectives set to date have been exceeded, with ongoing and increasing concentration on point of sale tastings, radio, television, radio and print media promotions built around quality and unique taste taking the place of the initial sponsorships. The brand will be valued globally in two years' time and at that time consideration will be given to capitalising it on the APMB balance sheet.

■ Is Commodity Branding Worth It?

In the case of ENZA and many firms in an increasing number of commodity businesses – blood collection products, replacement motors and steel strapping among them – the answer to the above question is obviously yes. Through knowing how and when to differentiate their products and seek cost leadership these commodity providers are becoming increasingly profitable.[17]

In the future we are likely to see increasing differentiation of products, a shrinking of the commodity markets for many products and increasing competition in what remains of traditional commodity markets.[18] Commodity producers will therefore need to be adaptable to market conditions and to learn to apply the strategies and techniques that best suit the product and the market. In some markets generic marketing may be the most appropriate and effective way to sell commodities, while in others the development of a differentiated and well-promoted brand may reap significant rewards.

■ Notes

1. J. G. Thomas, and J. M. Knoonce, 'Differentiating a Commodity: Lessons from Tyson', *Planning Review* (1989) September/October, pp. 24–9.
2. D. H. Buisson, *Commodity Marketing*.
3. Thomas and Knoonce, 'Differentiating a Commodity'.

4. J. Mejia, 'Dole Sets Out to Brand Nearly All Its Vegetables', *Supermarket News* (1990) 22 October, p. 52.
5. 'New Marketing Mix for Stella Cheese: Turning a Commodity Into an Upscale Brand', *Food Business* (1992) August, p. 16.
6. P. B. Brown, 'The Product is the Message: How to Convert a Commodity Into a Brand Name', *INC* (1990) June, pp. 104–5.
7. J. G. Smith, Chairman of Uxtoby-Smith Inc., a New York City market research firm, cited in INC (1990) June, p. 104.
8. A. Kominik, 'Farm Products Goes into the Battle of the Brands', *The Dominion* (New Zealand) (1995) February, p. 23.
9. D. A. Aaker, *Managing Brand Equity: Capitalizing on the Value of a Brand Name* (Maxwell Macmillan) (1991) p. 7.
10. 'Balancing Act on Water (Highland Spring Ltd)', *Super Marketing* (1993) 1057, 2: 36.
11. H. Ware, 'Venison: Brand Focusing Reaps Rewards', *Food Technology in New Zealand* (1994) 20–1 April.
12. D. A. Aaker, *Managing Brand Equity* (1991) p. 272.
13. Ibid., p. 20.
14. M. W. Lawless, 'Commodity Bundling for Competitive Advantage: Strategic Implications', *Journal of Management Studies* (1991), vol. 28, pp. 267–80.
15. Buisson, *Commodity Marketing*.
16. USDA 1995 estimates.
17. V. K. Rangan and G. T. Bowman, 'Beating the Commodity Magnet', *Industrial Marketing Management* (1992), vol. 21, pp. 215–24.
18. Buisson, *Commodity Marketing*.

CHAPTER 17

Branding in the Pharmaceutical Industry

Andy Milligan

Interbrand

■ Introduction

Branding as we understand it in the fields of fast-moving consumer goods and services has rarely been welcomed or much used in the pharmaceuticals industry. A new drug would be given a name and packaging, but historically there have been few if any genuine pharmaceutical brands.

What made branding such a rarity in this industry? A number of factors can be seen as contributing to the relatively late adoption of branding by the pharmaceuticals industry:

- Drugs were seen as a 'rational purchase', unlike fast-moving consumer goods goods, and hence were not perceived as a suitable subject for branding.
- There was felt to be no real audience for branding, because the 'consumer', the patient, was not the purchaser of the product, which was purchased in the main by health services and prescribed by doctors or pharmacists.
- Regulatory controls were perceived as making the type of creative brand development used in other industries impossible to implement in pharmaceuticals.
- Pricing controls on drugs were seen as invalidating branding, since the investment that would be required to create and develop the brand could not be recouped through higher pricing of the branded product.

However, one of the most significant recent changes in the pharmaceutical industry has been the growing use of branding techniques to build awareness of and interest in a new drug. These techniques are designed not only to establish a product in a competitive therapy area (for example Valtrex in the highly competitive antiviral market) but also to help protect the drug post-patent.

What is driving these changes? A number of factors can be identified that either singly or working in combination have made the pharmaceutical industry worldwide reconsider the value of branding.

The first factor that has led to a reconsideration of the value of branding is the need for pharmaceutical companies to prolong the life of their products as they come off-patent, in order to help set off ever increasing research costs. Historical analysis shows decreasing exclusivity periods between the launch of innovative drugs and follower drugs, as the industry becomes ever more sophisticated. The costs of bringing a new drug to market are on average now £100 million or more and the effective patent life approximately 8 years. Given these figures, the development of brands for the innovative drugs is a critical tool in extending their value to the company.

Also of relevance to the branding debate is the increasing number of products that are switching at some stage in the product lifecycle from prescription to over-the-counter (OTC). Once in the OTC arena, branding becomes critical to guide the consumer's choice of product. There is therefore a strong benefit to establishing the brand in the patient's mind while the drug is at the prescription stage, so that they can identify with the brand and continue to purchase once the drug comes off-prescription. A successful example of this type of trading development can be seen in Glaxo Wellcome's license extension to sell the 75 milligram dose of Zantac over-the-counter.

The increasing availability of previously on-prescription products OTC, caused and driven by the move to self-medication, is also supporting the growth of pharmaceutical branding. The emergence of patient lobbies (such as the groups lobbying for patients with MS or AIDS) who have an ability to argue their cause strongly is, given their consumer rather than health services background, creating a target group likely to appreciate and react favourably to brands. Once consumers themselves are making the decision on the drug, branding is acknowledged as more relevant. The new consumer is much in need of branding to steer him or her through a difficult and important purchase decision. However, branding in this area needs to be particularly sensitive to the peculiarities of the OTC market, where 'relief' rather than enjoyment drives purchase and the purchase is of low interest but high involvement.

Also, finally, underlying all these issues is the need of pharmaceutical companies to differentiate themselves in an increasingly competitive and commercial environment – where branding is now being taken seriously because it is seen as a potential source of competitive advantage.

■ The Importance of Strong Brand Names

One of the most noticeable features of this increased interest in branding is the use of strong brand names on new drug products.

In the past, brand names generally reflected the generic compound, but today trade marks are becoming much more innovative. Two brand names that stand out as excellent examples of this process, and that happen to be in competition even with each other, are the anti-emetic with the generic name of granisetron, sold by SmithKline Beecham under the brand name Kytril, and another anti-emetic with the generic name ondansetron, sold by Glaxo Wellcome under the brand name Zofran. Neither of these brand names bears any resemblance to the generic name. This innovative approach allows both brand names to be more easily protected by law, and also discourages generic intrusion through substitution. In addition, the names are creative and different, yet are not difficult to pronounce, write or spell. Since physicians will have to write and pronounce the brand name many times in their daily routine, a company must make the trade mark as easy to remember as it is to spell and pronounce.

Another trade mark philosophy that has surfaced with the advent of generics has been the development of brand names indicative of the disease the product treats. For example, in recent years, a new chemical entity has been developed for use in the treatment of asthma that has been launched under the brand name Serevent – 'sere' suggesting 'serenity' and 'vent' indicating that the drug should be used for patients with breathing difficulties. Another example of a brand name that indicates clearly the use of a drug is Imigran, for the treatment of migraine. These are two powerful examples of pre-emptive pharmaceutical branding – differentiated, international and a 'tough act' for other pharmaceutical and generic companies to follow.

■ International Brand Names

A relatively new philosophy is the development of a single brand internationally. Many of the major pharmaceutical companies operate in fifty or more countries around the world; clearly there are sizeable economies of scale that can be achieved through the promotion of one brand in all markets. It is not an easy process; for example, incidences of a conflict with an existing trade mark obviously multiply with each new country. A brand name for a product may be extremely appropriate in English but may be totally unacceptable in another language. In those cases where there are insurmountable difficulties, a letter or two will have to be changed in one or two languages to solve the problem and, in effect, the brand name will be seen as a worldwide trade mark. However, when the exact brand name cannot be used in three or more of the major pharmaceutical markets of the world (the US, the UK, Italy, France, Germany, Japan, Spain, Switzerland, Sweden, the Netherlands and Austria) then it is likely that the manufacturer will prefer to adopt a different trade mark with wider applicability.

Techniques for developing worldwide trade marks are very complex, but the result can be well worth the effort, particularly in the event of any future trade mark infringement cases. If a trade mark has been established on a worldwide basis, the ownership of it and rights to it are much more protectable.

Further, a worldwide trade mark ensures familiarity with the brand name and with the product, as well as with the manufacturer, which is particularly important as people continue to travel to and live in different countries. The combination of an innovative, worldwide trade mark makes for an exceptional marketing and legal product franchise in the pharmaceutical industry, as in other product sectors.

■ Stages of Naming a New Drug

The brand name tends to be developed relatively late in the product's lifecycle. So before the brand name exists there must be another way of referring to the product during its development. First the product is given a laboratory code. This is usually an alphanumeric identifier comprising initials indicating the developing laboratory and a serial number, for example BRL (Beecham Research Labs) 54321. It is wise to keep to this convention and not to make the code name indicative of the drug under development or too 'user friendly'. Should news of the development be leaked, the company might find that everyone refers to the code number and builds up such familiarity with it that it pre-empts the role of the trade mark. For example, Glaxo Wellcome are still working hard to ensure people refer to Retrovir rather than AZT.

Then there is the generic name for the compound, which indicates its chemical structure and sometimes indicates the broad therapy area. The generic name must be approved by an independent committee or regulatory body in each country – the approved names committee – to ensure that it is not misleading or too similar to other generic names. The appropriate committee in the UK is known as the British Approved Names Committee, or BAN for short, an apt acronym on occasions!

Once the generic name is fixed, a trade mark can then be developed. This too will ultimately have to be approved by regulatory bodies.

■ Creating and Developing New Brand Names

The most common methodology employed by pharmaceutical companies that have international divisions is first to create a trade mark that is acceptable to the domestic marketplace – frequently the UK or the USA – and only then, after registrability is established, will the name be checked for availability and suitability in other countries. The reason for this action is simple. The USA, for example, represents about a third of the world in terms of worldwide pharmaceutical sales, Japan another third, and the rest of the world the final third. Clearly, therefore, the USA and Japan are likely to be the two nations that are most important to any international pharmaceutical corporation.

As has been pointed out, there are several new strategies being employed in the development of international pharmaceutical trade marks, and each company must decide which method is best for its situation. Many corporations have established what are known as trade mark committees. These each have several members, representing various divisions of the corporation as well as various disciplines. It is the duty of the committee to recommend to upper management possible brand names for new drugs that are suitable and have been legally searched and found to be clear and therefore registrable all over the world. Finding a new trade mark is no easy task because there are so many already registered (over 40 000 in the UK alone!).

Since the task of developing a worldwide trade mark is so complex, and involves considerable work, many of these committees have looked to outside agencies to develop an acceptable worldwide trade mark for a specific product. An agency listens to the committee's description of a specific drug, and the corporation's intended marketing position, as well as its ideas for types of prefixes or suffixes that are preferred or disliked. The agency then conducts group panels in key cities around the world to seek the preferences of doctors and consumers. They also use computer programmes to develop shortlists of names for presentation to the client. Many corporations have found this method to be very satisfactory, but the process is still quite complex, particularly when it becomes involved in the area of searching and registering trade marks in countries around the world.

As mentioned, Japan is a very significant market for international sales, and therefore it is mandatory that a worldwide trade mark be accepted in the Japanese market. Owing to the great difference between Japanese, for example, and English it is advisable always to test potential names for pronunciation and use with Japanese physicians.

Another basic problem, particular to US pharmaceutical companies in developing worldwide trade marks, is that most drug products following development and clinical testing are first marketed abroad, before ever being approved in the USA. This makes the process even more complex, since the time constraints are much more severe internationally than they are in the USA. Therefore the brand name will be chosen many years in advance of the drug's approval and introduction into the US market. Agreement between the various corporate divisions (domestic and international) is often difficult to achieve in terms of a worldwide trade mark but, in terms of value to a pharmaceutical corporation, it is essential to move in this direction. Zofran and Kytril are both excellent examples of worldwide trade marks.

■ **Conclusions on Developing Brand Names**

Today, and for as long as generic drugs are sold, the development of trade marks for new pharmaceutical products will be one of the most important tasks facing the pharmaceutical industry. It is by no means a job that should be taken lightly, for it could very easily make or break a product when it enters the marketplace.

■ **The Importance of Strong Brand Identities**

The increased interest in branding has been seen in a focus on developing strong brand names, but equally important for the development of a new brand is the creation of a strong visual identity. In parallel with the rise in focus on developing effective brand names for drugs has been an upsurge of interest and creativity in the development of strong pharmaceutical brand identities through design.

Recent research by Interbrand carried out on an international basis looked at the views of key prescribers (specialists, general practitioners and pharmacists) on packaging design. The research helps to explain why prescribers are increasingly receptive to branding as expressed through design. Although efficacy and price remain critical factors in choice, branding (by means of not only name, but also packaging design and even delivery system) is seen as useful for three reasons:

- It improves compliance.
- It makes products easier to stock and dispense.
- End users are increasingly asking for products by reference to brand clues (name, colour and shape).

Effective compliance is a vital issue for prescribers, particularly among their elderly patients who make up an increasing percentage of those under their care. Good design – in product packaging, in dispensing equipment or in the shape or colour of tablets themselves – can help support compliance. Although many patients cannot remember drug names they can remember shapes and colours. Therefore products that are properly differentiated by colour and shape and are packaged in distinctive, attractive and informative packs, which are seen to be of immense value in improving compliance.

One of the major problems currently facing pharmacists is that too many products look the same. In response to this problem, pharmacists frequently create their own differentiation by putting potentially confusing products in different drawers or creating their own labels. Pharmaceutical companies can help pharmacists by developing better packaging designs and labelling, which is functional as well as attractive. Pharmacists, we know, will specifically choose those products that are recognisable, differentiated, and hence easy to stock and dispense, over those that are not. This creates a powerful opportunity for a strong and distinctive brand identity to create real added value at the point of sale or when being dispensed, and therefore increased sales for the product.

■ Key Issues for Pharmaceutical Brand Identities

The issues discussed earlier in this book concerning the creation of strong brand identities in other fields are almost uniformly equally important for the creation of strong pharmaceutical brand identities. However, the nature of the pharmaceutical industry also means there are a number of additional factors to consider. Pet hates of prescribers include inconvenient pack sizes, unclear expiry dates, unclear dosage strength and over-complex usage directions. Dysfunctional packaging (for example difficult-to-open childproof caps) is also a recurrent issue. The pharmaceutical market is also relatively conservative and unnecessary design innovations are not appreciated. Wastage is a major concern. There is therefore a clear dislike of packaging that is seen as gimmicky, frivolous or wasteful.

On a positive note, effective upfront functionality, for example well-used colour or specially shaped tablets, is highly appreciated, as is branding carried through the whole product (inners and outers).

■ Branding the Delivery System

It is not only through packaging design and tablet shape and colour that branding can work in the pharmaceutical market. Increasingly, as drugs themselves come off patent, manufacturers are seeking ways of prolonging patent life through branded or differentiated delivery systems. Examples include innovative asthma inhalers, distinctive, attractive dispensers for HRT products and contraceptive pills, and insulin pens with improved functionality. If a particular delivery system has a benefit over and above the standard product in that area, it is more likely not only to be prescribed by doctors, but to be requested by nurses who find the product easier to explain and to administer. In many therapy areas, such devices are also likely to be requested by patients – whether repeat patients or those who know someone who uses the product. This is especially true of those therapy areas with which patients feel very involved – for example, chronic complaints or, in the case of contraceptive pills, active choices.

For the pharmaceutical company, branded delivery systems represent a substantial benefit because they can be used to continue to sell off-patent or generic drugs even when substitutes are widely available. Certain target markets would benefit especially from the development of tightly targeted delivery systems or dispensers; for example, children (witness the attractive insulin pens and asthma inhalers available today) and the elderly, for whom it is possible to envisage an entire range of branded, generic products.

■ Conclusions on the Development of Strong Pharmaceutical Identities

From our research and experience in developing pharmaceutical packaging and identities, we would recommend the brand owner to follow these key rules:

- Brand everything (outer, leaflets, blister packs, tablets, ampoules and so on).
- Make the product strength clear.
- Make the best-before date obvious.
- Leave room on ethical packs for the pharmacist's label.
- Make instructions and other on-pack copy easy to read.
- Use pictograms whenever it will help comprehension.
- Think about the particular needs of the end user.

But in the end the most important of the rules for building distinctive brand identities in pharmaceuticals are those that are true across all industries. Opt for distinctive and protectable names; be consistent in branding across all applications; use colour typefaces and symbols to maximise convenience and user friendliness; and differentiate, differentiate, differentiate!'

Note: Zantac, Zofran, Valtrex, Imigran, Retrovir and Serevent are registered trade marks of Glaxo Wellcome.

CHAPTER 18

Brand Revitalisation and Extension

David Andrew

Interbrand

■ Introduction

Every branded goods or services company has one or more brands that are underperforming. Not that long ago such a brand would in due course have been stripped of its marketing support and relegated to cash flow status. Today, however, the prohibitive cost and effort involved in establishing new brands has made brand owners much more conscious of the equity in their existing portfolios, and much less inclined to jettison a brand that isn't living up to expectations – as long as its equity is robust. Indeed, exploiting existing equity for all it is worth, while rationalising the brand spectrum to permit concentration of resources behind key brand properties, has become a major focus of marketing management.

There are many avenues one can take towards revitalising a brand, but it is not our intention here to discuss the individual marketing initiatives that can be undertaken in pursuit of improved brand performance. Instead we concentrate on how brand assets can be viewed, understood, managed and ultimately leveraged by the organisation, and how improving brand *management*, in the broadest sense, is the key to unlocking brand potential.

There are five stages of thinking that any company faced with this challenge needs to undertake, as follows:

- Know thyself.
- Stretch the thinking.
- Recognise the changes.
- Identify and manage core values.
- Leverage the assets.

■ Know Thyself

Interbrand's work in conducting formal evaluations of over 1200 of the world's leading brands has revealed that, despite ostensible success, many are either underperforming or simply not living up to their potential. While such shortfall is usually attributed by their managers to a range of external factors – new sources of competition, new competitive formulations and configurations, shifts in consumer lifestyles and behaviour, economic conditions, and so on – the reality is that the seeds of the erosion of competitiveness often lie *within* the corporation, rather than outside. In fact, it is a combination of internal factors that is most often responsible. Specifically, the following preoccupations are alarmingly prevalent in major branded goods companies:

A preoccupation with:	*Rather than*:
• What *is*.	• What *could* be.
• Research.	• Intuition/imagination.
• Risk-avoidance.	• *Calculated* risk.
• Process.	• Ideas.
• The tried-and-true.	• The opportunity horizon.
• Managing brands as products identified by brand names.	• Managing brands as key assets of the company.

Of course, brand managers should not ignore the left-hand column, but they should not stop there either. The sad truth is that brands are often locked into tightly defined products, positionings and markets as a function of the following:

• Historical experience and past brand practice.
• The conventional wisdom of the company – even in the best-managed organisations.
• Resistance to change.

The longer this mindset endures, the more the *status quo* is entrenched, and the less likely it is that the innovation essential to achieving (or restoring) competitive advantage can take place. Thus the very first step to reviving the brand is an acknowledgement by those responsible that rather than seeking solutions through better management of the 4Ps – product, price, place, promotion – i.e. doing the same sorts of things they've always done, only better – they should be taking a long hard look at the brand management culture that exists in the company and the limitations it may be imposing on strategic innovation.

■ Stretch the Thinking

Typically, marketing management has sought guidance on strategic issues through consumer research. But while research is reasonably good at answering the 'What is?' question, the fact that respondents are not much help with 'What if?' or 'What could be?' limits the ability of conventional research to contribute where strategic *innovation* is required. The reality is that shortfall against potential usually has less to do with problems of how the brand is *perceived* by consumers than with how the brand is *managed* by those responsible for it.

Often the brand team is simply not ambitious enough about its goals for the brand. Instead of searching aggressively for ways to reinvent the brand for greater competitive advantage, they settle for initiatives that do little more than tinker with next year's marketing plan. Revitalising a flagging brand is not easy, and *the* essential prerequisite for success is getting the team to think much bigger than it has been used to doing.

One way to start the process is to put in place a mechanism by which every aspect of the brand can be systematically challenged – particularly the tried-and-true thinking and practices that have served well in the past. Theoretically it should be possible to do this entirely from within. However, the vested interests of those responsible for earlier brand decisions – and the difficulty those who know the brand well have in breaking free of inward-looking preconceptions as to what the brand stands for, what it can do, and where it can go – means that such an approach is unlikely to be productive. Indeed, if there is genuine commitment to unlocking the potential of the brand then there should be no hesitation about introducing a change agent from outside the company, one who owes no allegiance to anyone in the organisation and can act as a catalyst to mobilise the resources of the brand team.

A proven method of shifting the frame of reference from *internal* to *external* standards is to subject the brand to the disciplines of benchmarking – assessing it against the key success factors that determine brand competitiveness and then comparing its performance with those of selected best-practice brands.

The format for doing so can range from a highly structured evaluative process to an informal workshop. But in any configuration brand benchmarking involves the following series of steps:

- Agreement on a range of criteria reflecting the factors that enhance competitiveness in the industry. While these factors should obviously include those reflecting functional performance and the delivery of tangible benefits to the customer, benchmarking is often most productive when assessing brands against their intangible qualities – the degree of *commitment* they enjoy from their customers, the brand's *relevance* to a wider as opposed to a narrower consumer base, the extent to which the perceived *values* of the brand are consistent with those of the target market.
- A scoring of the brand that is the subject of the exercise against these criteria – by each member of the team. This can most easily be done by plotting the brand's position on each of a series of matrices made up of two sets of polarised attributes – for example, low commitment/high commitment and low relevance/high relevance.
- A comparison of the individual scores and the resolution of any differences of opinion through discussion until a consensus is achieved.

- The selection of best-practice brands from within the category if they exist, but also from other categories and even other industries if such brands obviously excel in terms of the competitiveness criteria.
- A scoring of each of these brands in the same way as was done for the subject brand.
- An analysis in detail of how and why the scores of the subject brand and the selected best-practice brands differ.
- Identification of the key areas of shortfall and opportunity.
- Based on these findings, a design of the optimum best-practice brand – the ultimate the subject brand could aspire to if it were truly to lead and dominate the category or industry.
- Benchmarking this hypothetical optimum against the same competitiveness criteria to set the best-practice goal.

Such a process serves not only to open up the thinking of the brand team but to raise its sights as to what is achievable. An integrated sequence of initiatives can then be put in place to take the brand from where it is today to where a newly defined goal demonstrates that it could be in the future.

In conducting a benchmarking exercise for purposes of brand revitalisation there are three key things to remember:

- Experience demonstrates that for best results the benchmarking team should be drawn from a range of disciplines, that is not just from brand management but from research, new product development, the advertising agency, and so on. The crucial criterion for selection is that participants must see themselves as agents of change, not wedded to (or defensive of) the past, but dedicated to making a real difference to the future of the brand.
- Since the whole thrust of benchmarking is to stretch the thinking of the brand team, it is essential that it be clear at the outset that the intent of the exercise is to push that thinking beyond its traditional limits, to aim not just to *match* category competitors but to *surpass* them.
- Experience also demonstrates that selecting benchmarking standards from other industries pays far richer dividends in terms of new perspectives on brand potential than does choosing the brand's immediate competitors.

■ Recognise the Changes

Part of the problem in breaking through strategic inertia is that today many of those with brand responsibilities still manage brands – though most would deny it! – as if nothing much had changed for the past five years, when in fact change, particularly in fast-moving consumer goods, has been dramatic:

- Product parity in many categories has eliminated functional attributes – even quality – as differentiators.
- Endemic price competition has marginalised the brand's equity and its role in driving customer choice.
- Promotional tactics designed simply to take share from competitors have diminished the brand's capacity and motivation to grow the category.
- Trade dominance has undermined the brand's ability to achieve a bond with the customer.

Many brands that once stood for a differentiated product attribute now find that their functional delivery no longer gives them any sort of competitive advantage. Faced with parity performance and price the customer, as soon as the *'what* I'm going to buy' decision has been made, will look beyond product performance to brand values as the basis on which to decide *'who* I buy from'. And increasingly we are seeing that in such a parity situation buyers will lean towards the brand whose values – or those of the company that stands behind it – are most consistent with their own.

Thus the game has changed. Irrespective of whether one is dealing with a product, service, or corporate brand, the management of brand assets – what the brand stands for, what values it owns, what sort of relationship it builds with the customer – has become the key to differentiation and enhanced competitiveness. Without serious consideration of these issues the brand will almost certainly find itself commoditised and degraded – a follower rather than a leader.

◼ Identify and Manage Core Values

There is no way a brand can be revitalised without a clear understanding of the soul of the brand, the brand's DNA, and the values it represents. This topic really merits a chapter of its own, but it will suffice here to outline a framework for establishing a vision and mission for the brand as a theme and focus for defining its intended area of competence and the values that will build a bond with the customer. Many superficially robust brands in fact offer little more than passive reassurance. What values they once enjoyed in the consumer's mind either have eroded with time or are no longer relevant.

Genuine revitalisation of a brand thus requires the creation of a *new* 'reality' that its customers can identify with and share. For in the final analysis a brand does one of three things:

- It fits into its existing marketing environment.
- It reorganises the perceptions consumers have of the category.
- It invents a new category.

Note that for the failing brand the first of these is no longer an acceptable option.

In order to establish a sound framework for brand development and communication, we need first of all to establish the brand platform. This is the centre of the brand and could be likened to the DNA or soul of a human being. Once we know the brand platform we can develop the physical manifestation of the brand; its name and visual identity, analogous to the skin, bones and hair of the human. The brand platform informs the physical manifestation of the brand and goes on to inform all brand communications. Just as human beings dress up in order to position themselves to different target audiences (we might put on different clothes to play tennis, to meet the vicar and to go to a rave) so brands, once they know who they are, can begin to communicate to different target audiences, via different advertising and promotional strategies and tactics.

Once you have a clearly defined sense of what your brand believes and what it is, you are much more ready to meet the challenges of the future and to work out for yourself where your brand wishes or needs to go. If you have no clear idea of what your brand's platform is, you will look at the marketplace around it and follow what others do – which is no strategy for leadership and success.

The first step in creating a differentiated and appropriate brand platform is to create a brand vision that articulates the brand's view on the world and on the context in which it finds itself – a way of looking at the product category, or the consumer experience, or the world at large – that strikes a chord with its target market *and is capable of genuinely differentiating the brand from its competitors.* To do so the vision must be challenging, with an element of dislocation relative to the conventional wisdom of current category thinking.

For example, Apple's original brand vision was what we might call 'voluntary' or 'defining' – instead of following the marketplace it stuck a stake in the ground and asked the marketplace to follow it:

Man is the true creator of change in this world. As such he should be above systems and structures, and not subordinate to them.

What the brand is going to *do* in the marketplace to fulfil the vision we call its mission. The mission describes the brand's direction and thrust – how it will act, what will guide its work, where it will focus its efforts. Because of this, whereas the vision is often negative or questioning, the mission is always action-oriented and positive. In the Apple example, the mission was as follows:

Apple is dedicated to the empowerment of man – to making personal computing accessible to each and every individual so as to help change the way we think, work, learn, and communicate.

The vision and mission provide the directional energy which will shape what we refer to at Interbrand as the brand platform – the structure of functional attributes and brand values that underpin the vision and mission and acts as the blueprint on which all marketing and communications strategy will be based.

Effectively, a brand is nothing but a network of associations in the consumer's mind. If an association – whether rational or emotional – represents something that is personally and/or socially preferable to the consumer we call it a value. Such values are the key drivers of consumer choice (see Figure 18.1).

CENTRAL VALUES	What kind of life do I want to lead?
EXPRESSIVE VALUES	What kind of person do I want to be?
FUNCTIONAL VALUES (benefits)	What kind of products/services do I want to have?

Central values: e.g. Successful, fulfilling, meaningful, stable, powerful

Expressive values: e.g. Active, contemporary, important, in control, socially responsible

Functional values: e.g. Natural, convenient, technologically advanced, safe, effective, quick, money-saving

Figure 18.1   Consumer values hierarchy

Source: © Interbrand plc (1997).

The corresponding brand values are shown in Figure 18.2.

CENTRAL VALUES	What the brand and the consumer *share* at a fundamental level
EXPRESSIVE VALUES	What the brand *says* about the consumer
FUNCTIONAL VALUES	What the brand *does* for the consumer

Central values: Reflect what the purchaser and the brand share in fundamental terms – philosophically, morally, behaviourally. Examples of brands with well-developed central values would be *The Body Shop, Benetton, Virgin, Nike*.

Expressive values: Reflect the nature of the purchaser – hence type, sex, characteristics, personality, status, etc. Examples of brands with strong expressive values would be *Marlboro, Porsche, Apple, Armani*, and the like.

Functional values: Reflect what kind of product or service the brand offers and/or what functional benefits it provides to the customer – hence composition, use, effect, appearance, cost, etc.

Figure 18.2   Brand values hierarchy

Source: © Interbrand plc (1997).

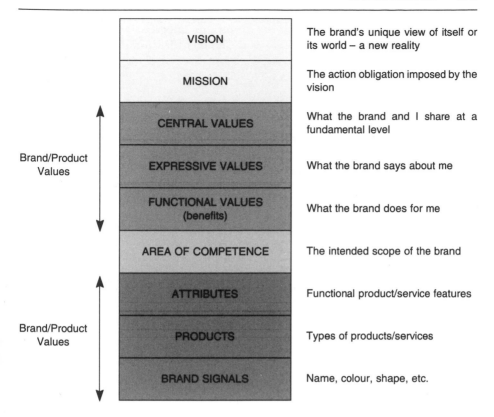

VISION	The brand's unique view of itself or its world – a new reality
MISSION	The action obligation imposed by the vision
CENTRAL VALUES	What the brand and I share at a fundamental level
EXPRESSIVE VALUES	What the brand says about me
FUNCTIONAL VALUES (benefits)	What the brand does for me
AREA OF COMPETENCE	The intended scope of the brand
ATTRIBUTES	Functional product/service features
PRODUCTS	Types of products/services
BRAND SIGNALS	Name, colour, shape, etc.

Brand/Product Values

Brand/Product Values

Figure 18.3   Brand platform structure

Source: © Interbrand plc (1997).

Ultimately, we predispose the consumer to our brand by linking *brand* values with *consumer* values – the hierarchy of values unique to each individual that guides every aspect of behaviour (see Figure 18.3).

While consumer associations can have their source at any level of the brand structure illustrated above, the further up the value hierarchy they are perceived the greater influence they have on creating preference.

When making a purchase decision the consumer looks for a particular combination of product attributes that provide him or her with a specific set of functional values. However, consumers will *prefer* a product–brand combination that expresses their ideal self-image – through its expressive and central values.

Finally it is necessary to extrapolate the implications of the brand vision into a definition of the intended *scope* of the brand – its chosen area of competence, outside which the mission is no longer valid or credible. If the mission is genuinely bold, that is has not fallen into the trap of defining the role of the brand too narrowly (as it might if relying too heavily on current product attributes), it will be apparent that the brand can embrace as broad a spectrum of products or services as is responsive to the identified brand values.

■ Leverage the Assets

Core values, once established, become core *assets* of the brand – assets that can not only serve as a basis on which to build greater competitiveness for the brand in its existing form, but that can also renew and revitalise the brand through a range of leveraging strategies –

- Line extension.
- Brand extension.
- Image transfer.

Line extension generally involves extending the scope of the brand within its product category, embracing products with functional, expressive and central values that reflect those of the original product brand. This course of action, if persisted with, eventually sees the transformation of the product brand into a range brand, spanning a number of different products – all of which share the core values.

Examples of line extension successes include:

- Marlboro ⟶ Marlboro Lights ⟶ Marlboro Medium
- Crest ⟶ Crest Gel ⟶ Crest Tartar Control

Of course, there are also many examples of Line Extension failures:

- Budweiser Dry – incongruent functional values.
- Crystal Pepsi – outside perceived area of competence.
- Cadillac Allante – shortfall against expressive values of original.

It is possible to provide some fundamental line extension guidelines:

- A line extension must be consistent with the core values of the original or 'parent' brand.
- In fact, no line extension should even be contemplated that does not both honour the core values of the brand *and* reinforce them.
- The source of line extension business and its impact on the parent brand should be carefully considered before embarking on the process. Will it take share from competitors or simply cannibalise the parent? Will it revitalise the brand by bringing in new customers, or simply enhance the brand's stature as perceived by its existing customers?

Brand extension, on the other hand, involves extending the product or range brand into an umbrella brand – sometimes referred to as a overbrand or banner brand. Here the process consists of taking the functional values of the brand and identifying other products – in *any* category – where the consumer seeks the same values. Hence, brand extension comes in many varieties:

- Same products, different form – for example Ocean Spray Cranberries →︎ Ocean Spray Cranberry Juice Cocktail.
- Distinctive feature or ingredient injected into product in different category – for example Mars Bar →︎ Mars Ice Cream.
- Natural companions in usage – for example Colgate toothpaste →︎ Colgate Plus toothbrush.
- Same customer franchise – for example Visa card →︎ Visa traveller's cheques.
- Perception of special expertise – for example BiC disposable pens →︎ BiC disposable lighters, razors.
- 'Owned' benefit – for example Palmolive mildness →︎ dishwashing liquid, bath products, shampoo.

Brand extension failures also exist:

- Levi's Tailored Classics – dissonant expressive/central values
- BiC Perfume – outside perceived area of competence.

Again, it is possible to give some basic brand extension guidelines:

- The key to determining the *direction* that brand extension should take is to identify product categories where the functional values of the parent brand are just as important to the consumer as they are in the original category.
- Consumer research is then required to determine the extent to which consumers will find the existing brand's participation in the target categories plausible and persuasive.
- Brand extension should be undertaken only when the parent brand is healthy, stable, and (ideally) growing – not when it is already on the decline.
- Once again, brand extension should be contemplated only if it will reinforce the existing vision, mission, and values. The extension initiative should in no way change the positioning of the parent brand. If the extension initiative will in any way change the positioning of the parent brand, then some form of new brand or sub-brand will need to be developed within the context of the overall brand architecture.

■ Image Transfer

In this case the brand is defined less by its functional values than by its expressive and central values, and thus is capable of transcending category boundaries and spanning a variety of product types. The best illustration is probably Virgin, with Virgin Records, Virgin Megastore, Virgin Airlines, Virgin Cola, Virgin Vodka and Virgin Financial Services, where the core values that are the common denominator effectively reflect those of Richard Branson himself – unconventional, entertaining, adventurous, entrepreneurial. But there are many other examples of successful image transfer:

- Marlboro cigarettes ⟶ Marlboro Country Travel, Marlboro western gear.
- Dunhill cigarettes ⟶ lighters and accessories, men's fashion, men's toiletries.
- Calvin Klein designer clothing ⟶ underwear, jeans, eyewear, fragrance.

And some image transfer failures:

- Harley Davidson motorcycles ⟶ wine coolers, men's cologne.
- Cadbury chocolate ⟶ soup, beverages, milk powder.

Again, we have provided some basic image transfer guidelines:

- The credibility of the brand in its new role is the single most important predictor of image transfer success.
- The greater the technical difference between the new product and the original the more difficult it is to effect the transfer, for example: Lacoste shirts ⟶ Lacoste tennis rackets.
- However, the Virgin example demonstrates that well-established expressive and central values can successfully carry the brand across major category barriers.
- Thus the other key success factor is the ability to position the new entry against a target market characterised by its responsiveness to the same core values as motivated the brand's consumers in its original format.

Figure 18.4 summarises the different approaches to leveraging the values of the brand.

■ Conclusion

Throughout this book, the theme of brands as creators of wealth has we hope been reinforced by the experts who have written so compellingly on their subjects. The majority of brand owners now openly acknowledge that their brands are assets in the true sense of the word and that without their brands their businesses would be immensely poorer. Indeed without brands, the 'magnets' of consumer loyalty, there would be little value in, or rationale for, any of the other assets in a business.

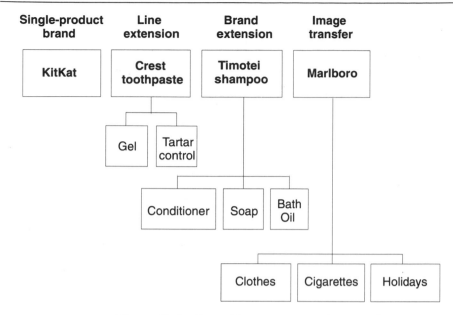

Figure 18.4   Brand leverage strategies

Also, like all assets, brands need to be maintained to preserve and grow their usefulness to the business that owns them. Advertising and promotion is essential, of course; this helps to ensure that the brand is constantly in the public eye and that its image remains fresh, authentic and relevant. As we have shown in this chapter, however, there are additional means by which the brand's attractiveness can be maintained and its potential enhanced: extension and image transfer.

Ultimately, however, opportunities to revitalise the brand through extension or image transfer are severely limited if the brand continues to be defined principally in terms of its current product attributes. The more this is so, the more difficult any kind of persuasive extension becomes. Conversely, shifting the emphasis of brand communications from what the brand physically *does* to what the brand *stands for* and *means to* the customer is the best possible preparation for eventual initiatives to broaden its scope and strengthen its influence in the marketplace.

CHAPTER 19

Managing the Brand

Andrew Seth

The Added Value Company

■ The Principles of Managing Brands

The principles of managing the brand have not changed during the thirty years I have been involved in the process. Given the level of marketplace change that has occurred, this might seem surprising. What has changed, however, is the capacity of some of our best companies to understand and implement those principles. A range of insistent pressures has made it difficult for some of the outstanding marketing performers of western business to maintain and develop their value systems, their mission statements and their strategies. Inevitably, this has been reflected in uncertainty of purpose in the management of brands and in these same companies' stated views of their own achievement of best marketing practice.

A recent study by the Marketing Council in October 1995 rated the marketing performance of the leading twenty marketing companies in the UK. It found that Mars, Kellogg's and Unilever had dropped more than ten places in the ranking; Procter & Gamble and Guinness by more than five places; while Cadbury, Nestlé, Ford, American Express and Shell had dropped off the top twenty list altogether. Virgin, Direct Line and Tesco now occupy the top five places along with Microsoft and British Airways. We can debate at length what these changes mean. What is certain is that it reflects apparent uncertainty among some of the great exponents of successful brand management as to how to manage the brand challenges of tomorrow. If the principles haven't changed, why the uncertainty? How have the sure-footed proponents of strategic advantage, with their sedulous, established methods of brand development and maintenance, so comprehensively lost their way?

The past, of course, was a whole lot simpler. When Procter & Gamble developed the brand management approach in Cincinnati and exported it round the world in the postwar years, the task of brand management seemed intelligible and coherent. Company value systems took time to establish themselves, but, once in place, changed rarely, and then by a process of gradual, almost imperceptible evolution. It was entirely possible to recognise these same value systems and cultures wherever you encountered these companies around the world. Strong, purposeful communication from headquarters, whether US- or European-based, ensured a high degree of uniformity. Stable management career patterns, often lasting a lifetime for individual participants, minimised the need for or likelihood of radical change.

■ The Brand Management System

Into this calm and structured world was born the brand management system. The identification of the brand manager as champion of the consumer brand in highly functional and well-controlled national enterprises has a been a strong feature of the best-run marketing companies during the second half of the twentieth century. The approach has travelled easily around the world, from New York to London and on to Tokyo.

The brand manager's calling card was invariably marketing expertise, found in one primary responsibility, namely the understanding of the consumer needs and aspirations in his brand's market. He – it usually was a 'he' in those days – had a remit to look at everything and go anywhere in the company, in the search for new and better ways to transmit better value to the consumer. His range was wide and ever widening. it encompassed the brand role or purpose; fully embraced brand performance in delivering that purpose; and axiomatically covered the image and personality of the brand, based on its approach to brand communication. His scope moved ceaselessly from core strategy, the fundamentals of long-term consumer success, to operational elements and implementation of strategy in all its aspects – price, distribution, trade features, for example. Necessarily, his definition of the competitive framework and of brand advantage was a crucial part of the company's everyday approach.

One or two other observations on the way the brand manager's job worked in the best-run companies seem necessary. He based recommendations and proposals for action, often made directly to the company's board of directors (the highest visible level of hierarchy) on appreciation and analysis of the consumer and on a series of tried and trusted research techniques. His brand's (product) development was close by, easily accessed, and under his company's control. Customer or retail considerations, while important, were well able to be managed by specialist sales teams who created strong business relationships with key customers. Finally, the brand manager himself was in regular touch with and close proximity to the most senior general management, the key decision-makers in his company. He made the recommendations; they took the decisions. They might not always agree with him or give him what he wanted, but if he was up to his job, and usually companies picked the best available people to fill the key brand jobs, he knew, in detail and in short order, exactly where they, and therefore his brand, stood on every important issue.

■ The Changing Global and National Environment

This brand management world, born in the fifties, is no longer recognisable in today's businesses. Some of them have eliminated the job entirely, finding themselves incapable of making it work in today's complex and fast-moving competitive world. The changes have indeed been immense. The search for competitive advantage, a requirement previously recognised only in the best-run companies, is now pursued, relentlessly, everywhere in the world, by companies of every shape and hue, manufacturing as well as service, and by small and medium enterprises as much as the very biggest battalions. National organisations have been replaced by transnational companies working in an increasingly transparent global village, with important strategic consequences. Time has become a key element where the new winners leverage innovative competitive formulas at speed. The primacy of being first is unquestioned; one study showed that while being six months late to market caused profits to fall by a third, having development costs 50 per cent above budget showed infinitesimal loss in profit potential.

The brand is increasingly having to operate in a hostile and precarious environment, well described by Will Hutton (1996) in 'The State We're In'. Declining western industries, weak and underinvested R&D, poor growth levels and national competitiveness, and short-term financial priorities dominate business decision-making. What chance is there for the brand champion, for brand strategic primacy, with this as a backcloth? Much too often companies have been prone to sacrifice strategic advantage to deliver short-term results and satisfy demanding stock market ratios.

'Tomorrow's Company', the RSA report, points out that a high percentage of Britain's most profitable companies nominated by *Management Today* through the eighties have now collapsed or been acquired. Cost reduction, while a crucial component of long-term company competitiveness, has been elevated to a degree of prominence that is unhealthy and underserved. *The Independent* in December 1995, under a heading 'Off with their Overheads', talks of the 'cut-cut-cut' mentality embedded in corporate cultures and asks what happens when costs can be hacked no further. Brand consistency and a secure platform of marketing expertise and commitment backed by appropriate consumer research has been relegated to second place. Moreover, the manufacturer–distributor pendulum has swung violently in favour of the retailer in many western markets, notably the UK, Scandinavia and most of northern Europe. This has diminished the resolve of yesterday's long-term brand custodians, who have compounded their brand problems by inserting their heads firmly in the retail noose and making 'own brands' for retail sale. Alongside, it has encouraged new retail brands to build their own franchises – Marks & Spencer, Body Shop, Virgin retail and Migros in Switzerland are good examples.

■ Brand Responsibility: Who Owns the Brand?

Finally and most importantly, however, the cultural environment in which the brand is now 'owned' and managed is hugely different. Sometimes one is tempted to ask, 'Who is the brand owner?' It is not always obvious that there is one around. Speed and global frameworks have effectively destroyed the simple structures and processes in which yesterday's strong brand properties were built. Simple hierarchies have been replaced by a matrix, itself often global, that removes the national brand management teams from key decision-makers. Organisational delayering has not always improved communication. While there is plethora of brand information available, it is often the key operational matters which the re-engineered company treats as its key priority. Preoccupation with immediate results and the removal of established career development patterns have exacerbated the problem. The brand has often become the first casualty. Collapse of the brand usually means goodbye to the business. It will be crystal clear, therefore, that management of the brand is a matter of long-term and company-wide significance, that it demands a unique and clear leadership view and that the issues are cultural. The brand is necessarily right at the core of the company's business and reputation, inextricably tied to long-term business success or failure. It will further be recognised that in today's fast-moving complex business world, where decisions need to be taken with speed, good judgement and often at many physical removes from the company HQ or centre, the key issues for the successful marketing company will be to 'own' an intelligible process, a level of teamwork and strategic commitment that empowers its management to make the right consumer judgements and take the right brand decisions. Business itself recognises this as a matter of principle. That the brand is at the centre is in no doubt – the brand sets the framework within which the entire activities of the company, its governance and its strategies will operate. Success depends on integrity of purpose at every level of association between the brand and its potential consumers. As Chris MacCrae (1995) points out in *World Class Brands*, as 'a channel of communications, the world class brand is a democratic one whose audiences are free to vote against it at any time'. Companies as significant and well established as Coca-Cola, Ford, Lever, Johnson and Perrier are living testimony to this reality.

The company vision, therefore, requires a clear and enduring statement; internally as well as externally, those concerned need to know the character of the enterprise that owns and manages the brand. Statements of mission and character abound: but it is by company behaviour, and over the long as well as the short-term, that one can genuinely assess their seriousness. Let us look at two examples of organisations that have 'voted with their boots' over many years.

Cadbury Schweppes is a British-based but increasingly internationally focused food and drink business. Its competitive edge

> derives directly from the excellence of our products, the relevance and vitality of our brands and the expertise, commitment and resourcefulness of our employees. Cadbury's commitment to its brands is palpable at all levels of its management team. Meeting them makes you realise they care deeply for their key brands. The company's main commercial assets are its brands and it is

our responsibility to develop the markets for them. They are a guarantee of quality and value to consumers and we must invest consistently in building their reputation.

The past chairman, Adrian Cadbury, wrote this in 1989 (*The Character of the Company*) and the present leadership was content to reissue it six years later, unaltered. Company style and values are a crucial discriminator in successful management of brands. Substance, the core fundamental proposition by which a company conducts its business, is equally important. Unilever's top one hundred worldwide managers reviewed the management of their brand equities recently at a management conference at Eastbourne. The key competence was agreed to be 'improved understanding of the consumer' and successful implementation to be dependent principally on 'breaching new innovation boundaries leading to greater satisfaction through the early identification of discontinuities followed by their acceleration and amplification'. It should be noted that the process of innovation is an active, radical and self-examining process, testing the boundaries of knowledge, sensitivity and experience: and that the result needs to be one where real and measurable progress for the brand can be made through adopting the innovation in question. This, in turn, will test the purpose and cohesion of the entire organisation.

This brings us to the matter of ownership of the brand, since it is ultimately this which matters. Written two centuries ago, Adam Smith's words from *The Wealth of Nations* still apply with force: 'The directors being managers of other people's money than their own, it cannot be . . . expected they should watch over it with the same anxious vigilance which the partners . . . watch over their own.' Brand ownership is a delicate matter. In some companies, where controls are primarily financial, brand responsibility is delegated to comparatively mundane levels; of course the 'delegation' is largely fictional, because the room for manoeuvre and the chance to progress strategically are themselves entirely circumscribed. In other businesses, with justification that 'only senior people know these brands in sufficient depth', all decision-making, including the most modest copy and operational changes, are taken to the highest levels in the hierarchy. The result is demoralisation of the imaginative younger people in the marketing teams and ultimately a total ossification of the process. Best practice will ensure that the vision is well communicated: 'Who we are, what we do and where we are going' is the Cadbury description. Honda describes the overarching vision as 'the Honda ideal' and its top management as 'romantics locked in its quest'. Second, best practice will require that knowledge and information regarding brand performance and particularly long-term brand health and security pass quickly everywhere. Motorola and many Japanese businesses have this down to a fine art. The simple truth is that 'It's what matters that gets measured', and vice versa; a company where the financial ratios are the key reporting element in board reviews will end up, to all intents and purposes, run by its bean counters.

■ Best Practice in Brand Management

Best practice needs to preserve a sensitive balance. Strategies to deliver the long-term brand vision are necessarily the property of the long-term business, and their guidance and protection the milieu in which experienced leaders should speak and be listened to. But it is, simultaneously, crucial that a strong cadre of committed and imaginative young managers is vested with the capability to innovate, develop and manage the brands forward, and it is equally crucial that their ideas are canvassed, tested and given room to breathe and succeed in a culture that rewards the differentiator and the radical. Brands are living evolving organisms; their consumers change from purchase to purchase and from year to year. The rewards of experimentation, of exploring brand potential and of pursuing the brand into new forms of relationship are very great, and vibrant business cultures will ensure that this kind of voyage can be accomplished and encouraged.

This brings us to brand focus and the need for brand selection and choice – very much a senior management task. A key role of senior management in a successful company is to determine the core brand range behind which resources will be marshalled and focused. It will need to recognise in a modern, fragmenting set of markets the significance of the corporate or banner brand. Nestlé's chairman summarised the logic as follows: 'The Nestlé name is now being introduced across all our brands, Maggi, Findus – everywhere. All have the Nestlé bird's nest . . . the advantage of a worldwide company comes from a common identity like Volvo or Coca-Cola.' It is a lesson that has not been lost on the emerging eastern companies as they have expanded rapidly. The corporate brands Hitachi, Sony, Hyundai, Toshiba and Samsung are widely displayed and well recognised the world over. Business will need to direct itself to manage a focused set of product brands or increasingly a single monolithic but carefully nurtured corporate brand that is the company. The choices are demanding and can, in the short term, be painful; short-term volume and result will often be sacrificed to generate defensible, strategic long-term positions capable of generating distinct advantage and long-term revenue.

Hamel and Pralahad (1995) confirm the need for choice, noting why some brands engender greater predisposition to buy than others. The four characteristics they describe as crucial to ultimate success are recognition (i.e. awareness), reputation (confidence that the brand will deliver against its claim), affinity (their word for the strength of the brand's emotional aspirations) and domain (the breadth of the brand's potential catchment market). Almost without exception, they have found the management of brand potential or stretching equally problematic, and have learnt the hard way, by attempting too great a degree of stretch for core brand properties. The best advice one can give a company is to get ahead of the market in brand selection, determining brand stretch and, where possible, establishing the worldwide banner brand properties. The risks of failure are considerable, but the option of inertia and complacency, of allowing too fragmented and too local a brand range to persist too long, represents an immeasurably greater long-term risk to a company.

■ The Search for Competitive Advantage

Alongside the need for choice, top management has an equally clear core responsibility to define accurately and consistently the competitive advantages behind which the company will evolve, extend and defend its brand range. In *Ten Golden Rules* Hardy (1995) emphasises the importance of 'sticking to your knitting' and underlines the core competitive advantage that he believes – and which the worldwide marketplace confirms – Procter & Gamble possesses:

> In all of these successes the Procter & Gamble manufacturing and marketing skills were exploiting the work of the research and development laboratory. In each case the laboratory had provided a product 'extra' which facilitated the development of significant competitive advantage.

Procter & Gamble may be described in the determination of core competitive advantages as an 'easy read'. So, significantly, are many of the strongest eastern competitors – Honda, Sony or Kao. But the search for genuine and enduring advantage to back the brands in western business has not yet been taken to the levels of stringency required. Hamel and Pralahad (1995) again –

> It is not enough for a company to get smaller, better or faster . . . a company must be capable of fundamentally reconceiving itself, or regenerating its core strategies and of re-inventing its industry. In short, a company must be capable of *getting different'* (my emphasis).

How many companies deliver against this criterion? The authors suggest, among the upstarts, CNN, Microsoft and Body Shop; might they have added Virgin? Among the well-established businesses they believe British Airways and Hewlett-Packard certainly pass the test.

The process of determining core differentiated competitive advantage is demanding and it is endless. It requires painful and objective appraisal of the likelihood of generating market leadership with your brand portfolio, not today or tomorrow, but many years ahead. It will need realistic, company-wide determination to deliver. It is a tougher picture of the Honda self-appointed 'top management charge' we described earlier; romantics in quest of the ideal they may be, but the process in which they are engaged is analytical, deep-rooted and will require special kinds of persistent, driving and objective leadership.

■ The Role of Top Management

Finally, in the core brand marketing tasks of top management lies the fundamental responsibility of generating and maintaining a culture, a business ambience, where improved understanding of the consumer is the driving force behind the entire team entrusted with the management of the brand. This is the key competence, which permits the protection and enhancement of brand equity. It is a live and evolving task, particularly because techniques to generate relevant consumer knowledge are themselves improving at an exponential rate, and the level and nature of information available is markedly greater than that which previous generations of management were able to command. It remains the key area of difference between the business which is managing its brands well and the business that isn't. It is a difference between brand strategy and operations; between thought followed by action and mere action. It is the sign of the well-run business that knows and cares about its brands and recognises they are the route to survival in tomorrow's market. Few western companies discharge it well enough, however; few view the task as one of potentially, or actually, 'reinventing themselves', which we saw to be the likely measure of best practice. Few charge their marketing teams, their brand managers or those entrusted with brand development and innovation with this level of challenge or responsibility. But this is the standard that tomorrow's successful brands will require.

It is easy to recognise the culture when you see and experience it working. Lever UK through the seventies and early eighties embodied this. Roles and responsibilities were exceptionally clear from young team members with a driving and entrepreneurial zeal, through wise, experienced operating managers who held the teams and the brands together, to a board of directors who refined the strategy and constantly re-examined among themselves whether there was a better way to compete. Constructive tension in this enterprise positively crackled. Ideas were continuously moving around the business; the only issue was which of them to pursue for most advantage, and about that there was constant, purposeful debate, review and decision. The same was true in the US Lever business I went to work in through the early eighties; because we knew we had the competitor's attention and, occasionally, deep anxiety, we were a strong, integrated team. Brand volume more than doubled in five years; shares were uniformly positive. Innovations that gained consumer attention were the brand manager's daily routine activity, even if many of them were the creation of smoke and mirrors – we did not have a strong R&D presence in the US at this time.

■ Culture and Vision – Crucial Determinants

Once again the east has taken this culture to its most highly developed philosophical level of embodiment in the business. Nonaka and Tageuchi (1995) describe it well in *The Knowledge Creating Company*. The belief in tacit, experiential knowledge and its transmission and integration through an entire culture is well expressed, for example in the case study describing Honda's approach to delivering key automotive innovation with the Honda City. Management says openly to everyone, 'Let's gamble', but with a tight and demanding brief for change; teams of experienced cross functional young managers drive the options forward; and the key bridge-building element is possessed by Honda's senior operational leadership. This is the way in which innovation with a fully integrated brand management team needs to be managed. It expresses one ultimate truth about the management of the brand: it's not only one person, one team, one function or even one board's task to manage the brand: it is the task for the business as a whole. To paraphrase the old song, 'The brand belongs to everyone'; or, as Drucker put it, marketing the brand in the best-run enterprise is everyone's job; it is far too important to be left to a single director or a single function.

A final point then on the nature of the leadership task involved in brand management. The brand, as Stephen King said many years ago now, is itself 'a complex set of satisfactions delivered' and, as his then London JWT boss, Jeremy Bullmore said simultaneously,

> If we are to be the custodians of a brand, we have to be scrupulously attentive to every minute item, hint, clue or cue from which our ultimate users will form their own images. Only through conscious control of every brand stimulus can we hope to achieve the desired brand response. Branding is a skill that requires the utmost subtlety and sensitivity.'

How strange that as today's information-driven society makes it possible to exercise even greater degrees of sensitivity in the strategic management of brands, the gauntlet is so rarely taken up by modern marketing business, which prefers to concentrate on operational matters, measurable short-term financial ratios and downsizing its marketing establishment.

In truth, we are far far away from the ideal in the structures and processes that we entrust to manage today's brands and markets. Consumers themselves are living in a world where ever accelerating levels of change are taking place. Change is endemic. The need internally could not be more obvious: it is to respond in kind and, through sensitive response, to create the longest term levels of competitive advantage, for our country, for our companies, for our brands, and indeed for ourselves. It can only happen (*vide* Drucker), of course, at the level of the whole organisation. Partial response will produce partial levels of gain. The requirement is for the 'learning company' to be, each and every-day of its life, an organisation that takes as its biggest priority the continuous learning of all its members, and as a result continuously transforms itself. We can be sure that there is a very great prize to be won, and it is, at its simplest, the provision of an enduring but ever developing level of consumer satisfaction, or delight, to use the TQ word: from which, if we do it first and right, our businesses can make the maximum levels of brand gain. Isn't this exactly where we started and isn't it among every marketer's personal goals?

■ The Brand – A Continuing Source of Advantage

Today's marketing people, today's brand management, are living in a very different world from that inhabited by the first brand managers. Since theirs was a new world, where marketing had aspirations to be the new science and 'the consumer as king' was at least a wholly new expression of philosophy, open-mindedness and learning were nothing less than axioms. Forty years on, our structure and processes exhibit a tightly defined, closed appearance; measures abound, but few of them are radical, open-ended even strategic. Marketing people, themselves uncertain about their careers or future and doubtful about the values and aspirations of their companies, concentrate on credibility, the here and now, on making it happen, on good current practice and defensible operating methods; mainstream consultants offer superficially attractive re-engineering panaceas to deliver slightly closer-to-inch-perfect levels of effectiveness. Viewed from the outside the organisation strikes the observer as a smooth, well-oiled machine, but one better suited to eliminating the possibilities of change, experiment or movement, than of facilitating the introduction of change.

Today's and tomorrow's brand managers, be they 25 or 60, junior managers, board members or chief executives, specialists or generalists, strategic or operational in outlook, all need to embrace action learning for themselves and their brands and then to make it happen. The systematic feedback of action to learning and back to action again is an approach, a habit and mindset. What has stopped marketing people doing it is what my erstwhile Lever and Unilever training colleague Ed Green calls 'The soft issues . . . of attitude, behaviour, values and culture. We rarely discuss them, hence the need to break the soft barrier.' It is never too late to start, and it's certainly not too late for a new generation of managers of brands to show that they can lead and that, above all, they really do care about tomorrow's brands.

■ References

MacCrae, Chris (1995) *World Class Brands* (New York: Addison-Wesley).
Cadbury, Sir Adrian (1989) *The Character of the Company*.
Mazur and Hogg, (1993) *The Marketing Challenge* (New York: Addison).
Hamel and Pralahad (1995) *Competing for the Future* (Cambridge, MA: Harvard University Press).
Hardy, L. (1995) *The Ten Golden Rules* (Windrush Press).
Nonaka and Tageuchi (1995) *The Knowledge Creating Company* (Oxford: Oxford University Press).
Hutton, Will (1996) *The State We're In* (London: Barry & Jenkins).

CHAPTER 20

The Future for Brands

Susannah Hart
Interbrand

Over the last two or three decades, the concept of brands and branding has developed almost out of all recognition. In the fifties and sixties, if you had asked a typical consumer to give some examples of brands, they would probably have responded with the names of household products: Ivory Soap, Fairy Liquid, Kellogg's Cornflakes. Now, they are just as likely to reply with the names of companies, like Nike or Body Shop. In another ten years' time, what will people be saying? Will they be giving the names of rock groups, actors or sports stars as brand names? We still speak of 'the branded goods arena'. Will that become anachronistic as all goods come to be considered as possible brands?

Reading through this book, it is possible to identify a number of trends and developments in branding, both as it is practised and as the authors believe it should be practised. As we have seen, it is already well acknowledged, in the boardroom and in the City, that brands are financial assets, every bit as much as plant, machinery and stock. Indeed, brands are arguably the most valuable assets of all in that, in theory, they do not have a finite life and therefore will not depreciate. The aim of this chapter is to highlight some of the more interesting topics covered by this book and to comment on how brands are likely to develop in the future.

■ The Changing Brandscape

We can see, from the examples given in this book and from data elsewhere, that traditional fast-moving consumer goods are to some extent falling from grace; in their place we are beginning to see new brands emerge as the most powerful and the most differentiated – among them many corporate and service brands. Interbrand's international review of brand power, 'The World's Greatest Brands', cites as the top ten most powerful brands in the world McDonald's, Coca-Cola, Disney, Kodak, Sony, Gillette, Mercedes-Benz, Levi's, Microsoft and Marlboro. While many of these are still product brands, it is interesting to see that for the first time in such surveys a retail service brand fills the top slot.

■ What Has Happened to Consumer Goods Brands?

Consumer goods branding used to be considered the model for all branding; it was where the belief in the brand was born and truly developed. Fast-moving consumer goods companies, like Procter & Gamble, Unilever and Mars, developed their own well-thought out models of brand development and monitoring, their own systems for brand management. As Andrew Seth has shown in Chapter 19 on this subject, it was in companies such as these that the traditional school of brand marketing was created.

Yet although companies such as these still guard and promote their brands zealously, and continue dutifully and with a good deal of inspiration to invest in research and development to bring new brands on to the market, very few people are talking about them any more. Why is this? Does the old brand management model no longer work, or is it simply that other types of company are catching up and generating more interest?

Recently in western markets, both in grocery and in other fast-moving sectors, we have seen the apparently inexorable rise of the retail brand and the increasing failure of packaged goods brands to make sufficient inroads. There is no one single reason for this; rather a number of factors are coming together to change the consumer landscape.

Much has been written about the way in which training practices in traditional fmcg manufacturers, though excellent in many ways, can lead to overemphasis on personal career development and corresponding short-termism. Bright people are moved on every 12 to 24 months and in their anxiety to prove themselves in each of their roles, they will seek to make some mark on the brand, even when this is not necessarily in the brand's best interests.

Retailers in the UK and other developed markets have invested in their brands every bit as much as have consumer goods manufacturers. To some extent this has been easier for them than for the manufacturers; they have one corporate brand to promote, rather than a dozen or more flagship or pillar brands. Nevertheless, real brand building, through added value, product innovation (particularly in growing segments in grocery such as cook chill) and consistent promotion has led to the creation of real brand equity.

Many fast-moving consumer goods represent a low-risk purchase to the consumer. Unlike a car or a costly piece of electrical equipment, they are not very expensive, and the consequences of making a wrong decision are relatively low – you don't like the taste of your breakfast cereal quite as much for the next week or your cat goes off its food. For this reason, own-label grocery products offer an easy opportunity for trial. Given the scale of brand building that has been carried out by the retailers, trust in the retailer has in many cases superseded trust in the manufacturer. Many manufacturers have not helped themselves by supplying own label and still expecting people to buy their product. At the moment this practice has largely remained within the grocery/consumer goods sector, but from our experience with other types of companies, from computing to healthcare, we would not be surprised to see many of the famous brand names of today across a wide range of industries turn into nothing more than own-label suppliers to retailers.

What is more, the packaged goods manufacturers have been remarkably slow in responding to this situation. They have reacted less than promptly and arguably with insufficient vehemence when retailers have launched surprisingly similar products with surprisingly similar brand names and packaging designs; they themselves have failed to be sufficiently innovative in the creation of distinctive and different packaging designs. An over-reliance in many cases on the corporate brand has led to the use of non-distinctive, descriptive names for even the most interesting of new products, allowing retailers to ape everything about the product, including the name!

The historical strength of marketing-led corporations has led to a focus on what is in our view an unsustainable product-based approach, benefiting no one but the advertising agencies, who have to think up new and creative ways of promoting relatively small product benefits. Big corporations the world over, and not just in the fmcg marketplace, are driven by fear and held back by complacency; sometimes it seems as if their belief that they know best stops them looking outside at the changing world.

■ From Products to People

In an environment where everything is equal and quality costs nothing, product differentiation really is no longer enough. In such a world, functional values and attributes will enable you to be a player in a marketplace, but will not make you a success. Many of the brands that are emerging today are succeeding because they do not focus on a specific product, but instead communicate clear values which can extend across a plethora of different products and services. It is here that the relative strength of the retailer and service brands lie; they have so much more opportunity to speak to customers, they exercise control over an entire environment and they also enjoy opportunities to spend money not simply on product development but also on providing additional brand value over and above this.

Again, much has been written about the shift from large-scale broadcast advertising to below-the-line, targeted promotions. With the proliferation of media, advertisers can no longer hope to catch the same percentage of the target market population as previously. One international food group, for example, decided for the launch of their new pasta that they would not develop a traditional TV advertising campaign, but instead would send samples of the product to people with the right demographic profile.

Once again, this growth in database marketing offers an advantage to those companies who develop loyalty schemes or 'brand clubs'; here too we see that service organisations (financial services and airlines among others), as well as retailers, are in an excellent position to begin really to understand what drives their customers. The Internet too, though much hyped and still somewhat 'uncontrolled', offers brand owners another opportunity to track and trap consumers.

■ Service Brands

What do we mean by a service brand? Traditionally we are referring to brands which bring a specific service to consumers, such as retail, fast-food restaurants, financial services, transport services and so forth. Brands such as McDonald's, Sainsbury and British Airways would all fall under this definition of a service brand. Historically, most service brands have developed from organisations or companies, and, although there has been some concentration on visual identity, there has not been until recently much attempt to establish a set of motivating and differentiated brand values.

However, the great service brands of today have distinguished themselves by concentrating on developing and maintaining a brand positioning which provides a competitive advantage. As with all brands, the strongest brands are built on emotional and intangible differences, rather than mere product differences.

It is often said that a service brand is only as good as its weakest link, which in the case of retailers or banks is often the checkout operator. These small cogs in the machinery of the whole are the individuals who have the most interface with the consumer and therefore those who need to be most motivated and to fit most closely the brand positioning. As a result, internal communications and staff training assume particular importance in a service brand, as Michael Jary points out in Chapter 15. British Airways, for example, runs special workshops for all employees as part of their 'breakthrough programme'. The aim of these workshops is to ensure that everyone within the organisation shares a common vision and purpose. If service excellence is to be delivered at the 'point of sale' then initiatives such as this will need to become more widespread.

Brand management for service brands therefore needs to become a much broader function, in order to ensure that each of the many experiences the consumer has of the brand is consistent; without this attention to detail, promises of service excellence will remain empty words.

■ High-Tech Brands

Currently, only two of the world's most powerful brands in the Interbrand top ten are high-tech brands, although clearly this area has seen massive activity and development. Several brands have emerged as winners, but there have also been many casualties. Moreover, many successful manufacturing companies have failed to turn their initial product advantages into brand advantages. This is partly because the rate of change of new product introduction in many high-tech categories has led to a heavy emphasis on product attributes and functional values. Products have tended to be aimed at the early adopter, and it has been hoped that other consumers will follow in due course, as the knowledge filters down. For this reason, differentiation between products and brands has been short-lived.

However, the market is changing. The proliferation of products has left consumers confused and bewildered. With such rapid falls in prices, choosing a product on price is no longer easy, either. With the blurring of traditional category boundaries, well-known brand names are also starting to compete in the high-tech sector. This has meant that high-tech companies have been forced to adopt more traditional marketing practices in order to avoid failure. For many high-tech companies, the message is the same as for packaged goods manufacturers; what is required is less emphasis on new products, and more emphasis on the overall brand. Sustained brand-building activity needs to be undertaken to ensure that consumers can choose on something more than bytes and dollars.

■ The Growth of Non-traditional Brands

We believe that over the course of the next decade we will see an increase in the growth of brands in non-traditional and even non-commercial sectors. By this we mean not just actors and sports stars, but also charities and non-governmental organisations. There is no history of branding in these areas, though the use of a name and logo has long been relatively widespread. In the past few years some organisations have begun to adopt the language of branding and even begun to operate as true brands – in the charitable sector, for example, there are Oxfam and Greenpeace.

A number of reasons exist for this shift. First, many non-commercial organisations have undergone, to a greater or lesser extent, crises of identity and purpose, due to regulatory, legislative, funding or political changes. A new awareness of the need to motivate interest from target audiences has also arisen; such organisations have become aware of their so-called 'competitive set'. Coupled with this is an increasing acknowledgement that the tools of brand development offer a 'best practice' model for commercial development.

Charities, for example, have now realised that they operate in a clearly defined marketplace and that they are competing with other charities for share of funds and consumer spend. In order to attract contributions, they must communicate a meaningful point of difference which target audiences can recognise and with which they can identify. Moreover, in the UK, for example, the *raison d'être* of many governmental and non-governmental organisations has been called into question as a result of recent governmental policy; some have been given agency status and set revenue targets. Again, to be effective, they need to understand what they stand for and communicate these values to their members or target market.

Figure 20.1   Nike
The price of Nike on the US stock market soared when it was
announced that Michael Jordan was returning to basketball

Sporting authorities are aware of the opportunities to raise revenue that new media and international interest afford; many are also aware of the need to compete against other forms of sport for audience interest. In addition, teams, players and rock stars have all become aware of their individual commercial value and, indeed, their ability to influence social behaviour. Manchester United has for example recently launched a beer, Red Tribe, which is a first attempt away from more traditional licensing into the launch of sub-brands. Two further examples illustrate the growing power of the personal brand: the price of Nike on the US stock market soared when it was announced that Michael Jordan was returning to basketball; more recently, the value to O. J. Simpson of his name has been considered as one of his assets for the purposes of assessing damages in his civil case.

At a time when commercial operations are seeking to establish brand values which are social or human, charities and other non-commercial organisations are ideally placed to exploit their inherent human and social values in order to extend their influence and increase their revenues. However, this means that they must restructure themselves into brandcentric companies, where line responsibility is given to a brand manager and where ultimate brand responsibility rests with the brand owner – CEO or DG. This, for many such organisations, will require a quantum leap in thinking.

■ Global Brands

Of course branding has not reached the same stage of development in all parts of the world. Here, in the product-and-brand saturated west, brands are having to move up the value ladder, away from functional values (what the brand can do for me) through expressive values (what the brand says about me) to central values (what the brand and I share at a fundamental level). In the newly opened markets of eastern Europe, functional and expressive values in many cases are still enough; to be able to buy western brands is in itself a statement about the individual. In less-developed countries, many brands are still desired and trusted for their functional values; in these markets, for many people, it is often enough that a brand has a guaranteed origin and a guaranteed consistency of quality.

But although new trends in branding may not have reached all around the world yet, this does not mean that the global brand has no meaning and no future. As Bill Tragos has shown in Chapter 13 consumer convergence is increasing rather than decreasing, and satellite television and the Internet are both breaking down borders and crossing boundaries with a speed and coverage unknown in the past. Developments in information technology are also likely to mean that more entertainment and shopping is done in and from the home. For the brand provider, the rise of international brands has helped by reducing production and promotion costs.

■ New Brand Launches

The cost of developing new brands, is, as we have read elsewhere, extremely high. It is also extraordinarily difficult. Creating new trade marks is costly and challenging, both because of the increasingly international application of many brands and also because of the cluttered nature of the world's trade mark registers. Finding a free, available name that is devoid of negative linguistic associations in 130 countries of the world has never been easy, but it is getting harder and harder. Add to this the cost of launching and promoting a new brand internationally and it is easy to see why only the brave or brilliant attempt it.

As companies increasingly acknowledge that their existing brands are extremely valuable, so we will see more attention turned towards managing and husbanding these. For all these reasons, therefore, we will continue to see an increase in brand revitalisation strategies – either by means of brand extension, or by brand licensing, or by the launch of carefully developed sub-brands or sister brands.

■ Brand Risk and Reputation

The brands we have described as the brands of the future are beginning to be aware that consumers in developed markets are becoming ever more discriminating and are looking behind products and services to the company beyond. This is illustrated amply by this quote from *Marketing Intelligence and Planning* (1993):

Consumers are increasingly interested in and concerned about corporate reputation and, although there is still far too little public information about the companies with which they do business, they are developing sophisticated ways of evaluating reputation, and affecting its behaviour if it falls short of their expectations.

Corporate public relations disasters of all types can have equally devastating effects on the reputation of brands – from the infamous Hoover free flights offer to the benzene in the Perrier incident.

Moreover, with the recent renewed interest in Shell's activities in Nigeria, attention has been focused on the responsibilities of brand owners not only to their consumers (after all, we have all known about outstanding customer value for years) and to their employees, but also to society as a whole. The immediate effect of such incidents on the brand is reflected by damage to the share price in the world's stock markets. However, who can calculate the effect that human rights issues such as this will have on the future of the Shell brand at retail? If we do not know how to assess such brand risks now, there is no doubt that the diligent brand owners of today are already focusing their attention on such issues.

■ Brands and Society

It should be clear from this that brands have a strong social influence on a society's sense of purpose, direction and economic growth. We could argue that brands, like politicians and the Church, are some of the influences which help us navigate through life. Moreover, from the Shell human rights issues to the Co-operative Bank's ethical policy, we can see that brand owners are becoming the new messiahs or pariahs of modern society. Table 20.1 illustrates how it is possible to paint an evocative picture of society at any particular time by naming the prominent brands then:

Table 20.1   Prominent brands in the UK, 1950s to 1990s

1950s	*1960s*	*1970s*	*1980s*	*1990s*
Hoover	Biba	Sex Pistols	BMW	Virgin
Persil	Mini	Adidas	Next	Nike
Ivory Soap	Mary Quant	Martini	Filofax	Orange
Kenwood	Oxo	Ford Capri	The Face	DKNY

Since brands play such a fundamental role in society, we believe it is the responsibility of brand owners to begin to ask themselves more wide-ranging and searching questions: rather than ask a straightforward question such as 'Will it sell?' they must ask a series of more complex questions: 'Will it make a contribution to our customer's success?' 'Will it improve the customer's and society's well-being?' 'Does it add to our country's cultural stock or bring pride to our nation?'

Such thinking is not new. David Packard, one of the founders of Hewlett-Packard, put it very succinctly when he spoke of his ambition for this company back in the 1960s: 'Why are we here? I think many people assume, wrongly, that a company exists to make money . . . we are here to make a contribution to society, a phrase which sounds trite but is fundamental. . . .'

What he envisaged for his corporation then will be true for many brands in the future; brands are not just about making money for their owners or their shareholders, not just about fulfilling basic consumer needs. Brands possess great power and the truly great brands will be those that learn to balance this power with responsibility.

■ Reference

Marketing Intelligence and Planning (1993).

Index